Teaching Reading

In Social Studies, Science, and Math

By Laura Robb

SCHOLASTIC
PROFESSIONAL BOOKS

NEW YORK · TORONTO · LONDON · AUCKLAND · SYDNEY
MEXICO CITY · NEW DELHI · HONG KONG

With love for the three educators in my life—my husband Lloyd and my children Evan and Anina
and
In loving memory of my brother, Dr. Eugene M. Seidner

I have used the actual names of teachers from Powhatan, Winchester City, Clarke County, Warren County Schools, and New York City. All other names are pseudonyms to protect the privacy of those teachers who were considering change or were in the process of change.

Cover design by Josué Castilleja
Cover photograph by Bonnie Forstrum Jacobs
Interior design by LDL Designs
Interior photographs by Bonnie Forstrum Jacobs.
(Photo on page 311 by Tom Hurst/SODA)

"History of My People" by Walter Dean Myers from *Soul Looks Back in Wonder* by Walter Dean Myers. Copyright © 1993 by Walter Dean Myers. Published by Dial.

"Traveling" by Eve Merriam from *Jamboree* by Eve Merriam. Copyright © 1984 by Eve Merriam. Published by Dell.

"Number Theory" by Lillian Morrison from *Overheard in a Bubble Chamber and Other Science Poems* by Lillian Morrison. Copyright © 1981 by Lillian Morrison. Published by Lothrop, Lee & Shepard.

ISBN 0-439-17669-7
Copyright © 2003 by Laura Robb
Printed in the U.S.A.
1 2 3 4 5 6 7 8 9 10   23   09 08 07 06 05 04 03 02 03

Table of Contents

Acknowledgments

My deepest appreciation goes to Wendy Murray, Editorial Director, who encouraged me to write this book, and who has been there throughout the process of revision and editing. I also want to express my gratitude to Mary Hofstra and Ray Coutu, whose input has been invaluable to the book's content and organization, and Terry Cooper, Editor-in-Chief, for her support and commitment to publishing professional books that speak to teachers and address their needs.

Thanks to teachers and students from Virginia and other states who have influenced this book, especially Dick Bell, Debi Gustin, Kathleen Hobbs, John Lathrop, Ray Legge, Harry Holloway, Josh Mosser, Jasper Oliver, and Nancy Roche, my wonderful colleagues at Powhatan School.

Thanks to the teachers of Quarles Elementary in Winchester, especially to Heather Campbell and Gail Johnson who refined many strategies with their students; to the teachers at Warren County Junior High School, especially math teacher Ginny Carnell; to teachers and students I've worked with at Daniel Morgan Middle School, Frederick Douglas and Virginia Avenue Elementary Schools in Winchester; to the sixth- and seventh-grade teams at Johnson Williams Middle School and the teachers at Boyce and Cooley Elementary Schools in Clarke County, Virginia, my sincere thanks for inviting me into your classrooms. Special thanks go to the teachers at Keister Elementary in Harrisonburg, Virginia, who helped me learn with them for five years.

I'm grateful to those who've read drafts of the book—Adam Berkin, Donna Cronin, Valerie Maxwell, Myra Zarnowski. The comments from each of you added so much to the vision in my mind. Special thanks to Lauren Leon, who made the book's design innovative, artistic, and reader-friendly.

Again, I'd like to thank every teacher and student who touched my life and impacted on my ever-developing theory of how children learn. What you have taught me has become part of this book.

Finally, my deepest thanks go to my husband Lloyd who never complained about the long hours I spent on weekends and evenings writing this book. His encouragement and support have never wavered and have been my loving beacon.

Laura Robb

Teaching Reading in Social Studies, Science, and Math

Foreword

By Donna M. Ogle

W hat a joy to open a book and find such a wealth of ideas for engaging students with informational texts. Too often the efforts of teachers who are committed to developing their students' reading abilities focus almost exclusively on narrative fictional literature—particularly novels and short stories. Yet, we know that the majority of materials students will read during their school years and throughout life are not stories but the kinds Robb invites us to explore in this book—informational books, newspapers, magazines, textbooks, and other content sources.

For teachers who know that students deserve help in reading content–rich texts this book provides a real "road map" of how to get started, how to involve students actively in the process, and how to address those "roadblocks" that often seem to daunt our progress. And it comes at an important time. With our national preoccupation on high-stakes testing and content standards, students are expected to learn and be able to use a great deal of information. Even large-scale reading tests now reflect a broad range of reading tasks that include informational reading, using multiple texts and manipulating graphic data.

Laura Robb is clearly a master teacher, coach, and staff developer. She shares a wealth of experiences gained from working with content learning in a very accessible manner. Her deep commitment to and empathy for her students is clear and she reminds us all of the need to listen to students and respond to them—not just teach "our" lessons. She knows the importance of helping students become engaged in learning and using the range of materials needed for their success. Therefore, this book is full of practical ways teachers can scaffold their instruction to build students' control over a repertoire of strategies that develops their confidence and independence in reading textbooks and informational materials.

As I read each chapter I was continually reminded of Robb's grounding in real classroom experience. She not only lays out good strategies in a practical lesson format, but shows us examples of each of the strategy lessons from an actual teaching experience. The voices of real teachers and classroom situations dominate. Robb also discusses how she fine-tuned these lessons to meet the needs of particular teachers and classrooms. Her practical orientation extends to her willingness to freely share times when even her expert instruction has gone awry—and what she does to "fix-up" such experiences. Teaching is a life-long learning experience and in this book Robb openly shares a wealth of knowledge gained on her journey.

The book is useful for beginning teachers as well as those with years of experience—and those who work with teachers in professional development. It can be read at a basic level to develop a general framework and learn how to use specific strategies. Veteran teachers, too, can gain a great deal, especially in the ways she fine-tunes strategies to meet specific student needs, suggests ideas for working as a coach, and encourages deeper thinking and reflection. The many examples of what can and needs to be done to improve both teachers' approaches to using informational materials and students' active engagement with their learning provide something new for every reader.

Some additional qualities of this book deserve special attention. First, the ideas are well-grounded in current research and best practice and her references are good guides for further reading. Robb explains her theoretical orientation in constructivism, schema theory and the work of Rosenblatt while focusing on classroom applications. The book format models her approach to scaffolded teaching; there are general strategy lessons, specific applications in content lessons, and reflections on those experiences. Teachers can easily take the model lessons and try them out and use her reflection guide to deepen their experiences. Robb has chosen strategies carefully; she knows teachers need to focus on and fine-tune the strategies that work most effectively for them, their content, and their students. Finally, she also reminds us that content reading begins well before middle school as teachers share their interest in books and learning and guide students to develop their own. The whole book clearly builds the case for, and illustrates the benefits of, responsive teaching.

Introduction

Writing this book has sometimes felt like solving a huge puzzle with hundreds of pieces…and not having a table large enough to put them together. As I read seminal works on content area reading by Alvermann and Phelps, the Vaccas, Estes and Vaughan, Gillet and Temple, and Tierney and Readence, and did classroom research on teaching reading in social studies, science, and math, I began to recognize the abundance of strategies and ideas available—and realized that I couldn't include "everything" in one book.

I've had to make hard choices about what to include and what to omit. My work with content area teachers greatly influenced these decisions. Most teachers have 40- to 45-minute periods to help their students learn complex concepts and teach the vocabulary that enables them to understand this information. I was aware that they would have limited time to devote to teaching reading strategies. So, instead of covering the wide range of reading and writing strategies that researchers have developed, I selected the strategies and management tips that teachers I've worked with in grades 3-8 have found effective, and that are not overly complicated and time-consuming.

I've tried to write a book that will work seamlessly in elementary school, middle school, and beyond. I do not propose that teachers overhaul their curricula or ways of teaching, but that they take short bursts of time each day to teach reading and learning strategies that will help their students "unlock" every kind of text and thus experience success with every subject.

What's the main engine that drives this book? Essentially, the book seeks first to dispel the myth that students enter grade 3 magically able to read for knowledge because they have spent their primary years learning to "decode" text; and then to provide teaching strategies to make comprehension happen. Comprehension and meaning making do not start in third grade but are part of excellent reading instruction in the primary grades (Clay, 1979b; Fountas & Pinnell, 1996). Students in grades four and beyond need and benefit from reading and writing instruction that refines their application of strategies to varied reading materials and introduces new strategies to their repertoires.

At the start of each new school year, we all step into our classrooms knowing that the 25 to 35 students facing us are a mixture of those who read below grade level, on grade level, and above. We've got to reach every one of these learners. My years of classroom experience, my research and my work with content area teachers have convinced me that we need to rethink the way we teach specific subjects and content area reading. In this book I share a three-part learning framework and strategies for utilizing this framework in your classroom and supporting your students as they learn. As you present the strategy lessons offered in this book, you will develop skilled readers and learners who will come to enjoy the subject you teach because you've provided them with the tools for success.

—Laura Robb

⤳ Chapter 1 ⤳

Rethinking the Way We
Teach Content Area Reading

*To try to make sense, to construct stories, and to share them with others in
speech and in writing is an essential part of being human.* — *Gordon Wells*

I looked at my watch. One hour to lunch—and freedom, I thought. The room, filled with more than one hundred staff developers and reading specialists attending a half-day in-service on reading and learning in science and social studies, seemed so much more inviting at 8:00 AM while we drank coffee, downed muffins, and chatted.

As the speaker lectured on about how to prepare students for Virginia's SOL (Standards of Learning) tests, I noticed the other teachers were as restless as I was. They looked at their watches, passed a notebook back and forth, gazed out the window at the blossoms on the dogwood tree, or stared down at their tablets—no longer taking notes. Like my colleagues, I could not concentrate. After two-and-a half hours of listening, my brain rebelled; I couldn't absorb another piece of information. Moreover, though I tried to subdue this thought, I didn't care.

One seventh-grader, Kawan, came to mind, his words chiding me now. "I'm not gonna pass history or science," Kawan told me the afternoon before. "I fall asleep every day. They [the teachers] give me an 'F' for participation. That's a joke. The only ones who participate are them."

"Why can't you stay awake?" I asked.

"I'm helping my dad on the farm. I'm tired. School makes me bored. We do nothing—nothing but sit and listen to stupid stuff. Sometimes they even read some pages from the book. [He rolled his eyes.] Yeah, and we're supposed to take notes. Who cares?"

Kawan read on grade level, and though he could read the textbooks in science and history, he chose not to read them. Shrugging his shoulders, he said, "I'll flunk even if I read the books. I don't remember half of what I read. I guess I'll be in summer school again."

Sitting in that in-service, I found myself in Kawan's "who-cares?" shoes, seeing learning from his perspective in a way I hadn't as I sat beside him just 24 hours ago. I fully understood why he didn't care, and I felt sad that I had not responded to him in a manner that honored the problem that he and students everywhere face daily: how to deal with a prevalent classroom practice that views learners as passive receivers of knowledge.

Kawan felt disengaged from learning. Or perhaps it's fairer to say, his teachers' lecture style *had disengaged him*. In this state of detachment, Kawan struggled with retaining information from his textbooks. "Too many new words and stuff to learn," he told me. Lacking the strategies for reading and gathering information from his history and science textbooks, and knowing that the teacher would deliver the information in a daily lecture,

Kawan decided not to read. Students like Kawan are not learning how to use textbooks, a resource and instructional tool that will be part of their learning in secondary school and college. It's for such students that I write this book.

Content Area Reading and Learning: Four Assumptions That Need to Be Examined

"What does content area reading and learning mean to you?" I pose this question at the start of study groups and when I teach reading classes for school districts. It's a great way for me to gain insight into teachers' ideas about learning, as well as their classroom practices. Here's what Danielle, a sixth-grade history teacher with two years of experience, wrote in her journal:

> I want my students to learn all the material I have to cover this year. I assign pages in the textbook for them to read. By sixth grade, they should all be able to read a grade-level text and answer the review questions. I give them time to copy notes from the board so they have the important ideas in their notebooks. I want my students to love history as much as I do, so I tell them all I know about topics we study.

Danielle's comments reflect the beliefs of most content area teachers. She is passionate about her subject and wants to transmit her passion and knowledge to students (Moore, 1996). And like many other middle-school teachers, Danielle had only one undergraduate class in reading. "Teaching reading is not my primary focus," she told our group. "Teaching history is."

The focus on having students learn information greatly influences the classroom model that many content area teachers develop. Some become dispensers of knowledge, while others integrate storytelling and projects, and orchestrate activities (Evans, 1988) but in a manner that doesn't deepen student understanding of the content. Danielle and others in the study groups framed their instruction around beliefs that developed from their own school experiences (Alvermann and Phelps, 2000). Following are four assumptions the groups said accurately reflected their beliefs. (In italics, I offer alternatives to these assumptions.)

1. The textbook is the main information resource for students.

The textbook should be one of many resources. Informational picture and chapter books, historical fiction, biography and autobiography, photo essays, magazines, and newspapers can all help bring greater depth and perspective to students. The Internet, videos, parents, other teachers, and community members are also valuable sources of content.

2. Lecture and copying notes are great ways to teach new information, especially for students who can't read the textbook.

Active participation in learning is also extremely important. In fact, learning by doing enables students to link their prior experiences and knowledge to new information and construct new understandings (Parker, 2001; Wells, 1986). However, this "doing" does not always occur when the child works alone (Vygotsky, 1978; Wilhelm, 2001). Such learning also requires effective teaching and working with more knowledgeable adults and peers. Therefore, paired, small- and whole-group discussions are also effective ways for students to learn (Alvermann et al., 1998; Gambrell, 1996).

3. The review questions at the end of each chapter help students study and determine what they understand.

Researchers have demonstrated that teaching students to ask their own questions and modelling notetaking strategies can improve comprehension of texts (Palinscar and Brown, 1984; Vaughan and Estes, 1986).

4. Students learned how to read in the lower grades, and they don't need reading instruction in middle school content subjects.

As readers mature, teachers can help them refine their knowledge and use of the in-the-head strategies Marie Clay described—strategies such as predicting, questioning, and retelling that enable students to make sense of texts (1979). When strategies are taught, teachers can improve students' ability to read and comprehend challenging texts and help them learn more information (Vygotsky, 1978).

CONTENT LITERACY

McKenna and Robinson define content literacy as "the ability to use reading and writing for the acquisition of new content in a given discipline" (1990, p. 194). Most educators agree that meaningful dialogue and writing are also necessary for students to connect to information in a text and make it their own (Alvermann, 2000; Alvermann and Phelps, 1998; Gillet and Temple, 2000; Vacca and Vacca, 2000).

Moving Beyond the Assumptions to New Understandings

So, how can teachers begin to incorporate alternative methods into their content area instruction? In Chapters 3 through 7, you'll gain insights into ways teachers can move away from these four assumptions about content area instruction, towards a more dynamic teaching and learning model. You will see how other teachers engage students in reading, writing, talking, and thinking to learn new information in a subject. You'll also discover how teachers develop and apply content area literacy strategies to textbooks and informational trade books (Alvermann and Phelps, 1998; McKenna and Robinson, 1990).

The process of weaving comprehension strategies into content area teaching takes time, especially if you are a new teacher. It's not a three-month "fix." I remember one of my professors at the University of Virginia, Dr. Estes, stressing this point. He believed content area teachers needed at least two to three years of classroom experience to relate to and understand how the reading process connects to their subjects. Teaching itself can create an awareness of the importance of modelling what good readers do to comprehend and learn.

Dr. Estes also described the relationship between a reader and a book that transformed my view of reading and resulted in the conviction that underlies everything in this book. "Come now, let us reason together," Dr. Estes said fervently, and with those six words, reading became for me an active, impassioned, and intimate event.

Come now, let us reason together still resonates with me. It so aptly captures the complex process that is reading. This process is more than personally reacting to a text; it is, instead, interacting with the text, reasoning with it to develop a hypothesis and justify it. By using accurate facts and inferences from the text, readers can transform interpretations into valid and reasonable thought (Rosenblatt, 1978; 1983).

Reading as Reasoning Together: A Classroom Example

Fourth graders in Sally Pearson's class struggled with personal reactions versus reasonable thought and validity while discussing "Night People" a chapter from *A Lion to Guard Us* (Bulla). The book was one of many texts related to their study of colonial America. Here's a part of one group's conversation.

LEROY: *They're* [the children] *afraid of the night people they meet.*
JAMAL: *It says on page 38 "They were in alleys and doorways. They were part of the shadows."*

DOMINIQUE: *How does that show they were afraid?*

JAMAL: *I'd be afraid of shadows and strangers in the dark.*

LEROY: *It's silly to be scared. Those [night people] are like the homeless. We need to help them.*

VINNIE: *I never knew that there were homeless in those days.*

JAMAL: *But they're little kids. And that woman scared them. She tried to touch Amanda and said she [Amanda] was her daughter.*

DOMINIQUE: *Maybe they shouldn't be scared, but the book shows they are.*

VINNIE: *Yeah. And they run back to the house they were thrown out of. I'd say they must be more scared of those night people than Randolph and Miss Trippett.*

LEROY: *Maybe we should say they're scared of both.*

JAMAL: *I think Amanda's scared of becoming a night person and not having a home.*

DOMINIQUE: *You have to prove that. I don't see proof of that. They're scared of the night people. That's it.*

The students support one another as they move from personal and/or initial responses to story facts to finding a reasonable interpretation of the characters' words, actions, and reactions. This conversation illustrates active reading, where four students first use their experiences and feelings, then relate and integrate these with the text to construct a reasonable interpretation of this chapter. These fourth graders were fortunate to be reading historical fiction that offered opportunities to search for meaning and justify interpretations.

Textbooks: How They Short Cut Critical Reading

Unfortunately, historical novels, biographies, and informational chapter books are not always used to teach or enhance a social studies and science curriculum (Woodward and Elliott, 1990). Students whose main source of information is a textbook laden with facts and written without voice and style have little opportunity to interpret and justify. Moreover, textbooks and trade books can contain information that is not true, and it's important to offer students strategies to discover these inaccuracies (Beck et al., 1997; Zarnowski, 1998b). Freeman and Person point out that "concerns regarding textbooks have also dealt with the inclusion of too much information on the one hand and the hesitation to include 'controversial' subject matter on the other," (1998, p.13). In fact, controversy stimulates thinking and inspires the desire to read, discuss, and debate (Vaughan and Estes, 1986).

Five Roadblocks That Affect Teachers and Students

Trying to reach the wide range of readers in a class can also be frustrating for teachers, especially when districts require that every student read, comprehend, and absorb the same material—and take state tests written for students reading at or slightly above grade level. When alternate materials are not available for teachers to use with struggling readers, teaching can feel like navigating an impossible obstacle course. Here, I will examine five roadblocks teachers of social studies, science, and math run into daily. Later, in Chapters 3 through 7, I'll explore strategies that can help you overcome these obstacles.

Roadblock 1: Students Avoid Reading the Textbook

When I work with grades 3 through 8 in various schools, I ask students: "Do you read assigned pages in your history and science textbooks?" "Never!" "Hardly ever," and "Why read stuff if you don't have to?" are typical of the responses I get from some students in grades 4 and 5, and the majority in grades 6 through 8. As one fourth grader put it: "I don't have to--she [the teacher] gives it all to us."

"If you listen in class, the teacher tells you everything that's in the chapter. Why read it? All you have to do to get your homework right is look up vocabulary in the glossary and read the parts that answer the questions," reasoned a seventh grader.

Of course, there are students who *do* read the textbook, usually high achievers who are proficient readers. However, too many students who *can* read the textbook have decided that it's easy to skip reading assignments (Tierney and Readence, 2000). By listening to lectures, and copying and studying notes from the chalkboard, many students can learn the required information to pass and even do well on quizzes and tests.

Sixth-grader Jason's self-evaluation of why he doesn't read his science text reveals the fallout of a teacher using only a textbook to try to impart information, rather than incorporating several texts to generate discussions that would foster critical reading, wherein students would evaluate the accuracy of information:

> At first, I read every assignment. Sometimes I read it twice, if it was hard.
> I even wrote some notes. Like we did in fifth grade. I worked hard. I got

good grades. But we never talked about it [the reading]. So, I listened to the teacher. I copied notes, did the questions. Defined the new words. I started looking up answers and using the glossary for the words. My grades only dropped a little. So I stopped reading it [the textbook].

A teacher's lecture style may aid and abet students' avoidance of textbook reading, but the dry, voiceless nature of textbook writing is at the heart of students' resistance. Below is a sampling of quotations I've collected that highlight students' responses to textbooks they find "boring and dull."

- Facts, that's all you get. It [reading the textbook] makes me sleepy. —*Lisa, Grade 4*
- I just read the parts that have the answers to homework questions. —*Jimmy, Grade 5*
- I read most of the time if it's a good book that I can't put down. The textbook is boring—I hardly read it. —*Chrissie, Grade 8*

These students have made a conscious decision to take their chances and not read even those assignments they *can* read and comprehend.

Roadblock 2:
Some Students Can't Read the Textbook

Many children find learning to read difficult in primary and intermediate grades and continue to struggle in middle school (Allington, 1998). Students who read below grade level struggle with or cannot read a textbook written on grade level. Often their choice is not to read. It's easy to blame the textbooks and say that they are too difficult or dull (because often they are), but we must also take responsibility and search for

---

FACING REALITIES

Many educators question using textbooks that are too difficult, that bore readers, that mention fact upon fact, or that leave out important, but controversial information.

My solution is to offer students the best nonfiction instead. Unfortunately, the reality is that there are schools that don't have libraries, and those that do often have a slim and poor selection of literature. Moreover, some districts require that schools use adopted textbooks, so it's necessary to teach students how to read and learn from them.

Teaching Reading in Social Studies, Science, and Math

ways to improve the reading comprehension of our below-grade-level students.

If we don't change our instruction, we perpetuate the terrible cycle of "losing" students. The teachers I work with have observed this cycle year after year, and truly want to stop it by improving their practice. Every year their classes include students who read at or below grade level, and who say the textbook is too difficult because "there are lots of hard words and facts." And every year, many of these struggling readers fail and fall further behind in reading because they aren't actually reading (Ciborowski, 1992; Graves and Graves, 1994; Gillet and Temple, 2000; Tierney and Readence, 2000).

Allington (1998) reminds us that many studies (Bond & Dykstra, 1967; Knapp, 1995; Shanklin, 1990) reveal "it is the quality of the teacher, not variation in curriculum materials, that is identified as the critical factor in effective instruction," *(Teaching Struggling Readers,* p. 4). Without a doubt, more reading classes in pre-service training and organized professional study in schools can improve the calibre of instruction, and help teachers meet the diverse levels of students (Robb, 2000).

Students who can't read the textbook must rely on lectures and other oral presentations. These students live on the edge of the map and teeter on the brink of failure when they don't know enough about a topic or concept to connect to the lectures and learn new information that way.

As a result, their self-esteem plummets. The more students experience failure the more they feel discouraged (Schallert and Reed, 1997). Often, like eighth-grader Jeremy, students develop disruptive, survival behaviors: "I like being sent out for talking," Jeremy confides, "It means I don't have to sit there and feel dumb." Students like Jeremy could improve their reading and learn new information if they received reading instruction in all subjects and had additional time to complete tasks that are diffi-

SPIRALLING INTO BECOMING AT-RISK: BEHAVIORS TO WATCH FOR

This list has been culled from my own experience and the observations of teachers I coach and mentor. Not all students exhibit every behavior. Use the list to help you reflect on students' academic indicators and behaviors to plan effective interventions (see pages 244–249).

Students who can't read the textbook don't:

- Improve as readers.
- Develop and refine strategies and skills.
- Pay attention during class.
- Complete homework.
- Believe in their ability to learn and progress.
- Earn good grades.
- Develop acceptable behavior.
- Feel empowered to learn.

cult for them (Smith, 2001). Unfortunately, by sixth grade, many teachers feel that students should have enough reading skills to learn from a grade-level textbook. And in addition to feeling the pressure to teach content, many middle school teachers do not have the background knowledge to teach the reading and writing processes because reading instruction was a minor part of their pre-service training.

Roadblock 3:
The Myth of Learning to Read vs. Reading to Learn

It was 7:00 A.M. The winter morning was chilly and gray. I sat at an empty, round table in a coffee shop, waiting for the teachers in our study group to arrive. Fifteen minutes later, six teachers in grades two to five sat around the table with me. We sipped steaming coffee, and I listened as they shared feelings about teaching reading in social studies and science using nonfiction books. "Our students take standardized tests in third grade," Betty said, "and the test passages are mostly non-fiction, so we *must* teach them how to read these books." Lots of nods followed Betty's comment.

"Textbooks, too," added Phil. "My fifth-grade students do so much better when they understand its [a textbook's] structure."

"The sixth-grade teachers," said fifth-grade teacher John, "expect us to have every kid reading perfectly so that every student can read any book they assign. It's like they think learning to read stops after grade 5."

"I know the feeling," agreed another fifth-grade teacher, Tim. "Last year the fifth-grade teachers in our district met with the sixth-grade teams, and they made it clear that it's *our job* to teach the reading—they teach the information."

When visiting middle schools, I hear this sentiment voiced again and again. It represents the myth too many teachers believe: that in the lower grades students are *busy learning to read*. Once in middle school, they must be prepared to *read to learn*.

In an excellent article in *The New York Times* that presents the results of scores for 8000 fourth graders in 40 states who took the National Assessment of Educational Progress reading test in 2000, journalist Kate Zernike discusses the widening gap among the best and worst fourth-grade readers, and the fact that the scores remain flat and show little to no progress since 1976. Ms. Zernike also writes that by the end of third grade, "classroom priorities flip: students stop learning how to read and begin needing to read

Teaching Reading in Social Studies, Science, and Math

to learn other subjects" (April 2001).

Obviously, it's time to abandon this idea and teach students how to read to learn in all subjects. If we want students to improve their reading and thinking, then teachers in grades 3 and above should help students construct meaning by modelling and teaching the strategies and techniques that support learning to read while reading to learn (Alvermann & Phelps, 1998; Tierney & Readence, 2000; Vacca & Vacca, 2000; Vaughan & Estes, 1986).

All readers, whether a five-year-old reading a simple patterned book about pets or a fourth grader reading a chapter in his history textbook about the Civil War, learn information by taking what they know and linking it to new ideas in order to construct new understandings. While reading, they apply strategies that help them solve the problems that print presents—problems such as figuring out the meaning of unfamiliar words, making sense of confusing passages packed with new ideas and concepts, or selecting the essential ideas and setting aside nonessential details (Gillet and Temple, 2000; Pearson et al., 1992; Robb, 2000b; Rosenblatt, 1978; Smith, 1978; Wells, 1986).

Whether young or old, all readers apply the same strategies (Clay, 1979b; Fountas and Pinnell, 1996, 2001) to prepare for reading, to monitor their comprehension, and to reflect on what they've learned after reading. The difference between the first grader and seventh grader is the depth of understanding of reading strategies and how they support learning as well as the complexity of reading materials (Keene and Zimmermann, 1997; Pearson et al., 1992). Throughout our adult lives, we simultaneously learn about language and then use language to learn, especially when asked to unlock meaning from a difficult text (Wells, 1986).

Roadblock 4:
Middle-School Reading Traditions

- *I don't know enough about reading to teach it with science.*
- *If I spend all my time teaching reading and writing strategies, I'll never cover even half the curriculum.*
- *I'm only allotted 40 minutes four times a week to cover everything. I have to lecture and write notes on the board.*
- *The parents or resource teachers need to help the kids who can't read my text—I don't have time.*

I understand these comments and can empathize with their frustration. Especially in today's climate, where in all states but Iowa, a required curriculum and standardized tests that measure what students have learned drive instruction (Glickman, 2000/2001). In some states, mandated standards along with state-wide testing reinforce the transmission model of learning, where the teacher delivers information through lecture and notes-to-be-copied and the student receives and processes the knowledge.

Roadblock 5:
The Transmission Model of Learning

Educators who develop lessons using the transmission model of learning believe that a body of knowledge exists apart from learners. They also believe that this knowledge can be transmitted to students through lectures, by copying notes, and by memorizing important facts and new vocabulary (Alvermann and Phelps, 1998; Tierney and Readence, 2000; Vacca and Vacca, 2000).

Many middle-school teachers cling to the lecture mode because that's the way they learned in elementary and middle school, high school, and even college. "It served me well," one eighth-grade teacher wrote on an exit evaluation of the first day of a class. "I learned how to read and think. It worked for me. Why should I change it?" Such honest words reinforce my belief that any call for change from transmission to constructivist models, or any call for adjustments in teaching practices, must be sensitive to and consider teachers' beliefs and theories, as well as provide ongoing support during the change process (Robb, 2000b).

For me, preparing lectures and writing notes on the board is far more demanding than handing the learning over to students. The pressure of capturing and sustaining the interest of a young audience—or an adult audience, for that matter—is great. I've often wondered if students feel like my son Evan, now a principal, who was in my fifth-grade class many years ago. A parent came to our class to share his trip to Egypt, and he talked at the children for 30 minutes. After our guest departed, my son passed me a note that said, "Gee mom, can you sing and dance to liven things up?"

How I wished I had been thoughtful enough to have coached this parent ahead of time and helped him make his presentation interactive. My expectations for a person with no teaching background were unreal.

To ensure that my teaching has enough "song and dance," as Evan might say, I always ask myself this question when planning a lesson: How can I make this lesson interactive, so my students and I *share* responsibility for their learning?

Help Students Become Active Makers of Meaning

Whenever I consider the transmission model, my mind flashes back to an afternoon in a sixth-grade classroom. Thirty students dutifully, passively copied pages of science notes from the chalkboard. The teacher sat at his desk, grading papers. Yawns abounded. In the back of the room, two students passed notes. Several drew pictures and cartoons. Circulating around the room, I bent down next to a student and asked, "What are you learning?" "How to copy from the board," he replied.

Filling a journal with notes does not guarantee that students will absorb new facts by connecting what they know about the topic to this information. In fact, if students lack prior knowledge of the facts they are transferring from chalkboard to notebook, the information will disappear from their memory as inexorably as waves upon a beach slide back into the sea.

But do we toss out the textbook along with the transmission model? Not necessarily. Instead of avoiding textbooks, I want students to learn how to read them to get the most out of them and informational trade books, magazine and newspaper articles as well. I want students to connect what they already know to new information and develop new understandings that they can retrieve as they continue to learn (Ciborowski, 1992; Gillet and Temple; Robb, 2000a).

Teaching Vocabulary Is Key

One way to ensure that students get the most out of their reading is to focus on vocabulary. Science, math, and social studies all require reading and learning new information along with unfamiliar vocab-

An eighth grader thinks aloud and models how she uses context clues to figure out a word's meaning.

ulary. Textbooks carry a particularly heavy vocabulary load. Leaf through just about any middle-school science or social studies textbook, and you'll discover that each chapter introduces 10 to 30 new words that students must comprehend in order to connect new information to what they already know—a daunting task for students and adults alike. (See pages 198–208, for strategies that help students cope with new vocabulary).

Modelling Strategies Is Key

As teachers in grades 3 and beyond, you can encourage students to shake off a passive stance toward reading and instead see reading as a highly active and enjoyable process. Through modelling your own use of strategies, you can help your students acquire and refine reading and writing strategies and skills that will enable them to make meaning out of informational texts. These strategies, discussed in Chapters 3 to 6, include posing questions, taking notes, selecting essential details, and self-monitoring recall and comprehension (Ciborowski, 1992; Gillet and Temple, 2000; Keene and Zimmerman 1997; Tierney and Readence 2000).

Learning as a Construction of Knowledge

When I reflect on how I best learn a skill, the image of myself in the process of learning is always active. It's of me, "doing" things. For example, a few years ago I was given an orchid, but I had no idea how to care for it. I checked out several books on orchids from the library. I read and formulated questions; then I read some more and jotted down some notes. Next, I applied the knowledge I had gained. I purchased plant food and a grow light, and fed and watered the plant. Then, I made adjustments based on what I observed, moving the orchid to a sunny window and giving up the grow light. In other words, I *constructed* my own knowledge. It didn't come verbatim from the library books, but from an interplay of the information there and my own experience—prior knowledge, my sense of the light and temperature in the house, as well as my experience with the orchid.

Engagement with a text—whether the text is written, oral, or visual—involves this same active, constructive exchange between the known and the new. The reader connects to the text by using prior knowledge as well as his or her present mental, physical, and emotional state to construct meaning (Rosenblatt, 1978).

Rebecca and William move deeply into their reading world.

Years ago, I took my mother to see *The Verdict,* a movie starring Paul Newman. In the final scene, the telephone rings, four, five, six, times, and the main character stands by the phone, struggling with the decision to answer or not to answer it. Finally, thoroughly engaged, my mom and several others yelled, "Pick it up, already!" On the walk back to my mom's apartment, she said, "I felt I was in the movie. I had to tell him to pick up that telephone." Just as my mom was "in" the movie, I want my students to be "in" the world of the texts they read, and "in" the learning.

Gordon Wells, in *The Meaning Makers: Children Learning Language and Using Language to Learn* (1986) concludes:

> It [knowledge] has to be constructed afresh by each individual knower on the basis of what is already known and by means of strategies developed over the whole of that individual's life, both outside and inside the classroom. On both these counts, there are bound to be substantial differences between the individuals in any class of students, and hence, a wide variation in the interpretations that are put upon the teacher's words. Unless students are given opportunities to formulate the sense they make of new topics in their own way, using their own words, an important means of gaining understanding is lost. In addition, the teacher loses the opportunity to discover what meanings the students bring to the topic and so is unable to make his or her contributions contingently responsive. (pages 218-219)

For Wells, learning is "the guided reinvention of knowledge," a phrase that I think beautifully describes learning. Wells' conception is the antithesis of the transmission model. Like Lev Vygotksy (1978), Wells believes the learner is guided to "reinvent knowledge" with the support of a more knowledgeable adult or peer. The chart on the opposite page compares the transmission model of learning to the constructivist model, a research-based approach that shows how we process and connect information and ideas (Boomer, et al., 1992; Rosenblatt, 1983, 1978; Short and Burke, 1995; Wells, 1986).

Bringing Teachers and Constructivism Together

When I introduce the constructivist model to teachers, I open with and explain these three short phrases: SHOW ME, HELP ME, LET ME.

SHOW ME invites you and me to model and think-aloud so students observe how reading and writing strategies and techniques work.

HELP ME means that you and I must reserve class time for students to practice and apply a strategy to different reading materials. While students do the work, the expert (you) circulates around the room, answering questions and guiding them. Before moving students to independence, pose questions to make sure that you and your students share the same understandings about a topic or process.

LET ME reminds you and me that it's our responsibility to release control gradually and move students towards independence.

I constantly try to remember my teen years because they remind me of the *doing* part of learning. Whenever my mom or dad wanted to "save" me from a bad experience or choice, my rebellious inner voice always said, "Let *me* do it." It's the same with learning. We have to release our students and let them do it.

Unfortunately, all roads that lead to constructivism are not straight and smooth. You'll have to learn to cope with and adjust to the potholes, bumps, detours, and challenges. And you will, especially if you learn together with colleagues in support and study groups, where you can share literacy stories, air frustrations, and celebrate successes (Robb, 2000b).

Teaching Reading in Social Studies, Science, and Math

Transmission Model	Constructivist Model
• Teacher and textbook are at the center.	• Learner is at the center.
• Teacher imparts knowledge. Learner passively receives information. Facts are seen as separate from the learner.	• Learner creates knowledge by linking new information to past experiences and knowledge. The contexts of learning also affect how students process information.
• Teacher focuses on input and specific outcomes, directing and controlling the learning.	• Teacher is a facilitator and co-learner who creates opportunities for active learning that consider students' prior knowledge.
• Curriculum and standards are dictated by state and district and delivered to students by the teacher.	• Teachers negotiate with students how to study the curriculum, even mandated topics.
• Teacher controls day-to-day planning.	• Teacher includes students in day-to-day planning.
• Teacher talk dominates.	• Students talk about their reading and writing in order to learn and connect ideas. Talk is often self-evaluative, where teachers and students strive to learn more about the process and the effectiveness of teaching practices.
• Assessment by objective testing. The purpose of assessment is to determine students' abilities, compare students' performances, evaluate schools, and find fix-it prescriptions to improve students' performance on tests. Assessment is separated from instruction.	• Assessment by subjective testing. The purpose of assessments is to evaluate students' strengths and needs. The main goal is to plan instruction, support students, and promote self-evaluation. Assessment becomes part of the learning process for teachers and students.

Three Challenges to Building a Constructivist Classroom

Challenge 1:
Classrooms and Class Schedules—
Self-Contained vs Subject-Specific Classrooms

I only have forty minutes! Many middle-school teachers feel that it's easier for teachers with self-contained classrooms to adopt the constructivist model because they have the entire day to involve students actively in reading, discussing, writing, and thinking, and to confer with and support students.

My answer for these teachers is that investing short bursts of time teaching reading strategies will pay off and can actually free up time for constructivist teaching and learning. Once students can read textbooks as well as other informational texts with greater ease and independence, they'll have more time to pursue research projects of interest, do further reading, and so on. And you'll have more time to work with students who need extra guidance, hold student conferences, and guide hands-on projects, etc.

Challenge 2:
Standardized Testing

I'm finished with stars. A colleague of mine told me this story about her son, who is in fourth grade. Christopher and his class were learning about the stars. When Christopher's mother tried to read him some legends and poems about this topic, he told her, "We've learned everything we need to pass the tests. I'm finished with stars." Christopher's comment highlights one of the dangers inherent in a system of mandated standards for all public schools. Because tests have become *the* measure of a school's success, teaching to the tests, and making the tests the focus of learning, builds stress among students and, as in Christopher's case, makes their natural curiosity and drive to know more degrade into "learning enough to pass."

Along with state standards has come high-stakes testing that measures student achievement, holding schools that don't meet minimum standards accountable. What standards and high-stakes tests don't consider is that children's background experiences and developmental levels differ widely, and a single curriculum does not fit or reach all children (Ohanian, 1999).

However, state standards along with standardized tests are currently required. When these test results are not used to judge, but are viewed as one set of results that can help educators determine whether programs and teaching strategies are effective for the school's population, then the testing can be helpful (Glickman, 2000; Routman, 1996).

In *Standards in the Middle: Moving Beyond the Basics* (2000), authors O'Neal and Kapinus state:

> For teachers, whether new or seasoned, it will be necessary to explore more content and new pedagogy. Most standards call for a deeper understanding of basics as well as learning more challenging skills and concepts. To help all students, including those previously passed up as incapable to meet the standards, teachers will need to have a better understanding of the content and skills themselves and will need to stretch their instructional abilities (page 111).

Carl Glickman, in his article "Holding Sacred Ground: The Impact of Standardization" (*Educational Leadership* 2000/2001) encourages educators to work around mandated standards and high-stakes tests and develop alternative, performance-based assessments that demonstrate students' progress in learning content through speaking, performing, and writing. Standardized tests assume that a body of knowledge exists that students can learn through drill and memorization (Serafini, 2000/2001). Assessment, however, must also consider students' daily writing, reading and speaking and link what students do to how and what we teach. We can reach all readers in grades 3–8, especially those who struggle, by discovering where they are and by teaching reading strategies that provide these students with the tools to learn in all subjects, gently nudging every child forward (Ivey, 2000).

MAKE STUDENTS TEST-WISE

Instead of focusing your entire curriculum towards these tests, reserve 8-10 minutes a day, several times a week from fall to spring to give students opportunities to practice and analyze specific types of questions (Calkins et. al, 1999; Fountas and Pinnell, 2001). During the year, practice five to ten minutes three to four times a week in order to diminish student and teacher anxiety and leave time for teachers to respond to students' needs by choosing the best strategies to support students' learning.

Challenge 3:
Adolescent Readers and Illiteracy

Only six percent of high school students are advanced readers. Adolescent illiteracy has been recognized by the International Reading Association (or IRA) as a nationwide issue that must be addressed. The 1999 National Assessment of Educational Progress (NAEP) Literacy Report Card from 1971 to 1998 supports the findings of the International Reading Association.

The testing done by the federally funded NAEP and mandated by the United States Congress assesses trends in students' literacy across the nation. The definition of literacy that NAEP offers is a reasonable one, relying more on performance-based tasks than multiple-choice questions to assess literacy. NAEP defines reading from the dual perspectives of purpose and response. According to NAEP, the tests measure three purposes for reading: the literary experience, gathering information, and performing a task such as using a train schedule. NAEP also measures four student responses to reading: constructing meaning, developing an interpretation, forming a personal response, and analyzing material.

The NAEP reading scores have changed little from 1971 to 2000. While NAEP data indicate that most students can decode words, there are serious problems with making meaning, analyzing, and drawing inferences. In 1998, *only 6 percent* of the high school students tested were advanced readers capable of synthesizing, inferring, making connections, and comprehending challenging texts.

This comes as no surprise to me, for as I visit schools, I find the emphasis is on recalling factual details instead of using facts to infer and make connections to the world, to other texts, to one's own experiences. I'm also still noticing round-robin reading as the main component of reading instruction, which is disheartening, since research shows the ineffectiveness of this practice (Opitz and Rasinski, 1998). In many of the sixth- to eighth-grade classes I've visited (even the so-called advanced sections!), students are asked 50 to 75 factual questions per class on details such as what a character wears or eats, or places he visits. History and science questions test students' ability to memorize new vocabulary and information, rather than their understanding of concepts. Too often, teachers don't ask students to analyze the information they read or use it to connect to their lives, nor to evaluate issues such as recycling, the greenhouse effect, or using historical hindsight to work for peace and eliminate poverty.

Almost all adolescents who took the NAEP were able to complete simple reading

Teaching Reading in Social Studies, Science, and Math

tasks. However, about 40 percent of adolescents could not read and comprehend specific factual information. What else can we conclude from 27 years of flat reading scores but that we practitioners need to re-examine our instructional practices?

Students in grades 3 and beyond need more and better reading instruction not only in language arts, but in all subjects. School districts need to develop ongoing, level-building professional study groups that keep all teachers abreast of and involved in the most effective teaching and learning practices (Birchak et al., 1998; Robb, 2000a; Santa, 1997).

Pause and Reflect on: Your Teaching Practices

Read the checklist of constructivist principles that follows, and reflect on your teaching style. How many of the seven principles do you see strongly playing out in your teaching? Would you say your current practice is closer to the transmission model or the constructivist model?

____ Talking and writing are part of reading to learn.

____ Learning, for students, is active and interactive.

____ Working together, students and teachers negotiate learning experiences and projects.

____ Reading nonfiction literature, magazines, and newspapers is part of content area learning.

____ Self-evaluation of learning experiences is vital for students and teachers.

____ Adjusting curriculum is critical to meeting students' diverse needs.

____ Offering opportunities for students to provide feedback to their teacher and one another improves student understanding and teacher instruction.

✎ Chapter 2 ✎

Responsive Teaching in a Three-Part Learning Framework

It takes a lot of courage simply to face the unknown every morning in a classroom of children, coming as they do from such varied and deeply troubled families.... For those of you who have decided to venture out into new ways of teaching, there are no charts for what to do.

—Katherine Paterson, from a speech at North Adams University, 1996

Responsive teaching requires an ever-increasing knowledge of how students read and write. In the context of this book, we will look at how teachers use their knowledge of the reading, vocabulary-building, and writing strategies to support learning in social studies, science and math. We will also see how they teach these strategies—and have students practice them—within what is called the three-part learning framework. The three-part framework supports students as they process information and consists of these phases: Getting Ready to Learn, During Learning, and After Learning (Alvermann & Phelps, 1998; Gillet & Temple, 2000; Tierney & Readence, 2000; Vacca & Vacca, 2000; Vaughan & Estes, 1986). But before we thoroughly investigate teaching within this three-part framework, I'll illustrate just what "responsive" teaching is.

For five years I coached members of the sixth-grade team at Johnson Williams Middle School in Clarke County, Virginia. Team members surrendered one planning period a week for professional study. We used a second planning period to consider how responsive teaching could improve the learning of content in all subjects (Robb 1993, 1994, 2000b).

Teachers shared stories about students who failed a test, started a fight, talked loudly, or didn't complete homework. I encouraged the group to offer suggestions for improving learning and addressing these problematic behaviors. At first, many teachers thought students should receive zeros for undone work, be sent to the principal's office, or receive an after school and/or in-school suspension for repeated disruptions. But as they talked further, the teachers began to look for reasons for the misbehavior: Perhaps it was because the student couldn't read the text or lacked prior knowledge of a topic. Heartened that they were entertaining new perspectives, I told them Kisha's story:

> *I met Kisha while coaching and team-teaching language arts and history with Cindy Hughes. Up until mid-February, this sixth grader completed most of her assignments. In response to Kisha's weak vocabulary and poor recall of information from the textbook, Cindy grouped Kisha with two other students and worked with them twice a week for 15 minutes. Cindy and I noticed that Kisha began to participate in discussions, and we were pleased. By the second week in February, however, Kisha shut down. She stopped participating. She turned in incomplete homework assignments or didn't do them at all. She yawned a great deal and barely spoke during paired discussions. Two to three days a week, by 9:00 A.M. Kisha complained of being hungry.*

When Kisha turned in a blank reading log, I suggested to Cindy that we invite Kisha to devote her next reading log entry to expressing why she hadn't been writing.

When I conferred with Kisha, I learned that her aunt was dying of cancer, and the family had no health insurance. Family members took turns sitting with the aunt, keeping her comfortable. They watched TV together. Sometimes, one of them read aloud parts of the newspaper.

After reporting Kisha's case to the principal, Cindy and I decided that it was important to meet with Kisha daily, offer emotional support, listen to her, and support her academic learning as much as we could. At one meeting,

Kisha's self-evaluation explaining why her reading log is incomplete.

Kisha told us that her aunt loved a good mystery. That day, I checked out several mysteries from the school library and said, "Try reading one of these out loud to your aunt."

When I finished this story, the teachers were silent for a few moments. "I never would have done what you did… I would have failed her," was one teacher's honest reaction. Then everyone talked at the same time, conversation flowing as quickly as water cascading down a mountain, and I knew I had nudged my colleagues to see their teaching in a new light.

Responsive Teaching Is Tuning-In to Students' Behaviors

These teachers came to see that middle grade and middle school students often beg for help and attention by acting in unacceptable ways. It's tough for them to verbalize feelings, so they misbehave by talking out of turn, using inappropriate language and, like Kisha, not doing their work. By listening to their stories without passing judgment, you can often gain their trust and eventually, though not in all cases, their cooperation. Once you and students have a trusting relationship, it's possible to start helping them succeed in school.

But it isn't an overnight transformation. As one teacher commented, "Now I see what responsive teaching really means. You could have lost Kisha. I know there are reasons for all the misbehaving, but it's hard to fight the old voices inside."

Fighting those old voices—those persistent and prideful thoughts that our teaching practice is fine, it's the students who are lacking—is what responsive teachers do daily. Responsive teaching requires us not to be overly invested in any teaching routine but to be ready to turn on a dime and, much like nimble dancers, try a new move when we sense that's what students need.

It's part tap dance, and part tenacity. Katherine Paterson observes that it's "sheer donkey endurance," and a desire to do better that drives writers to continue to work hard in the face of rejection and failure. Teachers, too, use that same, stubborn endurance to discover students' ever-changing needs and respond to them. There is no step-by-step plan to follow, but by combining an understanding of how children learn with feedback from colleagues and students, teachers can respond to and support students rather than react to and punish them.

Responsive Teaching Is a Problem-Solving Process

Responsive teachers recognize the unique background, experiences, and reading ability of each child. They also know that in any class there's a considerable variation in students' reading and learning levels. These teachers notice what students do and say and write, then rummage through their knowledge of reading and writing strategies, select the one they sense is the next best move for their students, and show them how to apply it (Goodman, 1985; Atwell, 1999). They work thoughtfully to discover where students are and slowly move them forward (Rudell & Unrau, 1997).

To maintain this "forward motion" for all students, responsive teachers set up their students to work in ways that are most productive. They balance the needs of those students who are at an independent level with those who need one-on-one or small-group support. Teachers like these constantly problem-solve to figure out how they can get to the students who need them most at a particular juncture in learning. For example, during a unit on explorers, sixth-grade history teacher Dick Bell recognized that most of the class had "gotten" the read-and-recall strategy and were restless to move on. So he organized these students to work in pairs on an information chart, which freed him up to support the three to four students who needed him to prompt and think-aloud how to differentiate between facts and author's point of view in a Jean Fritz book.

As you can see from this example, a responsive teacher tunes-in to each stu-dent's needs and recog-

Explorer	Dates	Country	Discovered	Problems	Changed Man's View of the World
Prince Henry	1421-1460	Portugeul	it wasn't the end of the world sent people who discovered Porto Santo	everybody was getting scared of the unknown	there was no unknown
Bartholomew Diaz	1487-1500	Portugeul	tip of Africa	storm on coast lost one ship	where Africa ended
Christopher Columbus	1492-1504	Spain	India's best route there and back	getting people to support him	
Pedro Alvanze Cabral	1500-1501	Portugal	Brazil	Brazil lost 6 ships	showed that Brazil was there made first Indian trading voyage
John Cabot	1497-1498	England	New Foundland	he disapeared	found New Found land
Amerigo Vespucci	1499-1501	Portugal	Brazil & America		added 3,000 miles map
Vasco Nunez De Balboa	1508-1513	Spain	Pacific Ocean	2 ships crashed	discovered new body of water
Ponce De Léon	1493-1513	Spain	Florida	shot with arrow & died	discovered new island or continent
Ferdinand Magellan	1519-1500	Spain	alot of, islands a route around the world	got killed lost ships like crazy	found an island strait to cross through south america

Jill, a seventh grader, completes an information chart about explorers she's studied.

nizes that these needs change as each student improves or moves to a new place in his/her learning. This recognition and response technique can help a teacher reach stu-dents and assist them as their needs change and develop.

Responsive Teaching Is Revising Teaching Practices

After the final meeting of a six-month professional study class on reading and writing strate-gies across the curriculum, a group of teachers and I chatted casually for a bit. Marty, a fifth-grade teacher lingered after the others departed. "Please, sit down," he told me, "I have some-thing to say. I took this class to earn re-certification credits. I planned on doing the mini-mum, getting out in May, and continuing to do what I've always done. I never thought I'd change." Marty's honesty startled me.

"What led you to change?" I asked, trying to sound casual.

"Several things," Marty replied. "At first I resented having to try these strategies in my class and then bring back student work to share with the others. But what really caught my attention were my students' reactions to the strategies. They loved talking and actually didn't mind note-taking, or collaborating to understand a concept, or even learning about the structure of their textbooks. And I found myself enjoying teaching science and math and history. Instead of droning on and then giving out worksheets, I was able to get my students to do the work—the research, the discussion, and I got to watch and listen.

"I learned from the others [teachers in the study group]. First, I thought, 'What could I learn from a third-grade or eighth-grade teacher?' Then, we all tried different things, and when I heard Janet talk about vocabulary mapping, I decided I could bring that to my class. And it worked."

"Wow!" I exclaimed, for that's exactly how I felt about Marty's outpouring. I encouraged Marty to share what he learned with his colleagues and invite them to visit his classroom. "You now hold the power to help others change," I added, as we walked toward the school's parking lot.

Change takes time. Change takes courage. Teachers who continually question, rethink, and revise their theories of how children learn are risk-takers and lifelong learners. They are communicators who share with colleagues. They are kid watchers and self-evaluators. They are responsive teachers.

Responsive Teaching in the Three-Part Learning Framework

As I mentioned earlier, responsive teaching requires a continually developing awareness of how students read and write. In this chapter, we will begin to look into how teachers use their knowledge of the reading, vocabulary-building, and writing strategies to support learning in social studies, science, and math within the three-part learning framework.

The three parts are often referred to as before reading, during reading, and after reading, and indeed many of the strategies taught within this framework relate to reading. However, within the context of this book, I prefer to use the term "learning" because in addition to reading texts, content subjects build on content area literacy experiences, such as conducting experiments, developing and testing hypotheses, solving math problems, and constructing models. Students benefit from instruction within each part of the model because they can:

Fifth-grade teacher Heather Campbell and I discuss possible interventions to support students

- Enlarge their prior knowledge before learning.
- Develop ways to monitor and improve their comprehension while learning.
- Apply new information to meaningful experiences after learning.

Getting Ready to Learn: An Overview

Preparing students to read, before the reading takes place, improves their comprehension because learners link new information and experiences to prior knowledge and events. This prior knowledge is stored in the brain in frameworks called *schema* or *schemata*. Researchers, such as Marvin Minsky (1975) and Richard Anderson (1984), developed the *schema theory,* which hypothesizes that a reader uses past knowledge and experiences and interacts with and constructs meaning from new information in written and spoken texts. For example, a student can use his knowledge of his train set and the tunnel he and his family have driven through to understand a new experience: an underground subway ride in New York City.

The schemata in our brain are never complete. Think of schemata as if they were a computer's hard drive, always ready to store newly acquired facts and ideas in huge folders. Learners make sense of written or spoken texts—or any new experience—by linking it to the schemata already "on file" that relate to the text or event.

The prior knowledge we bring to the text as we read goes far beyond the facts we've stored, of course. As Louise Rosenblatt (1978) posited decades ago, the reader uses his/her internalized culture, mood, personality, and memories, making each learner's experience with and understanding of a text unique.

Louise Rosenblatt: A Prophetic Thinker

In the first edition of *Literature as Exploration* (1938), Louise Rosenblatt observed how readers interact with texts. These observations greatly influenced schema theory. To Rosenblatt, a word on a page is simply a set of marks; it becomes a word, capable of carrying meaning, only when the reader links it to knowledge and personal experiences. Rosenblatt saw reading as a transaction. She notes:

> The reader's fund of relevant memories makes possible any reading at all. Without linkage with the past experiences and present interests of the reader, the work will not "come alive" for him, or rather he will not be prepared to bring it alive (Literature as Exploration, p. 26).

Forty years later, in *The Reader, the Text, the Poem* (1978), Rosenblatt explained that personal, aesthetic responses to literature precede literary analysis; these reactions might not be supported by the text. For Rosenblatt, the text is the source of valid interpretations of meaning.

Rosenblatt believes that a reader reads a text in two often intertwined ways: *aesthetic* and *efferent*. In an aesthetic reading, a person willingly submits to the alchemy of the author's imagery, metaphors, and language rhythms and to the reader's own experiences. An aesthetic reading is a personal response. In an efferent, or factual reading, a person concentrates on gaining information from the text, focusing his attention on gathering a body of facts or studying form and structure. Often, according to Rosenblatt, efferent readings mingle with aesthetic readings.

Teachers of social studies, science, and math can deepen students' engagement with nonfiction by modelling both aesthetic and efferent reactions to the text.

Getting Ready to Learn Instruction:
A Sixth Grade Example

Jim Stevens taught sixth-grade science for a decade before our paths crossed in a study group I led for history, science, and math teachers. The teachers wanted to learn more about integrating reading and writing into their curriculum. At our first meeting, Jim summarized his teaching methods in his journal:

> The textbook is always too hard for some kids, so I read the important parts with them. I do experiments to get them excited and sometimes this works. But my students seem bored.
>
> Some do okay on unit tests. Many do poorly. They don't study — and they don't remember information after the test. I'm here to try to do a better job with helping my students learn. I want my students to learn, but I also want them to feel that science is the best subject. I have never prepared my students to read a chapter, observe an experiment, collect leaves from school grounds, or watch a video clip.

Jim's candidness touched me. Others shared similar experiences. At our second class, I had teachers try a "getting-ready-to-learn" activity for themselves. I asked them to browse through the books and magazine articles about bats that I had provided. Next, I asked them to brainstorm what they knew about bats and then come together as a group to categorize this information on chart paper. Here's what Jim wrote:

> I had a great time with everyone. My list had six items. When we shared information, the list filled a large chart. I kept to science, but some had info about Dracula and vampires and that old TV show, The Adams Family.
>
> When we put everything in categories, we argued about where items should go. Then we agreed that an item could go under different headings as long as the person could give reasons. That's how bat sonar went under the heading "physical characteristics" and "finding food." I can't wait to do this with my class when we start our study of sound waves.

At the end of class, I encouraged them to try this "book browse, talk, and write" approach with their students before actually reading in the textbook. At our next meeting two weeks later, I asked teachers, "How did it go?"

Jim's hand shot up; his expression looked somber. "It didn't work," he said. "The kids

Some Key Getting-Ready-to-Learn Practices

When I visit schools, I have noticed that many teachers feel great pressure to cover content so students can pass state-mandated tests. To gain time, teachers often eliminate the pre-reading work students need to comprehend their textbooks. Resist this temptation. Use the following ideas to make the getting-ready-to-learn phase of your teaching a top priority.

- Activate students' prior knowledge of the topic you're introducing, including its vocabulary and concepts. Also preview with students the structure of the text you'll be using. Teach students how to brainstorm and categorize, use graphic organizers, such as maps and webs, and have them do free writes during which students record all they know about a topic in a short span of time. (See Chapter 4.)

- Assess students' prior knowledge to see if they are ready for the study. Listen to their discussions, circulate, and read their notebooks as they jot down ideas. This kid-watching will enable you to determine whether students know enough to connect to and comprehend their texts.

- Build students' background knowledge if necessary. When students demonstrate that they know little about a topic, find ways to enlarge their knowledge before plunging into the study. You can use photos, short passages from magazines and books, several read alouds, an experiment, film clips, or you might invite a guest speaker to share information.

- Establish a clear and meaningful purpose for reading. Research suggests that having a clear purpose for reading improves comprehension (Armbruster, 1991; Dowhower, 1999; Ogle, 1986; Blanton et al., 1990). Setting a purpose directs students as they read, by helping establish guidelines for how to approach the reading and what information is essential. At first, you can set the purposes, then later move into collaborations with students on purpose-setting. Finally, once your class has enough experience with this approach, you can turn setting purposes over to the students (see pages 117 and 121).

- Name the strategies that students will be practicing so they can deepen their knowledge of how specific strategies support learning (Dowhower, 1999).

didn't know much about sound waves." He held up a chart with only three words: music, waves, ears.

"What did you do?" I asked.

Jim grinned. He slowly unrolled a second chart packed with ideas and explained: "I checked out books about sound from the library. We browsed through them, talked about the pictures. I read some short passages. Students wanted to do this again the next class. So we did. They would have gotten very little out of the unit chapter if I started the old way."

Jim's experience with his students underscores Rosenblatt's insight: what readers bring to a text definitely affects their comprehension. The more we can "frontload" students with information before they read, the deeper their comprehension will be (Wilhelm, 2001). While reading, the learner stores this information and continually adjusts her knowledge as new understandings develop (Rosenblatt, 1983).

During-Learning Instruction: An Overview

Understanding is often described by researchers as the *click of comprehension,* the feeling of "Aha, I've got it!" These "clicks" let readers know that it's okay to continue (Garner, 1992; Gillet and Temple, 2000; Vaughan and Estes, 1986). The parts of the text that confuse are referred to as *clunks*.

When my reading gets derailed, I know that I must reread these pages differently. For example, if I read a few pages of a textbook and realize I haven't absorbed much information, I might reread the headings and captions to get the gist, and study the charts and graphs and think about the data they

TEACHER RESOURCES

PROFESSIONAL BOOKS WITH GETTING-READY-TO-LEARN STRATEGIES

These research-based books contain a variety of strategies that use talking, thinking, and writing to preteach vocabulary and concepts and to activate students' prior knowledge.

Teaching Vocabulary in All Classrooms by Camille Blachawicz and Peter Fisher, Englewood Cliffs, NJ: Merrill, 1996.

Teaching Vocabulary to Improve Reading Comprehension by William E. Nagy, Urbana, IL: National Council of Teachers of English, 1988.

Prereading Activities for Content Area Reading and Learning, 3rd edition, by John E. Readence, David W. Moore, and Robert J. Rickelman, Newark DE: International Reading Association, 2000.

Easy Mini-Lessons for Building Vocabulary, by Laura Robb, New York: Scholastic, 1999. Strategies to support students' learning.

present. Then I would slowly read one section at a time, retelling after reading to make sure that I understand enough to recall many facts and details.

Like all good readers, I am using metacognition—monitoring what I read so I know what I understand and what confuses me, and calling forth strategies to keep my reading on track. Teaching students these self-monitoring strategies is the main thrust of during-learning instruction. These strategies help students to recognize when their understanding is faltering; to identify what in the text is confusing, and to choose the mental moves (such as rereading) that will help them make sense of the passage (Alvermann and Phelps, 1998; Dowhower, 1999; Keene and Zimmerman, 1997; Pearson et al., 1992; Robb, 2000a; Tierney and Readence, 2000; Vacca and Vacca, 2000; Vaughan and Estes, 1986).

The key is to teach these strategies in such a way that students can easily apply them to a text and not feel bogged down by them. We will explore each of these strategies in more depth in Chapter 4; here, let's take a look at how one teacher recognized the need to provide explicit during-learning strategy instruction for a student.

During-Learning Instruction:
A Seventh-Grade Example

It's the second week of school, and Mrs. Hilton circulates around the room, watching her seventh graders to see who can self-monitor their comprehension and who needs assistance. She asks students to complete parts of a study map that shows the causes of the French Revolution. In the center, students place the words "French Revolution." Along the spokes that branch out from the center of this graphic organizer, students note a cause and details that relate to it (see page 43).

Irene dutifully reads the section on the French Revolution in her social studies textbook. But she does not work on the map. "I'm done," she announces and takes out a small, rectangular mirror to reapply pink gloss to her lips.

"Let me help you start your map," Mrs. Hilton gently suggests.

"I'll do my map at home," Irene tells her. "It's easy." Mrs. Hilton moves on, for several students have hands raised. She mentally notes to check Irene's work tomorrow.

Irene does not have her map completed the next day. When the teacher asks Irene why she hasn't completed her map, Irene shrugs her shoulders and says, "I left my book at school." During a short mini-conference with Irene, Mrs. Hilton discovers that Irene can read the words, but has no recall of what she read. That's why she was unable to complete the study map, Mrs. Hilton thinks. What Irene didn't comprehend, she could not write about. Yet Irene was unaware that not remembering resulted in her inability to complete the map. "I read it," Irene repeated many times. "It was just too much stuff to remember." Mrs. Hilton assured Irene that she believed the reading had been completed. She worked closely with Irene, having her read several sentences, retell them, reread, if necessary, and complete parts of the map. (See pages 235–236 for guidelines on working independently.)

Classed Society
- 3 estates: clergy, nobles, middle & lower classes
- Nobles - rich, big houses, own land
- Middle Class - worked for money
- Clergy - owned 10% of land
- peasent farmers - poorest about 80% of people

French Revolution CAUSES
✓ vive la France!

Empty Treasury
- No money in treasury
- France in debt from helping colonists in American Revolution
- 3rd estate says they are National Assembely and they represent the French people.
- People hungry - 1788 grain harvest was bad
- tennis court oath - 3rd estate - not leave untill France had a constitution.

Taxes Unfair
- riches - clergy & nobles paid NO taxes.
- taxes paid by 3rd estate - they didn't have enough money. peasents paid half they earned in taxes.
- Middle class wanted to change tax system. wanted a revolution.

King's Power
- middle class questioned divine Right to rule middle class said government
- is an agreement thats ruler and people share
- Louis XVI - apsolute power

Some Key During-Learning Practices

- Invest in teaching students to self-monitor their learning. Like Irene, many students are unable to self-monitor their reading and pinpoint the passages and words that confuse. In their minds, they "did the work," or as one eighth grader put it to me, "What's the big fuss? I read the pages. That's what you told me to do." In essence, they aren't even aware that they're missing anything.

    Speaking more generally, we need to teach students how to monitor their learning, regardless of the content area. Too often, kids speed through a math problem or a science experiment without pausing to evaluate, observe, or check their work. To combat this, I provide my students with what I call "process checks."

Post these on chart paper for students to refer to. Encourage them to add to the list throughout the year.

Process Checks

— Did I copy my homework assignment?

— Have I noted my observations?

— Did I check and note the progress of my experiment?

— Can I recall all the details?

— Does my answer relate to the question?

— Have I elaborated each idea?

— Does my answer make sense?

— Did I give the number of examples that were required?

— Do I understand new words/concepts?

— Is my actual answer close to my estimate?

— Did I read and follow directions?

- Use the terms of metacognition with students. In addition to defining and using "process checks," I share many other terms with my students, such as self-monitoring strategies, think-alouds, and fix-it strategies. For students to think, talk, and write about their learning process, they need the language that describes it. Once students know this vocabulary, it literally helps them think in new ways and have meaningful conversations with their peers and teachers.

- Model each self-monitoring strategy in strategy lessons. Unless you demonstrate how you use a reading strategy—talk aloud your thinking process—all of the terms you share will be pretty meaningless to students. In Chapters 5 and 7, you'll find many examples of strategy lessons to help you learn how to model for kids and then guide them to use the strategies independently. Here is a basic overview of this kind of strategic teaching, as it applies to instilling metacognitive behavior:

1. Invite students to read short chunks of text silently.

2. Clearly identify the strategy that students will practice.

3. Using this chunk of text, model for students how to self-monitor what they understand, and what confuses them, through strategies such as questioning and summarizing, and by checking to see if an answer is logical.

4. Model fix-it strategies that will help them repair their comprehension when it flags. These strategies include rereading, connecting to what you know, using clues in

charts, diagrams, and pictures, in-the-head think-alouds, estimating, and note-taking strategies (see Chapters 5 and 6).

5. Organize small-group and whole-group discussions.

6. Repeat steps 1 to 5 as students read each new section of a text.

7. Have students practice self-monitoring for 8 to 10 minutes a day for a week or two. Continue if students need more practice.

8. In brief meetings, support students who require one-on-one help.

- Teach students to think with the facts. In the midst of this information age, it's crucial for us teachers to remember that our goal is not to impart information, but to help students to "work" the facts, to think through them, assess them, question them, synthesize them, apply them. The more students monitor their reading to determine what they do and do not understand, the better equipped they are to do this. As strategic readers, they can access and use information in texts to think, analyze, and connect (Alvermann and Phelps; 1998; Harvey, 1998; Pearson, 2001; Robinson, 2001; Vaughan and Estes, 1986; Vacca and Vacca, 2000).

Let's look at how this played out in Dick Bell's class. Dick had previously modelled for his students how to make connections, and in a later lesson he emphasized this strategy of thinking with the facts. His students responded, making rich comparisons between the exploration of the Americas to the Westward Movement, and to astronauts exploring the moon and living on the Meir space station. Then Dick had them work in groups to discuss common personality traits of present and past explorers.

Sixth grader Winston pointed out that Prince Henry the Navigator never gave up his dream of sailing around the tip of Africa and discovering what Africa was like. "People back then said Prince Henry was spending too much money on his expeditions. They [people] complain today about the billions poured into the space program," Winston said. "But complaints by people living during Prince Henry's time never bothered him [Prince Henry]."

Johanna pointed out how persistent Prince Henry was. "It was like he was wearing horse blinders. He knew what he wanted and he stuck to it. I think that's a quality all explorers have."

"Yeah," Clint agreed. "And they have to not be afraid of unknown things like space and never-seen oceans. Maybe it's like having a strong faith in your idea and it keeps you going and believing."

Once the students had the facts and details, an energy, born of the thrill of connecting and thinking with information, infused their discussions. Students were able to move from the minutiae of facts to broad understandings of what these facts imply about the people who made—and make—the history, science, and math content they study.

At the end of class, Tim turned to Winston and said, "Boy, that was fun." Tim's words celebrated the pleasure all students felt that day as they used what they had learned to connect the past with their world.

After-Learning Instruction: An Overview

I board an airplane in Washington-Dulles Airport and settle in for the seven-hour flight to San Jose, California. My briefcase brims with reading materials: a book on struggling readers, four professional journals, two thick mysteries and three young adult novels. Enough to keep me occupied now and on the flight home. When I read professional materials, I keep a pencil and sticky notes nearby, for I'm always jotting notes on these and sticking them to pages as reminders for me to return and reread. Frequently, I reread sections or slow my pace down to make sure I absorb the details.

When I pull out a mystery, I stuff the sticky notes and pencil in my briefcase, press the metal button that angles my seat into a relaxed position, and prepare to be entertained by one of my favorite genres. A month later, if someone asks me to tell them about the book, I'll recall very little. Not because I'm a poor reader, but because I did not take the time to think about the plot, clues, and characters, to talk about it to a friend or my husband, to revisit favorite parts. (Moreover, my purpose was sheer entertainment.) To learn new information, simply reading a text once is not enough. Yet it's what students like Angel do all the time.

Angel is a seventh grader who fails many tests in science and history and occasionally scores a "D." During a conference, I asked Angel to tell me how he learns and prepares for tests and quizzes. "I read the pages, but I hardly remember anything. [Before a test] I leaf through the chapter and try to remember stuff."

"Do you do anything else?" I ask.

"Yeah," he says. "I pray that I'll pass. But most of the stuff on the tests—it's like I never heard of it even though I read the chapter."

"Do you take notes in class?" I ask.

"No. I don't write fast enough, so I listen. But then I get bored. And my mind goes to soccer."

Relying on a single reading, without follow-up experiences that invite students to return to the text to gather information and review important details, puts many students in Angel's situation. On the other hand, engaging students in after-study experiences, such as paired or small-group discussions, helps students learn and recall information (see Chapters 6 and 9).

Writing summaries, taking notes, or placing details in a graphic organizer also helps students retain information. When students cannot write about what they know and have learned from a text, an experiment, or constructions, such as building a kite or polygons, they have not yet made the new information their own (Atwell 1987,1999; Graves, 1983; Murray, 1984). A student's inability to write about her learning is a red flag. When you see this, you need to meet with the child to discover why. Reasons stu-

- "I never read the chapter."
- "I can't read this; it's too hard."
- "I left my book at school."
- "I thought it was due tomorrow."
- "It's on my desk. I forgot it."

- "I thought I packed it, but I guess I didn't."
- "Left it on the bus."
- "It's in my locker. I'll bring it at lunch." (Most never bring it that day.)

dents might offer include:

We've all heard comments like these, and it's easy to toss them off as excuses. Instead, try to see them as calls for help. Invite students to meet with you one-on-one, and draw them out by asking questions and listening hard. Offer support and extra-help sessions during lunch, recess, before the school day starts, or after school.

The after-learning part of the framework offers teachers many assessment opportunities to determine those who can move on or extend their knowledge and those who continue to need extra help (Alvermann and Phelps, 1998; Gillet and Temple, 2000; Moffett, 1981, 1983; Tierney and Readence, 2000; Robb, 2000a; Vacca and Vacca, 2000). Reflection invites learners to contemplate new information and experiences, clarify and use concepts, connect them to other ideas, and claim, "This new information is mine."

After-Learning Instruction: A Sixth-Grade Example

After Charlie flunked three science quizzes, his teacher asked me to help him. I negotiated times with Charlie and his father, and agreed to work three mornings a week before school started. Charlie's father dropped him off at Johnson Williams at 7:30 A.M. During those sessions, I showed Charlie how to use his textbook structure to take notes after reading a section (see pages 308–311) and how to prepare for tests. On his next vocabulary quiz, Charlie scored a 78—quite an improvement on the 42 he got on his last quiz. I praised Charlie, pointed out what he had done to improve, and let him know that with additional practice, he could ace a test. Three weeks later, Charlie scored 86 on a unit test. "I did it! I did it!" he shouted, brandishing the papers in my face as he ran up to me in the hallway. The indifferent, discouraged sixth grader had been transformed into an engaged learner in a relatively short period of time.

Some Key After-Learning Practices

There are dozens of Charlies out there who can do the work, if we give them the additional emotional and academic support they need. As responsive teachers, we need to find a way to get that help for each one of these students.

And beyond these students, all our students need rich after-learning experiences to cement their understandings. Here are some practices that encourage reflection, comprehension, recall, and analytical thought.

1. **Organize discussions** so students clarify new information and deepen understandings.
2. **Reserve time for students to write** the highlights of their discussions in a learning log or journal.
3. **Show students how oral presentations work** and ask pairs or groups to give oral talks on trade books that relate to their studies and to use drama or to recreate in a simulation an historical event.
4. **Have students complete experiments and projects** that invite them to use and apply their learning.
5. **Teach students several note-taking strategies.** Jotting down key points helps students remember material and is a great resource for test preparation.
6. **Ask students to use new information to craft news articles,** diary entries, or information cards for younger students.
7. **Engage students in self-evaluation** that includes debriefings of how a strategy worked and benefited them, and evaluations of oral presentations and written work.

For the rest of the year, I tutored Charlie, teaching him reading and study strategies to apply in all content areas. By May, as Charlie continued to be successful, we were meeting only twice a week.

A Final Word: Give It Time

The time you reserve for talking and writing after learning will differ with each topic. Throughout the three-part learning framework, remember to take your cues from the students. They'll signal you, through their work and their behavior, when you are moving too fast. In general, they need time to absorb the facts and the new vocabulary of the topics they encounter. Only then can they use this knowledge to make connections to self, community, and world issues, and to solve problems.

Heather Campbell supports a fifth-grade student by practicing read/pause/summarize.

Now that you have an overview of each part of the three-part framework, let's look at how one teacher makes it come alive.

Three-Part Learning Framework in Action: Grade 3 History

At Powhatan School, where I teach, students get their first history textbook in third grade. They study Colonial America, the settling of Jamestown, and the French and Indian and Revolutionary Wars. Their teacher, Nancy Roche, says, "Teaching history is hard because the children have so little background information—the textbook is really tough going for them." Nancy presented many strategy lessons to her students (see pages 298–301) on the structure of their history textbook. When she came to me for help in improving her history lessons, she told me she had done a lot of "telling" about the text, and had a hunch that was why her students didn't seem too engaged with these lessons. And so we planned three 45-minute lessons on the section about the French and Indian War, recording our ideas on a Unit Planning Guide (see page 55).

Materials: *Virginia USA,* Silver Burdett and Ginn, 1997, pages 186-191.

Note: Because these were third graders, Nancy and I broke the six pages of text into two lessons. We taught each part using the three-part framework.

Lesson 1
Getting Ready to Learn
(20–30 minutes)

1. I invited students to study a map that showed the land and forts that the French owned and the land Virginia claimed. Next, the children looked at two maps that compared land controlled by the British, French, and Spanish in 1700 and in 1763. The last two maps showed how much land France had lost and England had gained as a result of their war. Studying the maps helped the children verbalize these ideas:

- England knew our land was big—"vast" and they wanted it.
- France wanted to keep the land it had and probably wanted more.

2. Nancy introduced and pre-taught these new words: *surveyor, tax.*

3. I posed a "concept question," which invites students to think beyond the issues in a text and make connections to their world. I printed the question on large chart paper: "Why do countries want land?" Students copied the question in their journals, groups discussed it for about five minutes, then jotted down all they recalled.

Then students shared ideas, and I recorded them on the chart. When students made general statements such as, "They get more power," I encouraged them to give specific examples, which appear on the chart. They were able to make these connections orally, though not in their writing.

Why do countries want land?

• Gives them more power. They get bigger—have more land to live on.

• Have more trees to build ships, houses, forts, weapons.

• More people — have more soldiers.

• More farmers mean more crops to sell to other countries — more food for soldiers.

148 avid   April

why do countries want land?

The Countries want land is because they can get more powerful get more welthry from gold tobacco, lumber and new crops, and fur

David explains why land is important to countries.

• ~~Get wealthy: grow tobacco, mine metals, trap~~
  ~~beavers for fur, have lumber.~~
• ~~Sell land and get more money for it.~~

During Learning (15 minutes)

Purpose for Reading pages 186–188: Why did Virginia's Governor Dinwiddie send a message to the French Commander, Legardeur?

After reading, students used the "purpose" stated above as a springboard for discussion. Here are some ideas that students shared:

• *Jay:* England wanted all the land in the Ohio Valley. It would make them rich and powerful.

• *Elizabeth:* England wanted to take the fur trade from France.

• *Grace:* The Indians liked the French better because the French left the land alone and didn't clear it like the English.

• *Conner:* The English believed the land the French claimed belonged to England.

For homework that night, Nancy invited the children to write the letter that Governor Dinwiddie might have written to the French.

After Learning (45 minutes)

1. Students shared their letters. As Nancy and I listened, we realized the children had no concept of diplomacy. Why should they? Their letters were fiercely patriot-

Dec. 1753

Dear Commander Legardeur,
This land belongs to the English. We settled here first. Get off this soil or we will attack. If you will please leave your forts, you can leave the country unharmed. I sent my faithful soldier George Washington to deliver this message.
                    Governor Dinwiddie

A third grader writes to French General Legardeur.

A third grader, Eliza, dramatizes writing a letter to the French.

ic and passionate.

2. As students volunteered to read their letters, we celebrated the way they had integrated new information.

3. Then I divided the class into two groups: the English and the French. Those role-playing the French discussed how they felt about the letters. Their comments showed that the French were angry. Students distilled their ideas into these notes:

> *English:* Get off our land.
> *French:* Make me. We were here first.
> *Result:* War

4. During the heated discussions, Nancy placed these words on chart paper: *compromise, treaty, alliance.* Students shared what they knew about each word. It was interesting that the students' definition for alliance came from a computer game some of them played, a game where group members form an alliance and promise not to fight with each other. Next to each word, Nancy printed the students' input.

---

compromise:
English could pay the French.
English could give French other land.
They could share the land.

treaty:
An agreement. England and France could agree on things.

alliance:
England and France could work together like in the computer game, "1602."

Lesson 2
Getting Ready to Learn
(pages 189-191, 10 minutes)

The third graders studied the picture of Washington and his soldiers that appeared on page 188. They discussed the kinds of weapons soldiers used, their transportation, and uniforms. Finn observed, "With those red coats, the French and Indians would see them from miles away."

52   *Teaching Reading in Social Studies, Science, and Math*

Then we returned to the maps that showed land ownership of North America in 1700 and 1763. Students predicted that the English won the war because they ended up with the most land.

During Learning (30 minutes)

1. I presented a 10-minute strategy lesson on "Jigsaw," (see pages 264–266).

- Each one of three groups was responsible for becoming experts on a particular section of text.
- Groups reread, discussed, and planned their presentations.
- Groups taught their sections to the class.
- The class raised questions and added information after each presentation.

2. Nancy organized the nineteen students into three groups and gave them time to read pages and prepare their sections from the textbook.

After Learning (45 minutes)

Each group chose a leader to present the information. Members added ideas, and those who listened asked questions. Nancy took notes on chart paper. Here is a transcription from my notes of one group's presentation and the discussion it stimulated.

Part D: General Braddock, pp. 189–190

DAVID: This tells about the way both sides fought. The English wore red coats. Washington wanted to fight like the French and Indians, but Braddock wouldn't let him.

MATTHEW: Braddock was killed.

GRACE: Washington got wounded.

Class Questions and Discussion:

JOSEPH: Didn't the British fight in the open?

MATTHEW: Yeah. They were easy to spot and kill. But Braddock wouldn't change.

ELIZA: I wouldn't listen to Braddock if I was Washington.

CONNER: You have to. Braddock was higher than Washington.

GRANT: The Indians knew how to fight by hiding.

MADELINE: That's why they won the first two battles.

CONNER: If you hide, you can fight better 'cause no one can see you but you can see them.

MATTHEW: With red coats you were sure to get killed.

JAY: But the English won the war. And France lost most of its land.

Evaluation of the Lessons by Nancy Roche and Laura Robb

Though students used more time than Nancy usually allotted to cover six pages, *they* did the work. Nancy noted that when her students read without the purpose that "Jigsaw" provided, they did not remember much. The strategy also required the children to reread their sections many times. And of course, it helped to have small sections to teach. We agreed that students read the maps well and were able to draw many important conclusions from these. Nancy liked the concept question because it focused students on a key issue for the English and French, an issue countries still wrestle with today.

I added our comments to the unit planning sheet that Nancy and I completed together (see below).

Using a Unit-Planning Guide

Before plunging into a four- to eight-week unit of study in math, science, or social studies, take 10 to 15 minutes to organize your teaching ideas into the three-part model. The unit-planning guide works for reading, research, experiments, a math topic, construction projects, and making posters. You should store these in a file folder or a 3-ring binder. Refer to them and any adjustments you made when you begin planning for each new group of students.

This form gives you a place to record your pre-thinking and allows you to note adjustments and changes as the unit study proceeds. You can use information on this form to plan strategy lessons.

Teacher's Name *Nancy Roche & Laura Robb* Date _____

Subject and Topic *French & Indian War* Grade *3*

Getting Students Ready For The Study

Experiences: *map - study & discuss*
Preteach: surveyor, tax
Concept Question: Why do countries want land?
discuss & write in journal.

Adjustments:
more time to build knowledge of what a tax is. more time to discuss concept question and write.

During the Study

Experiences: *Read pages 186-88 & discuss*
Read pages 188-191 & discuss
Divide sections among groups - each present - Jigsaw

Adjustments:
Class loved Jigsaw - wanted more time to make their presentations more creative

After The Study

Experiences: *Write letters to French General.*
Read to class - volunteers only

Adjustments: *Time was always an issue - it helps to slow down and let children absorb new material and reflect on it.*

Plans for a study of the French and Indian War with third graders.

Teaching Reading in Social Studies, Science, and Math

Unit Planning Guide

Teacher's Name _____   Date _____

Subject and Topic _____   Grade _____

Getting Students Ready for the Study

Experiences:

Adjustments:

During the Study

Experiences:

Adjustments:

After the Study

Experiences:

Adjustments:

The Role of Strategy Lessons in Content Subjects

Integrating reading and writing strategies into your teaching of science, social studies and math prepares students to study new information, helps them learn new vocabulary, improves students' comprehension of textbooks and trade books, and enables students to learn and think with new ideas, concepts, and facts.

The strategy lesson is the vehicle for modelling these strategies. The lesson improves reading and supports students as they study a unit or theme. (Pearson et al., 1992; Harvey, 1998; Keene and Zimmermann, 1997; Tierney and Readence, 2000; Robb, 2000a). Short and focused, these lessons allow you to model, in 5 to 15 minutes, the content area strategies listed on page 58.

Once you've made the positive and powerful decision to integrate reading and writing into your subject, the strategy lessons you present will support students in these ways:

- Your demonstrations will model *how* to learn the material.
- Your demonstrations will *present content* in a manner that is accessible to students.

  These demonstrations can help students learn from textbooks, trade books, magazines, and discussions.

About the Strategy Lessons in This Book

I've framed the strategy lessons in this book—which begin in the next chapter—so that you can manage them within the time limitations of a 40- to 45-minute period. In later chapters, you'll explore research-based reading and writing strategies, such as paired reading and questioning, pre-teaching concepts, and finding the main idea, that are easy to present in short periods and are equally effective in block schedules where teachers have 90-minute classes. In self-contained classrooms of grades 3, 4, and 5, scheduling is more flexible, and teachers can add extra time to a lesson or return to the lesson later in the day, and support students who struggle.

I want to stress that the lessons aren't meant to take over your class time! They're meant to be brief, so that you'll still have most of your class period for students to do math problems, read texts, research, take notes, discuss material, complete quizzes, conduct experiments, and so forth.

Following many of the strategy lessons, I've included "Strategy Snapshots," in which I describe the strategy at work in a specific classroom. As you will see from these examples, the most effective application of these strategies occurs when teachers invite students to use the knowledge they have absorbed to "do" something—to involve themselves actively in history, science and math (Parker, 2001).

Tips for Planning the Lessons

Deciding which strategies to present and when can be daunting. To begin, I suggest that you choose two to three strategies from each part of the learning framework and present these until students demonstrate that they can apply the strategy to their reading and learning experiences.

The content area teachers I coach might present and then review a strategy lesson every day for one or two weeks. Other times, they offer a demonstration once or twice a week. Be flexible about the number of strategy lessons and let the material, the unit plan, and students' responses to the demonstrations help you decide how many to present.

Whole-class presentations: Sometimes, it makes sense to present strategy lessons to the entire class, especially when your observations tell you that just about everyone will struggle with the learning because they need one or more of the following:

- more background knowledge (Chapter 4);
- instruction on how a strategy works and supports reading and recall (Chapters 3-6);
- concept building (pp. 66–74);
- pre-teaching of tough vocabulary (pp. 197–208);
- study skills and test-taking practice (pp 160–161);
- organizational and time management skills (pp. 243–244).

The list of strategies that follows can help you plan and

THREE KINDS OF STRATEGY LESSONS

Planned Strategy Lessons: Prepare and think through the lesson before presenting it. Record the lesson on chart paper or an overhead transparency so you can reuse it for review. I prefer chart paper, since a chart can be visible for students' reference as they practice in class.

Review Strategy Lessons: Before you wrap-up a study, if some students have not learned to apply a strategy, re-teach parts of the lesson that still confuse students.

Peer-Led Strategy Lessons: Students can coach one another and review in pairs or small groups.

prepare lessons that respond to the needs of your students. One by one, isolate a strategy and show students how it works. However, keep in mind that once students understand this and other strategies, they will naturally choose and integrate those strategies they need to comprehend a text.

A List of Strategies in the Three-Part Framework

Strategies to Use Before Learning

These activate prior knowledge and experiences.

- Think Aloud
- Browse Through Texts
- Brainstorm/Categorize
- Use Graphic Organizers

- Pose Questions
- Pre-teach Vocabulary, Concepts
- Preview and Analyze

- K-W-H: What Do I Know? What Do I Want to Know? How Will I Find Out?

Strategies to Use During Learning

These enable students to learn information, self-monitor understanding, recall information, and start to learn new vocabulary.

- Visualize
- Use Graphic Organizers
- Take Notes
- Pose Questions

- Think Aloud
- Use Context Clues
- Identify Confusing Parts
- Summarize

- Retell
- Reread
- Infer
- Make Personal Connections

Strategies to Use After Learning

These foster connections to other texts and issues and deepen students' comprehension of new material and experiences.

- Skim
- Reread
- Think Aloud
- Pose Questions
- Connections: Other Texts, Self, Community and World Issues

- Visualize and Other Sensory Responses
- Reflect Through Talking, Writing, Drawing, Music, and Movement
- Drama
- Note taking

- Use Graphic Organizers
- Infer: Compare/Contrast, Cause/Effect, Main Ideas
- Summarize
- Retell
- Synthesize
- Self-evaluate

Following your lesson, reserve time for students to practice the strategy you've demonstrated using their textbook or a trade book they're reading. This also gives you an opportunity to observe who "gets it" and who needs more support.

The Role of Writing and Thinking in Content Learning

Writing in the content areas is embedded within many of the strategy lessons and ideas in this book, and you'll find samples of student writing throughout, but honestly, it deserves a book of its own. Writing is profoundly vital to effective content area teaching, so as you progress through this book, be sure to give the writing strategies full weight.

Writing in the content areas is not a separate, optional activity; it is integral to the thinking process in social studies, science, and math. Donald Murray in *Write to Learn* (1984) says that writing is "the most disciplined form of thinking." Like discussing, writing is a way of processing and remembering information and key elements of strategy lessons. By writing, learners transform printed or oral texts, science experiments, historical events, observations, and math problems into their own language to make meaning with new information. That's why scientists, historians, and mathematicians take meticulous notes to form hypotheses, document observations, conduct experiments, and solve problems. Writing for them is much more than data collection; it is exploring, revising, and thinking on paper. Writing helps them learn facts, work out what the facts mean, and use facts to make new discoveries and refine old theories.

TEACHER RESOURCES

TAKE RESPONSIVE TEACHING FURTHER

For more subject-specific strategies, check out these resources:

Drama for Learning by Dorothy Heathcote and Gavin Bolton, Portsmouth, NH: Heinemann, 1995.

Exploring Values Through Literature, Multimedia, and Literacy Events: Making Connections edited by Patricia R. Schmidt and Ann W. Pailliotet, Newark, DE: IRA.

Math Is a Language, Too: Talking and Writing in the Mathematics Classroom, NCTE & NCTM, 2000.

Science Workshop edited by Wendy Saul et al., Portsmouth, NH: Heinemann, 1993.

Seeking History: Teaching with Primary Sources in Grades 4-6 by Monica Edinger, Portsmouth, NH: Heinemann, 2000.

Social Studies in Elementary Education by Walter Parker, Englewood Cliffs, NJ: Merrill, 2001.

Thinking Like Mathematicians: Putting the NCTM Standards into Practice by Thomas Rowan and Barbara Bourne, Portsmouth, NH: Heinemann, 2001.

Journals: A Place to Think on Paper

The point of having a writing journal is to help students monitor their understanding of learning strategies, to collect data, then reread and analyze the findings in order to discover what they mean or how they can be used. The data collected can come from reading textbooks, trade books, magazines, or by making observations, talking to an expert, conducting an experiment or exploring several ways to solve a math or science problem, trying to understand an historical event, even by viewing a movie or television program, or using the Internet.

Whether you call these writing books journals or learning logs, their function is the same—giving students a place where they can note down questions, explore ideas, draw conclusions about their learning, self-evaluate, and keep a record of their thinking.

Tips for Reading and Grading Journals

Reading students' journals can be overwhelming, especially for middle school teachers who have five classes, each with twenty to thirty students. I remember the days when I brought a carload of journals home each weekend. I became more and more resentful each time my husband and children went hiking, to a movie, or visited a museum, and I sat at the dining room table reading a mountain of student work. Experience taught me to modify the way I read journals. Here are my suggestions:

- Over one week's time, collect the journals in two classes if you teach middle school. Take a few home each night, or every other night, over a period of weeks.
- If you teach a self-contained classroom, read four to five a day.
- Review journals after the first four to six weeks of school. After that, review them every eight weeks. If your classes are overcrowded, try to read the journals of students who struggle first so you can work in time to offer support.

Teaching Reading in Social Studies, Science, and Math

- Circulate and read while the students are writing in class; you'll quickly pinpoint students who need to work with you. Daily observations can help prevent tackling a huge problem later on, including staring at a series of blank or near blank pages at the end of six weeks.
- Ask students to select a page they want you to read.
- Occasionally select pages at random to read.
- Write your responses on a sticky note. The sticky note will mark the start of the new section I must review, and will remind me of some of the observations I made last time. Since I insist that students write the topic, their name, and the date each day, I look for accurate headings when I read journals. Dates and titles enable me to refer students to a journal page students need to review or make connections to new data.
- Make your responses short and positive. Praise what students did well. Phrase a concern as a question; questions are less abrasive than statements and extend an invitation for students to think about your concern.

I suggest that you not correct spelling and punctuation in these journals, for this writing represents students' first-draft thinking. Lots of corrections inhibit students from writing and elaborating on their thoughts. "He grades everything. There's no slack," a sixth grader said of his science teacher. "I write short sentences and as little as I can get away with. The less that's on paper, the less chance for making mistakes." Peer and teacher editing are best reserved for writing that will be revised and published. Instead, focus here on the ideas and content; and praise these in your responses.

Pause and Reflect on: Responsive Teaching

Responsive teachers tune into their students' learning process in order to celebrate progress, decide what strategies to teach, and to discover which students need additional support. Refer to the checklist that follows to see how many of these practices you employ.

_____ I watch one or two students each class to get a better understanding of how they are learning.

_____ I hold mini-conferences with students to discover strengths and needs.

_____ I involve students in writing to understand and learn.

_____ I read a sampling of students' journals.

_____ I encourage students to raise questions for discussion and to clarify information.

_____ I accept the differences among students and try to understand the unique needs of each one.

_____ I build learning around the three-part model.

_____ I develop strategic learners by presenting strategy-lessons before, during, and after learning.

_____ I present strategy lessons that respond to the specific needs students reveal.

∾ Chapter 3 ∾

Strategies That Span the Three-Part Framework

Strategies refer to conscious and flexible plans that readers apply and adapt to particular texts and tasks. The strategies readers use change when reading different kinds of text or when reading for different purposes.

—Pearson, Roehler, Dole, and Duffy

At a school I visited in Virginia, scores in reading comprehension over a period of three years had been poor. To deal with this problem, one instructor devised a way to teach comprehension in seven steps. She presented this approach to me and to her colleagues one day, leading us through a sample lesson with her students. The seven steps she modelled are:

1. Put a rectangle around the title.
2. Outline the shape of the paragraphs on the left hand side.
3. Number the paragraphs.
4. Read. Then circle the key words in each paragraph.
5. Read the questions.
6. Mark out the two answers that won't work.
7. Check the correct answer.

The teacher had students apply the steps to a reading passage. The passage was from a basal unit test. Even students who had struggled with reading grade-level material checked the right answers. Her colleagues were impressed and eager to adopt the formula. I wrestled mightily with my inner voice to censor my desire to say, "That's not teaching comprehension. That's teaching to a test format."

I know this teacher and her colleagues worked long hours; I know that they wanted their students to succeed; I know that they feared another year of poor scores because their school's scores would not meet state standards. This seven-step magic bullet was the direct result of high-stakes testing. It had little to do with teaching comprehension strategies because there was no invitation to students to think about the text deeply—to consider the title, look at the question-answer structure of the passage which spotlighted the main idea, and read the questions before reading the selection. Moreover, not every piece of reading is regimentally structured to respond to a formula—that's the danger of such formulas. Indeed, the best writing for children, whether fiction or non-fiction, is created by authors who write beautifully but who are not necessarily "education" writers. The reading and writing strategies we will explore in this and the next three chapters are those students can use with any text and that can be applied before, during, and after reading.

First, we will focus on four strategies: Building Concepts; Posing Questions; Observing; and the K-W-H-L Strategy (for What Do I Know? What Do I Want to Know? How Will I Find Out? and What Have I Learned?) All four strategies are easy to

Teaching Reading in Social Studies, Science, and Math

implement and support these content goals because they teach students to:

- Understand new concepts;
- Pose questions that self-monitor learning;
- Pose questions that reflect and deepen engagement with texts;
- Reflect on and recall what they have learned;
- Actively learn content by applying what they have learned to projects, drama, experiments, and writing.

Tips for Presenting Productive Strategy Lessons

When developing strategy lessons, try these suggestions:

- Name the strategy, then show and explain why it's important and how it can help comprehension and recall.
- Make clear the purpose for accessing and using each strategy.
- Make the strategy concrete by thinking your concerns and solutions out loud, modelling how it works for you.
- Show students how the strategy works by using it with texts they are reading in your class. If your textbook is too difficult, find a selection that all students can read and comprehend.
- Invest five to fifteen minutes in several class periods to help students internalize the strategy.
- Set aside a few minutes for students to question your demonstration and trade ideas about how they can apply the strategy to texts and learning experiences.
- Reserve time for students to practice with classroom texts and share what they have learned with their classmates. Using texts and magazines that are part of your curriculum

TO RECAP THE BENEFITS

Teaching reading, writing, and study strategies provides students with:

- Improved comprehension
- Better note-taking skills
- Greater recall of information
- Independence in coping with confusing words and passages
- Deeper understanding of new words and concepts
- Development of strong study skills

ensures that you will move forward while helping improve students' reading and thinking.

- Teach fix-it strategies, such as rereading and using context clues to figure out tough words, that enable students to solve reading problems independently (see pp. 142–151).
- Praise students' improved ability to read and learn new material. Build their self-confidence and make firm their understanding of how strategies improve learning.

STRATEGY LESSON:
Building Concepts

How It Helps You

"I can't do these problems," fifth grader Carol said. "I don't even know what a negative number is." Then Carol wrote a huge zero on her blank paper, turned it over on her desk, took out a book, and started to read. Discouraged and frustrated, more than half of the 25 fifth graders said the same thing: "I can't do this."

It was clear that Carol and her classmates lacked the background knowledge necessary to complete the problems. Later that day, when I conferred with Carol's teacher, I suggested that he take some time to explore with the students how negative numbers exist in every day life. So, on one day, the teacher presented a 15-minute discussion of temperature below sea level and altitude, and on the next day, he set aside 15 minutes for students to practice adding and subtracting negative and positive integers on a number line. These two concept-building sessions made this topic accessible to everyone in the class.

Before plunging into a study with your students, pause and think about the underlying concepts required to grasp the new information. When you build a concept foundation *before* stu-

Teaching Reading in Social Studies, Science, and Math

dents study a topic, and then continue to strengthen that foundation during and after the study, you offer students the knowledge necessary to learn and think with new information. Without this, your students, like Carol, will shut down or memorize information they "don't get" and will quickly forget.

Purpose

To help students understand concepts when they have little to no background knowledge

Materials

Science, history, or math textbooks, informational trade books, magazine articles; also, chart paper and marker pens

Guidelines

Before Learning

1. Organize students into pairs or small groups of three to six.
2. Identify a concept students must know in order to understand the unit.
3. Ask students to discuss the concept.

> Jackie Bowers asked her fourth graders to think and talk about this concept question: What are simple machines?

4. Circulate and listen to students talk. Determine how much they already know about the concept.

> Jackie's students talked about cars, microwaves, stoves, refrigerators, and compact disc players. After five minutes of tuning into students' responses, Jackie knew that she would need to build students' knowledge of how we classify a machine as "simple" before they could begin to think about the ways these machines affect our lives. She decided to read a Big Book about simple machines to her students. Jackie also brought in a shovel, hammer, screw driver, nutcracker, nail cutter, and an ice cream scoop for students to handle and discuss. Finally, she introduced the term "levers" to them, and together she and students related each simple machine to a category of levers.

5. Build concepts by reading aloud or experience the concept first-hand: invite students to look at photographs and illustrations, browse through books and magazines, observe items, try math manipulatives, etc.

> To help fifth graders understand the concept of automation, I invited them to fold a paper airplane from start to finish, then create the same airplane by dividing the folding tasks among students.

6. Reserve time for students to talk about and share their experiences so they start developing an understanding of the concept.

7. Set a purpose for studying the concept.

> Jackie sets this purpose for studying simple machines: How are simple machines useful? How do they affect our lives?
>
> Here's the purpose I set for my fifth graders: How did automation change the lives of American workers?

During Learning

1. Ask students to read the chapter (more than once, if possible) over a span of two to four days in order to gather information about the concept and purpose. The time this takes depends on the amount and complexity of the reading material.

2. Set aside 5 to 10 minutes each class and record the information the students have absorbed on chart paper.

3. Reserve 10 to 15 minutes after reading and discussion for students to jot down notes in their journals.

4. Return to key sections, reread these, and relate passages to the concept and purpose.

After Learning

1. Call for a discussion of the concept and reading purpose after students complete the chapter. Do this with the entire class, pairs, or small groups. Make the rounds and listen to students to assess what they understand.

2. Ask students to explain the concept in their journals. Students who don't write anything are sending the message that they need more support. This one explanation of assembly lines from Richard's journal also reveals a need for additional concept building: Assemble line is when machins do all the work.

> That day I carved out 7 or 8 minutes to sit next to Richard and engage him in talk about automation. His talk contains good details, which I jot down as bulleted notes in his journal.
>
> When I invite Richard to rewrite his explanation of automation, I tell him that he can use these journal notes.

3. Have partners explain the concept to one another, then write what they've learned in their journals.

4. Give students problems to solve that relate to the concept. This helps you see whether they have learned the information sufficiently to apply it on their own. In math, for example, students can set up equations using variables.

> In an eighth-grade math-history project, students followed a stock they chose to "invest" in for one month and graphed its variations in value.

5. Pose a concept question that invites students to link new knowledge to related issues or problems in their lives, their community, their environment, and the world.

> One seventh-grade math teacher asked students to consider: Where do you see the principles of geometry at work?
>
> A sixth-grade science teacher asked students to talk about the following: How does dumping chemicals into rivers and streams change plants and organisms in the water and ultimately affect our lives?

Building Concepts
Strategy Snapshot: Grade 3 History

Topic: Causes of the American Revolution

Time: Three or four 45-minute periods

Materials: *Virginia USA,* Silver Burdett and Ginn, pages 195–200.

Background Information: Nancy Roche and I met to discuss the background concepts students would need in order to understand why the colonies rebelled against England. We both agreed that students needed concrete experiences to help them understand the meaning of the colonists' angry cries of "taxation without representation," and the reasons that governments levy taxes.

Getting Ready to Learn: Two 30- to 40-minute classes.

To facilitate an understanding of the colonists' anger over the heavy taxes levied by England, I had third graders experience "taxation without representation." Each student received a bag of colored chips to pay taxes on items I arbitrarily chose. The children paid taxes for two consecutive days. Here's a copy of the chart explaining the tax system.

```
THIRD GRADE TAXES
Eat your snack:          10 cents
Drink water.            10 cents
Sharpen pencils:        25 cents
Recess:                 $1.00

CHIP VALUES
Yellow:                 10 cents
Green:                  25 cents
Red:                    50 cents
Blue:                   $1.00
```

Nancy and I used a large plastic container, marked "Teacher's Treasury" to collect taxes. Each time we collected chips, we gloated about all the money piling up in the treasury.

During the day students grumbled about paying taxes and complained to Nancy and me. Taxes were the dominant lunch and snack topic. "This is unfair. What are we getting out of this? I'm almost out of money. I don't want to give them [the teachers] anymore." Students felt it was unreasonable to be taxed on drinking water and recess. "We all have to go to recess in the morning and lunch and that's the highest tax. Not fair!" Hattie said to me as she added two red chips to the treasury.

Homework after the first day of taxation was to discuss taxes with their parents and discover how parents feel about paying taxes.

During Reading: One class

Before reading the textbook, students shared what they learned about taxes from conversations with parents. The consensus was that parents disliked paying high taxes but felt taxes were necessary to build roads, schools, bridges, help poor people, and provide public education. Students again griped at being taxed and getting nothing for their money.

I reminded students of their purpose for reading the section in the textbook on the Stamp and Townsend Acts, the Boston Tea Party, and the colonies declaring their independence from England.

Discussion revealed that students were now grasping the concept of taxes and especially "taxation without representation." Here's an excerpt of one group's conversation that shows students connecting their class experience with the colonists:

MATT: *England wanted money because they had no more after the French and Indian War. They used the colonies.*

GRACE: *The colonies should make their own taxes and build roads and stuff.*

JAY: *It's like us. You pay taxes and get nothing for it.*

MATT: *They [the colonists] got really mad and wanted to break away.*

EMILY: *Maybe if the king did things for them [the colonists] they'd feel not as mad.*

A sense of unfairness was growing among students—precisely the emotion I'd hoped would develop.

During the last fifteen minutes of class, I discussed slogans with third graders. First we talked about familiar ones such as "Virginia Is for Lovers" and "It's the Real Thing!" as well as the purpose of slogans. Then I connected familiar slogans to the one the colonists shouted, "No Taxation Without Representation." The next day, the children role-played colonists and came up with anti-tax slogans and posters (see photo at right). These also reveal their growing knowledge of the concept and purpose for this study.

Conor, a third grader, objects to British taxes.

Homework that evening was to step into a colonist's shoes and write a letter to King George III protesting the English taxes. Students' letters illustrated their understanding of why the colonists felt the Crown's taxes were unjust.

After Learning: Two classes

Third graders shared their posters, read their letters, and still complained about the taxes I levied. On the last day of this study, Nancy and I brought in cookies for an untaxed snack and popsicles for lunch dessert and explained that these were surprise tax benefits. Then I invited groups to talk about "taxation without representation" and paying taxes—how it made them feel, act and react. After groups discussed what people in our country receive for tax dollars, they helped me construct the web on the following page on large chart paper.

"We did our best to get out of paying and save our money" was the class mantra. Students' motivation for not wanting to pay taxes was clear:

- To beat the system I had unfairly established.
- To keep as much "money" as possible for themselves and give as little as possible to the teachers.

Nancy and I then invited students to write us a letter explaining what they had learned from their reading,

> Dear King George,   1763
> The colonys dont think the taxes are fair. They dont think the taxes are fair because we think the money is more needed on are colonys then being sent to Egland. The House of Burgesses are recommending that the colonits not pay the taxes of the Townshend Acts.
>   from,
>   Joe Stiider

Letters to King George reflect these third graders' understanding of "taxation without representation."

> John Henry   April 18, 1767
> Your Roral Hines I do not think that theys taxes are fare. So if you dont get rid of them the colonys will stop biying tax goods.
> PS: its no good to rais taxt good prises or mack nooow taxes.
>   sincirly
>   John Henry

Teaching Reading in Social Studies, Science, and Math

```
┌─────────────────────────────────────┐
│  FEELINGS                            │
│                                      │
│  • it's unfair                       │
│                                      │
│  • had no more money left            │
│                                      │
│  • felt good about cookies           │
│    and popsicles                     │
│                                      │
│  • mad that teacher took             │
│    away students' rights             │
│                                      │
│  • we won't like paying when         │
│    we grow up                        │
└─────────────────────────────────────┘
```

```
┌─────────────────────────────────────┐
│  WHAT YOU GET FOR TAXES              │
│                                      │
│  • money for gov't jobs--senators,   │
│    president                         │
│                                      │
│  • build roads and bridges           │
│                                      │
│  • army, weapons, tanks, airplanes   │
│                                      │
│  • schools                           │
│                                      │
│  • welfare                           │
│                                      │
│  • Medicare                          │
│                                      │
│  • parks like Yellowstone            │
│                                      │
│  • zoos—like in Washington, D.C.     │
│                                      │
│  • museums                           │
│                                      │
│  • some money to hospitals           │
└─────────────────────────────────────┘
```

TWR

```
┌─────────────────────────────────────┐
│  REACTIONS                           │
│                                      │
│  • tried not to pay                  │
│                                      │
│  • took a drink when went to bathroom, didn't pay │
│                                      │
│  • brought own pencil sharpener, didn't use class's │
│                                      │
│  • suffered and did without drink of water │
│                                      │
│  • used a mechanical lead pencil     │
│                                      │
│  • didn't sharpen pencils, brought extra │
│                                      │
│  • went to bathroom just before recess, then │
│    slipped in line without paying    │
└─────────────────────────────────────┘
```

talking, and experiences.

Students' letters showed the connection between their experiences with paying taxes, why our government levies taxes, and what makes taxes fair. Letters were composed without the use of textbooks. Taking the time to develop hands-on experiences combined with reading, talking, and writing, enabled third graders to relate to a challenging concept.

A third grader explains his feelings toward taxes levied by his teachers.

Dear Mr. Rook and Mrs. Robby

I learned a lot about how the colonists felt about taxes. I also learned that taxes are very important because they pay for all the roads, hospitles and schools. I also felt like the taxes were unfair but I changed my mind when I got those gnarly cookes.

Sincerely,

King Singer

Possible Concepts to Build in Science and Math

The better students understand a concept, the greater chance they have of remembering, applying, and connecting this concept and new information to their learning. Here are some examples of typical science and math concepts that students will need exposure to and concrete experiences with before reading about them in a text.

Science Concepts

- migration
- velocity
- space
- recycling
- water cycle
- fault
- weathering
- chemical changes
- physical states of matter
- photosynthesis
- water tension

Math Concepts

- variables
- negative numbers
- fractions
- decimals
- commutative property
- place value
- inverse relationships
- equations
- rate of diffusion
- different bases
- factors, multiples

STRATEGY LESSON:
Posing Questions

How It Helps You

Years ago, a fifth grader's comment reinforced my belief that students, not teachers, should pose questions before, during, and after a study. A week after I gave fifth graders inquiry notebooks, I invited students to write their feelings about this strategy. Here's what Katy wrote:

> I love asking <u>my questions.</u> I never thouht Id do it again. I think questions in the book are dumb. The teachers make up questions, but there not mine. I use to ask questions when I was little. I still ask my mom and dad. But not at school.

Using Inquiry Notebooks

A spin-off of writing questions in a journal, inquiry notebooks are a top-notch way to record what students are pondering and wondering about. Here are some suggestions for creating and using inquiry notebooks:

- Use colored construction paper to make a four-by-six-inch cover.
- Fill each booklet with six to eight pieces of paper. Staple at centerfold.
- Give each student an inquiry notebook one to two weeks before a study begins.
- Reserve fifteen to twenty minutes for students decorate the cover and print their name on it.
- Pass out notebooks at the start of each day; have students keep them on their desks.
- Ask students to write the date on a blank page of their notebooks, then record questions for that day.
- Encourage students to write the questions (see below) about the topic that pop into their heads. You can reserve short bursts of time, about 5 minutes, two to three times a day for students to record their wonderings. Encourage students to jot down questions at any point during your class or the day.
- Collect notebooks at the end of the day or class and store in a shoe box or plastic crate.
- Read through notebooks at the end of the first week. Check with your librarian to make sure you have materials available to

help students answer their inquires. If you have budget money, order some books and magazines. Otherwise, check resources out from your public library. Keep library materials in class to avoid losing them.

- Type questions from inquiry notebooks that relate to your study two days before you officially start the topic. Students can use these to guide their reading, research, and discussions.
- Have students continue to record additional questions during the study.
- Save questions that don't directly relate to the topic and invite students to discuss and research these if time permits.
- Point out that time and resource limitations can result in unanswered questions, and that this is okay. One or two students might want to pursue research independently and later share these with the class. You might also invite an expert from your school or community to visit and respond to students' queries.

> 5-3   After browsing
> What is blood plasma?
> What does the spleen do?
> What are lymph nodes?
>
> 5-7
> What is the longest organ?
> What is the heaviest organ?
> How long is the longest organ?
> How Heavy is the heaviest organ?

Posing Questions

How right Katy was! With more education and life experiences, the questions adults ask and the questions that writers of textbooks pose, usually aren't the same as those of a middle grade or middle school student. Research indicates that students who are taught to generate questions acquire higher levels of questioning ability than those who receive no training (Alvermann and Phelps, 1998; Pearson and Johnson, 1978; Pearson et al., 1992; Vacca and Vacca, 2000).

By turning the questioning process over to your students, you value and ignite their inquiries, giving them a reason to reread parts of the text and revisit important sections. You engage them in the study because *they* create the questions for discussions, writing, and research.

Purpose

To jumpstart and record students' inquiries and investigations of a topic or unit; to teach students how to write questions worth thinking about and discussing

Materials

A topic and texts, such as the weather, decimals, or the Great Depression, that students are studying; students' journals, chart paper, markers

Guidelines

Getting Ready to Learn

If students know little or nothing about a topic, they cannot generate questions. Offer them experiences that build enough background knowledge to wonder about a topic.

1. Organize your class into pairs or small groups (three or four students).

2. Discover what students know about a topic by asking them to talk to a partner or their group for three to five minutes.

3. Engage the students in one or more experiences that can build their prior knowledge. If students possess no prior knowledge, set aside fifteen minutes of two to five class periods to use some of the suggestions in number four.

4. Read aloud, ask students to browse through books and magazines, have them preview their textbook (see pages 105–110), show a video, film strip, or a clip from a film, or create relevant experiences.

Fifth graders in Jasper Oliver's class know about pond life. Most live on farms or in the country;

in second grade they investigated plant and animal life in the stream behind our school. Here are some of the questions fifth grade students posed: Which plants thrive? Why? How can we test the water for purity? Can we identify and classify the organisms in the pond? Are there leeches? Are leeches harmful or helpful to pond organisms? How can we improve the water quality? What effect will improving the water have on the organisms? How can we make sure our investigations are accurate?

Sixth graders will study diffusion and have no understanding of the term. Minda Parks, their teacher, sets up three experiments that groups complete over three days:

- Put blue food coloring in a beaker or clear dish of clear cold water; observe it.
- Spray perfume into the air and discuss what happens.
- Put red food coloring in a beaker or clear dish of boiling hot water; observe it.

5. Invite students to talk about their experiences for 15 to 20 minutes, then raise questions.

6. Ask students to record their questions in notebooks.

Here are some of Miss Parks's students' questions: Why did the food coloring mix on its own? Why did the red coloring mix faster than the blue? Why did the room smell like the perfume? Does it matter what color you put in the water? Should we test other colors? What would happen if we put the food coloring in oil? In alcohol? In beaten eggs?

7. Collect students' questions on chart paper and use for discussions during and after reading, to focus observing, or to plan an experiment.

8. Set purposes for reading with some of the questions.

Sixth grade math students preview a chapter on decimals and use these questions to drive their study of decimals: How can decimals be fractions and whole numbers? Can you change decimals to fractions and fractions to decimals? How? How are decimals in our lives?

SHOULD STUDENTS' QUESTIONS RELATE TO THE READING

When I invite third and fourth graders to pose questions while reading, I observe that many wonder about things the text sparks but does not answer. It's frustrating to students who have compiled a long list of questions and can't take notes from their reading.

Adapt the strategy and ask students to compose questions that relate to their reading and add one to two wonderings the reading generates.

During Learning

1. Have students read their textbook and/or informational trade books, and/or conduct interviews.

2. Ask students to generate more questions while they read and/or observe an experiment; this gives them incentive to read closely and critically.

3. Use students' questions to set up additional experiments.

> Miss Park's students tested green and yellow food coloring. They dropped food coloring into beaten eggs and oil and noted their observations.

4. Select questions from the chart and invite pairs, groups, or the entire class to discuss them.

After Learning

1. Select questions for discussions. Make sure students include specific details to support their answers. Students can answer questions in journals or retell the high points of their discussions.

2. Ask students to draw and write about one experiment.

3. Invite pairs or groups to give an oral presentation that explains one or more of the questions posed before and during the study.

A sixth grader's pictures and text demonstrate an understanding of her experiment on diffusion.

> In Dick Bell's history class, groups of three to four sixth graders study Renaissance artists. They use their questions and the knowledge gained by investigating them to prepare a lesson for first graders.
>
> Sara starts with a brief biography of Michelangelo's childhood, "because we thought first graders would connect to that." Then Noah, Teddy, and Will give one of the four 1st Grade teams a picture of a Michelangelo painting and one of a sculpture. The sixth graders ask the first graders to pose questions, and then use the reproductions and their own knowledge to answer the first graders' questions. The presentation closes with each first-grade group choosing their favorite work of art and trying to express why. When Will asks his group to select their favorite, Jill asks

him, "Do you really, really like these?"

"Yes. I like to paint myself," says Will. "What do you think?"

"They're so-so," says Jill. "Not that great." As the group walks back to its classroom, Sara says, "I bet this was the first time these guys saw a Michelangelo. It takes time to like this stuff. I'm glad we let them—the first grade—have the books for a couple of weeks."

4. Write responses to several questions in learning logs. Make sure responses include reasons. Have students share these.

> **BOOKS SIXTH GRADERS USED**
>
> *Art For Children Series* by Ernest Raboff presents the lives and works of artists. Books contain full color reproductions. Published by Lippincott.
>
> Da Vinci
>
> Dürer
>
> Michelangelo
>
> Raphael
>
> Rembrandt
>
> Velasquez

Teach Students How to Ask Analytical Questions

Use the suggestions that follow to show students how to ask high-level, analytical questions:

- Make clear that a factual question has one correct answer, such as: Who was the first president of the United States?

- Explain that analytical questions compare data, apply information to a problem, or use it to make connections. Examples are, Why was George Washington chosen to be our first president? Can you compare and contrast three issues Washington and Jefferson addressed?

- Help students see that the answers to analytical questions are not explicitly written in a text. Such answers require that students make connections and inferences, compare and evaluate information.

- Teach students the words that signify analytical and open-ended questions:

compare	design	contrast
categorize	evaluate	examine
judge	why	connect
design a model	analyze	create solutions

- Model how you create questions with these verbs.

- Introduce three to four such verbs at one time.

Posing Questions

PROMPTS THAT LEAD TO ANALYTICAL DISCUSSIONS

Introduce three to four prompts and reserve time for students to practice applying them in class:

Connect to another situation...

Connect to a community issue...

Connect to a world issue...

Show how this (person, idea, issue, data) changed our lives...

Use hindsight, to explain how this (problem, war, shortage, waste) could have been avoided...

Show more than one way to solve this problem...

Use the data to suggest a change...

Persuade us to take your stand or position...

Show how this information can help future generations...

- Allow time for students to practice writing questions.
- Permit students to use any verb/phrase as long as the questions moves beyond one correct answer (see list of verbs and phrases, left).

Open-Ended Questions for Informational Texts

The questions that follow can be used with topics and themes your class is studying in science and social studies. Set standards for supporting ideas and ask students to include specific details to back up points.

- Does the author try to persuade you in any way? How?
- Can you identify the facts? The opinions?
- How do statistics and data support the author's perspective?
- Do you find the author's evidence convincing? Explain.
- What new information did you learn? How can you apply this information to an issue or problem in today's world?
- How did this new information change your way of thinking about this subject?
- What words, phrases, statements does the author use that caught your attention? Why? How did they make you feel? What did they make you think?
- Did the author weave opinion and fact statements into the piece? Find examples of each.
- Were there any photographs, illustrations, charts, graphs, or diagrams that were important? Select two or three and show what you learned from them and explain why you believe each one was important.
- Did the reading leave you with unanswered questions? What are these?
- How did you connect to the piece? Was it personal? Was it an issue that affects your community and the world? Explain.

Posing Questions
Strategy Snapshot: Grade 7 Science

Topic: Soil

Time: Three to four class periods

Materials: *Earth Science* by Ralph Feather, Jr. and Susan L. Snyder. Glencoe/McGraw Hill, 1997.

Background Information: Seventh-grade science teacher Kathleen Hobbs is also a certified reading specialist who works closely with me at Powhatan. At a meeting in February, Kathleen said, "I don't think everyone is reading the textbook. I think it's a habit some have developed, and it's worked for them so far. But I want them to see how interesting the book is and how much more they can learn." We decided that the questioning strategy might help engage students with the text because it tapped into *their wonderings.*

Getting Ready to Learn: 20 minutes

First Kathleen had students preview the chapter on weathering. Pairs discussed boldface headings and words and studied pictures and diagrams. Then she invited students to pose some questions. "Some kids looked at me blankly, so I gave them a few examples such as: What exactly is weathering? Does weathering occur in all climate zones?" After Kathleen modelled questioning, students came up with some "great questions" that ended up establishing the purposes for reading the section on soil: How does the environment affect how soil develops? Why is soil important?

During Learning: one to two 45-minute periods

Kathleen prepared her during reading lesson the day before her class met. She decided it would be easier for students to understand the process if she read, shared thoughts, and raised questions for one paragraph at a time. Here's what she wrote in her journal about demonstrating the during reading questions:

> I modelled this for my students, too. When I told them they were going to read a section in their text and write down any questions they had about what they read, I got a panicked look from several kids! "What? I don't get it!" was a comment several were making before I even had a chance to explain. Slowly, I guided them through this process by reading aloud the first para-

graph and thinking aloud as I read. The section we were reading was on soil, and the first question I asked out loud was, "Where did the term 'dirt' come from?" I also wondered, "How long does it take soil to form?"

Then I had my students read the first two pages of the soil section silently and write down questions as they read. I did the same thing! My students had come up with some wonderful questions and sharing them generated excitement for the topic among students. Some of their questions included: How does soil help vegetation? How can you measure the thickness of soil? Is sand in desert soil? How does rock become soil? What would the world be like without fungi and worms and insects?

After Learning: 30 minutes

Kathleen encouraged students to think critically about the questions by having one student ask a question and others answer. "The most incredible part of this lesson was the students' answers. They returned to the textbook and gave solid reasons to support their answers. They used the diagrams and photographs. They painted a picture of an earth without decomposers. Zach said, 'I'll never look at a worm the same way.' Three students even volunteered to find answers to questions that the book did not explore."

What Students Had to Say

After the discussion, Kathleen invited students to share their take on the strategy. "I found it really helpful," Bobby said. "The questions made me understand the reading better. I kept trying to find answers as I read." All agreed, though Andrew thought it took a lot more time, and Richard said it was hard and time-consuming. About two thirds of the class said that to do this assignment *they had to read the book.*

Several students said the strategy was helpful if they practiced it with sections and not the whole chapter. Students agreed that

Rachel   Science   February 15
Before
What exactly is soil?
What are dif. types of erosion?
What causes erosion?
What is weathering?

During
Where did we get the term dirt?
How does soil help vegetation?
How do they measure thickness in soil?
What is the max amount of horizians?
How is horizon A different from the others?
What is leaching?
Is soil everywhere?
How does time change the chara. of soil?
What are the dif. types of soil?

6-3
is any soil on the top layer topsoil?
What is the rate of soil erosion?
how does soil become infertile?
What is killing?

1. Are water, glacier, wind and gravity the only types of erosion?

After
2. What type of soil do we have?
3

Raising questions before, during, and after learning.

Teaching Reading in Social Studies, Science, and Math

Math tour questions help students discover geometry in their school environment.

the point of practicing was to build the habit of posing questions in their heads as they read.

Use the questioning strategy judiciously, and focus on key sections of text, so students don't build long, never-used lists of questions.

History and Math Applications

Students can pose questions before, during, and after any topic studied in history and math. The quality of students' questions depends on the amount of prior knowledge they have and their understanding of how to compose analytical questions. For example, teams of seventh graders collaborate and compose questions that sixth graders will use to connect geometry to their school buildings and surroundings. It's an excellent way for seventh graders to review what they know about geometry and make connections to how geometry functions in the real world.

STRATEGY LESSON:
Observing

How It Helps You

Careful observation is at the heart of virtually every human endeavor, so it's no surprise that in the classroom, it can be used to stimulate all kinds of research and exploration. Here's how my fifth graders used their powers of observation to generate a study of one year: After students ate their lunches, they switched desks and put on detective hats. With magnifying glasses, students investigated crumbs on the floor and desktops and listed the foods their classmates ate. Then students shared their lists, offering reasons for their conclusions, and compared their findings with what the students actually ate. Here is Patrick's list and his reasoning:

- potato chips—a mushd chip under the chair—she stepped on it
- sandwhich—tiny piece of brown crust on desk
- grape jelly—purpel blob on desk—Kennis ate peanut butter and jelly
- part of a candy wraper—think its a milky way has "Mil" on it.

Having students observe supports your teaching because it stimulates thinking and reasoning (Saul et al., 2002.)

Purpose

To teach students how to observe closely, describe, and draw conclusions

Materials

Various kinds of objects such as plants or a terrarium, fish, animals; microscope slide with a hair or leaf; documents, such as "The Bill of Rights," letters, diary entries; a kite, a model of a bridge

Guidelines

Getting Ready to Learn

Take 10 minutes of four to six periods so students can practice observing different items.

1. Think-aloud and show how you observe an item such as a garden slug. You can put the slug in a glass jar or show students a drawing or photograph like the one in *Bugs* by Nancy Winslow Parker and Joan Richards Wright (Morrow, 1987). In my class, I would first think-aloud, then jot down notes on the chalkboard and draw a picture of the slug:

    It's about 3 inches long. Brown with black spots shaped like ovals. Has two feelers and dots on the round end of each feeler. It looks gooey and leaves a slimy path after it moves. Moves slowly.

2. Raise some questions that drive the reading:

    What are the dots at the end of the feelers? Why does it leave a slimy trail? Does it help soil? How long is the biggest slug? How do slugs breath? My goal is for students to see how closely I look, how objectively I describe what I see, and show students how I discover answers to the questions by reading aloud the section on the "Spotted Garden Slug."

3. Organize students into observing partners.

4. Instruct students to take turns thinking-aloud, then jot down notes, drawings, and questions in their journals.

5. Offer several warm-up experiences where students can practice the process: observe,

think-aloud, write.

6. Have a whole-class discussion of the object or experiment you want students to observe.

> I invite fifth graders to tell me what they know about spiders from their reading and observations. They're mostly country children with daily experiences outdoors. I make time for city children who might have little knowledge of spiders to browse through books, see a film strip, or visit an insect zoo.

During Learning

1. Invite pairs or small groups to observe, think-aloud, write notes, raise questions and draw pictures if appropriate.

2. Have students continue to observe the item if it changes over time.

> Third grade partners observe their tree each month; fourth graders watch the growth of bean seeds in a sunny window and in a dark closet daily; eighth graders observe a boa constrictor swallowing a mouse and watch the snake's shape during the next five classes.

3. Encourage students to draw conclusions and make inferences based on their observations.

> Fifth graders note that spiders repair their webs because "the bugs they catch rip parts." Anthony said, "I think rain that's hard hurts webs and spiders have to rebuild then." Observing can also stir the analogous thinking that Anthony did.
>
> Fourth graders observe that "water and good soil won't make the seeds grow right. They need sun too." And when Maria wonders what about the sun makes plants grow, Miss Grey knows the teachable moment for introducing photosynthesis has arrived.

After Learning

1. Have pairs or groups share their observations and information learned.

2. Conduct a whole-class discussion where pairs and groups exchange what they've learned.

3. Collect students' unanswered questions and use these as the basis for further reading or interviewing an expert.

4. Invite students to think about and share the qualities of a good observer.

    Here's what one group of eighth graders thought:

    - Watch silently at first.
    - Look at every detail.
    - Think-aloud to your partner or yourself.
    - Jot down notes that are objective. Don't put your opinion in.
    - Look again. Compare your notes with the item.

- Add more information.
- Draw a picture if you need to.
- Think about your observation and ask yourself questions.
- Record your questions.
- Share with a partner and compare what you've done.
- Read your notes over the next day. Add more.

Observing
Strategy Snapshot: Grades 4 and 6 Science

Grade 4

Topic: observing a monarch from caterpillar to butterfly

Time: three to four class periods during the process

Materials: monarch caterpillars; large glass tank with milkweed; students' journals; colored pencils

Background Information:
Debi Gustin's fourth graders observe monarchs from caterpillar to maturity. At the end of September, students release the butterflies while the entire school watches. In years past, Debi had students read trade books and articles, watch a video; this year she wanted to develop more completely the students' ability to observe, col-

A fourth grader observes, draws, and writes about a monarch caterpillar.

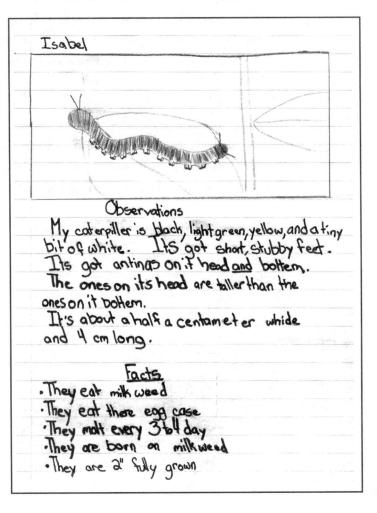

Isabel

Observations

My caterpiller is black, light green, yellow, and a tiny bit of white. Its got short, stubby feet.
Its got antinas on it head <u>and</u> bottem. The ones on its head are taller than the ones on it bottem.
It's about a half a centameter whide and 4 cm long.

Facts
- They eat milk weed
- They eat thier egg case
- They molt every 3 to 4 day
- They are born on milkweed
- They are 2" fully grown

Teaching Reading in Social Studies, Science, and Math

lect data from observations, and create scientific drawings.

She begins the study with a whole-class "Meet the Caterpillar" observation period, followed by some reading and discussion of several articles.

Then, on chart paper, Debi models what has to be done. Students create sketches, record observations, and collect facts. Isabel's work illustrates how much students learned by observing.

Grade 6 Science Field Trip

Topic: animal habitat around a stream

Time: two hours

Materials: observation sheet

Background Information:

Sixth graders have been studying habitats, the animals that live in different environments, and how the environment affects survival and the ability to gather food, mature and reproduce. Since our rural school has a stream on the property, Ray Legge, the science teacher, takes the students on a field trip to observe the stream and the land surrounding it. Field trips provide opportunities for students to develop their observation skills.

Ray divides twenty-eight students into groups of four and five. Students discuss what they see as a group and complete a "Habitat and Animal Life Description" sheet individually. Back in the classroom, students compare their findings, draw conclusions about why the habitat is changing, and predict how changes will affect animal life and how animals will cope with changes.

Group members Adie, sara, kierstin, John, Jill

Habitat and Animal Life Description

I. General: Circle one: Forest /(Stream)/ Vernal Pool / River

Shady, open, or both?

Vegetation-(None,)woody, or non-woody?
        If woody, large or small?

Terrain- Flat (rolling) or steeply sloped?

Soil- dry, (wet) or in-between?

Habitat conditions generally steady or (changing?)

II. Animal Life:

Vertebrates or vertebrate signs?

1. cray fish   5. frog
2. hole   6. frog eggs
3. Mayfly   7. baby black snake
4. tad pole   8. Fish

Invertebrates or invertebrate signs?

1. Worm   5. gnats
2. Cranefly   6. spider
3. water spider   7. ~~bee~~ Lacewing
4. tick   8. fly

Five sixth graders take notes on their outdoor field trips.

Observing

History and Math Applications

Students can observe artwork depicting clothing, homes, people, industry, and so forth, from an historical period and learn about that time.

Math students can study and think about a problem that's incorrect and try to find the error. Teacher Heather Campbell leaves one incorrect problem on students' tests ungraded. She asks her students to study their process, find their error, and redo the problem.

A fifth grader studies incorrect problem, then explains and corrects her work.

STRATEGY LESSON:
K-W-H-L

How It Helps You

This strategy was developed by researcher Donna Ogle, who called it the K-W-L, shorthand for the three questions designed to engage students in their learning: What Do I Know? What Do I Want to Know? What Have I Learned?

These questions enable students and teachers to evaluate the level of prior knowledge, support research, pique learners' curiosity about a topic, and provide a strong inquiry foundation for motivating students to seek answers to their wonderings.

Many teachers have added the "H" so that students engaged in research can also ask themselves: How Will I Go About Learning? This question encourages students to explore ways to collect information, such as interview an expert, conduct a survey and/or experiment, use the Internet, take photographs and, of course, read and ask a librarian.

Purpose

To enable students to see what they know about a topic; to encourage students to discover what they want to learn; to stir a discussion of ways to go about collecting information; to reflect on what has been learned

Teaching Reading in Social Studies, Science, and Math

Materials

Textbook, library books, magazines and newspapers, chart paper, markers

Guidelines

Getting Ready to Learn

1. Ask students to jot down in their learning logs what they think they know about a topic. Collect ideas and display on a chart; by sharing, you enlarge students' background. At the end of your study, you'll return to this chart and ask students to adjust their original thoughts.

Here's what I collected about the Middle Ages from fifth graders:

- It's after Rome fell.
- There were knights and armor.
- Everyone lived in castles.
- Lots of wars and fighting.
- No bathrooms then.

2. Enlarge students' prior knowledge by reading aloud, having them browse through books and magazines, showing a video, or giving them a series of experiences.

3. Ask students to jot down what they want to learn. Collect these questions on chart paper so everyone can use them during the study.

Here's a partial list of what seventh graders wanted to learn about factors and multiples:

- How do you find a factorial?
- What makes numbers relatively prime?
- How do you find the greatest common factor?
- Why isn't one a prime?
- What's the difference between the greatest common factor and the least common multiple?
- Why isn't zero a factor of every number?

4. Ask students to think of *how* they can find answers to their questions.

Seventh graders use <u>Math On Call: A Mathematics Handbook</u> (Great Source, 1998), their peers, and their teacher to investigate factors and multiples.

Fifth graders study the Middle Ages by moving through four film strip centers, reading parts of library books, listening to medieval music, and studying charts about monasteries, convents, castles, and weapons.

K-W-H-L

5. Have students choose one or two questions or invite groups to select a topic, such as castles or primes and composites.

During Learning

1. Allow enough time for students to read and ask additional questions. Students can collect data on Post-its, index cards, or on a page in their journals.

2. Set aside the last 10-15 minutes of a period for students to share and discuss questions. This process often raises more questions.

3. During the study, collect on chart paper any questions the text doesn't answer. Explain that texts won't have answers to all questions. Help students think of ways they can explore these questions. If time permits, research these questions or call for volunteers to find and present answers. There will be occasions when time won't permit delving into unanswered questions, and that's fine—invite those who are interested in the topic to pursue it independently.

After Learning

1. Have students discuss what they've learned. Use students' questions as a springboard for discussions.

2. Invite students to compose, in their journals, a list of what they have learned. Collect students' ideas on chart paper.

3. Ask students to use their knowledge to adjust their *What Do I Know?* lists or collaborate to adjust the ideas on the *What Do I Know?* chart.

> **Fifth graders adjusted their list:**
> - Only the king, lords, ladies, and some knights lived in castles.
> - Serfs lived in dirty, smelly, one-room huts--animals slept in the huts, too.

4. Negotiate with students how they can show what they have learned. You might have them choose two questions to answer in their journals, or you might select one and let students choose the second. Students can also write a list of four to five things they learned, retell the main points of their discussion, write a letter or diary entry, illustrate or dramatize an event or experiment, complete a double-entry journal (see pages 164–165 and 180–182).

> Some of Josh Mosser's fifth graders show what they've learned about ancient Rome by putting on a puppet show about Romulus and Remus. Some students built a model of the

Teaching Reading in Social Studies, Science, and Math

A third grader writes in her journal.

Coliseum and showed how Romans used it, recreating an event with a "You Are There" mini-play, and others created a drama that shows daily life. For, Josh, this is a great way to assess students: "I don't have to grade a stack of tests, which I find boring and not as helpful as asking students to become the history. This way my class gets to recreate and experience the past, then discuss it again."

In another class, third graders write letters to family in England about their life in Jamestown after reading their history textbook, watching a video, and reading Clyde Bulla's <u>A Lion to Guard Us</u>.

5. Give a test or quiz.

February 29, 1611

Dear Father,

I curse the Virginia Company for sending me her. All our food is gon. 5 men where shot to day by Indians. and I hade a rat for lunch. The horribistict thing you ever ate. Jamestown is dieing. 40 peple are left. I hade to tore don my home for fire wood. I've whnt to go back to London. Have a cup of tae and sit in front of the fire.

Love,
Chris

A third grader's letter to his father in England.

Building Concepts
Strategy Snapshot: Grade 4 Science

Topic: the human body

Time: three to four 45-minute periods a week.

This study lasted five weeks: Week 1—logging questions into inquiry notebooks, getting ready to learn; Weeks 2 and 3—reading, questioning, taking notes, starting projects; Week 4—completing projects; Week 5—presentations.

Materials: library books, inquiry notebooks and science learning logs for students, chart paper, markers

Background Information: A seasoned first-grade teacher, Debi Gustin had moved to fourth grade and invited me to team teach a science study of the human body. After completing the "K" part of the K-W-H-L approach, Debi and I created tentative plans for the study—plans that tapped into students' wonderings and continually included students' input and feedback.

Getting Ready to Learn

A week before the study officially began, Debi's fourth graders had fun making inquiry notebooks so they could log in questions (see page 75).

To start the study, Debi and I ask students, who sit in groups of four, to talk for five minutes about what they think they know about the human body. Then students jotted down a list of thoughts in their journals. Here are just some of the notes from the two groups:

Group I:

McKenzie: We have lots of organs.

William: We make gas. [giggles]

McKenzie: We lose our baby teeth.

Robert: The heart beats. You can hear it.

McKenzie: I can wrinkle the skin on my face.

Sudie: Bones are calcium.

William: Blood is in our body.

Robert: Boogers are dirt in the air that go in your nose.

Group II:

LIZZIE: We're 80 percent water.

KEVIN: You lose brain cells every time you kick a soccer ball hard.

SALLY: You taste with your tongue.

LIZZIE: The brain has different parts.

JOE: Your eyes see upside down.

SALLY: New babies have blue eyes.

JOE: Ears are cartilage.

LIZZIE: Skin has different colors.

JOE: That's the pigment in it.

When Debi and I reviewed the chart of what students know, we agreed that they had lots of information, but had no idea that the human body consisted of many systems working together. That was a concept we wanted to build before groups became experts on a specific system.

I started the next class by writing the words "browsing through books" on the chalkboard. The children thought browsing meant you only read certain pages, so I modelled how to browse:

- look at the pictures and diagrams
- read the captions
- read the bold face and colored words
- read a paragraph that looks intriguing

For 25 minutes students browsed, sharing titles and showing each other great pictures. Quiet but excited talk filled the class.

After browsing, students filled their inquiry notebooks with questions (see page 75). Then I listed the systems we would investigate on the chalkboard: Muscular, Digestive, Circulatory, Skeletal, and Nervous. I invited the children to tell me what they learned about the digestive system first because children had daily experiences with it. The list included: mouth, teeth, tongue, stomach, liver, intestines, rectum. Using the list, I helped students understand the term *system*—a group of organs working together. Each group then chose a system to study. Throughout the study, either Debi or I took five minutes to add organs to each system, then discuss the main job of each system. For example, the group studying the digestive system explained that this system changed the food we eat so our body could use it to grow.

During Learning

When Debi and I asked, "How will you go about learning?" the children said they would read parts of books and interview Mr. Legge (our science teacher). Here's how we structured class time:

- For 20 of the 40 minutes, students read, then took notes. They returned to the text to clarify an answer, but closed the book before writing. This way, students put their notes in their own words (see pages 178–184).

- During the last 15 minutes, groups discussed their notes.

- Interviews with Mr. Legge took place after students gained background knowledge and could pose questions books did not answer.

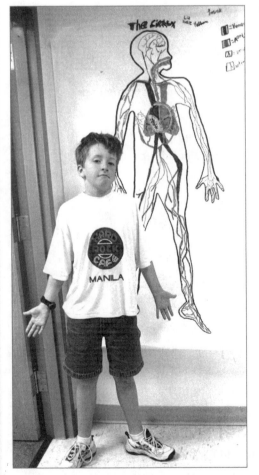

Lowell, a fourth grader, poses with his group's circulatory system drawing.

> Robert
> 1. These are some bones that are important because they protect other parts of the body
> A. The crannium (or the skull) protects the brain
> B. The rib cage protects the lungs
> C. The septum protects the heart
> D. And the spinal cord protects nervs
> 2. This is how bones grow
> A. The first thing that happens when a bone grows is osteolbasts go's across the bones growth surface which makes a layer of collagen. Then minerals of calcium phosophate stick to the collagen which crystallize to make new bone. On to you William

When students can jot down notes after reading and rereading, they demonstrate what they understand.

After Learning

Students suggested possible ways to share what they learned: make a life-size model, an illustrated calendar, a picture book, an illustrated dictionary, do and explain an experiment, perform a play of a system doing its job.

Ultimately, each group chose the same main project: a life-size drawing of the system they had studied. On butcher paper, students traced the body outline of one student whose name was chosen at random from a paper bag.

Groups taught classmates about their particular system. Some pretended they were a program on the

Teaching Reading in Social Studies, Science, and Math

"Discovery Channel," others presented information through an interview or a rock-and-roll song. Listeners asked questions, added information, and as Jen said, "It was funner than memorizing stuff!"

Science and Math Applications

The K-W-H-L is a strategy that teachers can easily use in all subjects. It does not have to result in a full-blown research investigation, but it is a great strategy for actively engaging students in their learning. Kathleen Hobbs uses this technique to enhance her students' reading of sections in a textbook. Once she feels her seventh graders have enough background knowledge about a topic, she has them read and complete a "K-W-L Worksheet" on two to three pages.

"I find that it engages students with the text and is a great note-taking tool, particularly the 'L' part, which invites students to reread and skim."

The K-W-L helps students take notes on their reading.

Pause and Reflect on:
The Importance of Practicing Strategies

Whenever you think, *But all this takes too much time; I need to cover content,* I invite you to *Stop and Reflect.* If we hope to develop independent learners, we must show students how to read well, how to study, and how to learn. To ensure that you cover content, use required topics to model the strategies that improve reading, writing, thinking, and observing. Have students practice and apply these strategies to themes you must complete. This way students can internalize a strategy and make it their own, and you can complete your curriculum.

Every time you present a strategy lesson and invite students to practice it during class, you offer them ways to problem solve to make meaning, link learning to their lives and the world, and to continue to learn beyond school.

✍ Chapter 4 ✍

Strategies to Use
Before Learning

*For maximum learning, students need prior knowledge about the
topic being studied and they need to relate that prior knowledge to
the contents of the passage.*

— Readence, Moore, and Rickelman

E ach day, Jerry Rich's eighth graders entered the classroom, headed to their seats in rows of desks, and settled in for a lecture on American history. Jerry usually stood behind a wooden podium at the front of the class to deliver his lectures.

A few years ago, Jerry invited me to coach him and team teach his class. In a letter he explained what troubled him:

> I love American history. Most of my students hate it or seem indifferent. I do have a few students who excel, but a few isn't enough for me anymore. Besides, I don't think I've gotten them to love history the way I do. I see 30 bodies in the classroom. Some listen, some take notes, many fail quizzes and tests. When I say something like, "You'll love the Civil War, it's an exciting topic," I get yawns and stares of disbelief. I want to, no, I need to change my teaching style.

On Tuesdays, I observed Jerry teach, then later in the day, we conferred. At our second meeting, Jerry and I discussed the three-part learning framework. I gave him chapters to read from content area textbooks as well as Readence, Moore, and Rickelman's book, *Prereading Activities for Content Area Reading and Learning.* Like his students, Jerry groaned. "Just tell me what to do," he said. "Why do I have to spend time doing all this reading?"

"A theoretical foundation will help you understand how kids learn and remember new information," I answered. At each meeting, Jerry and I discussed his reading. He bombarded me with questions. I urged him to observe a science teacher at his school whose students are active learners. However, I never felt I convinced Jerry how important it was for him to build background knowledge of how children learn.

After several meetings, Jerry and I sketched out some plans for a study of The Great Depression. Jerry planned to activate students' knowledge by inviting them to brainstorm what they know about the Depression. While the two of us shoved desks around his classroom, rearranging them into groups of six desks, he commented, "The kids will laugh and think I've lost it when they see the room this way."

When his eighth graders shuffled in, Jerry directed his students to their places. The class hummed. "What's up, Mr. Rich? Hey, where's the lecture stand? What's goin' on? You feelin' okay?"

I passed Jerry a hastily written note: "Ignore. Get them settled and move on." After directing students to take out their journals, Mr. Rich showed them how to head their page: name, date, and topic, What Do You Know About the Great Depression? Then he invited groups to talk about the Depression for about five minutes, recalling what they know. At first, there was silence. Total silence. Then, I jumped in and said that Mr. Rich and I would model how we talk about this historical period, and so we began. Soon, student talk dominated, and we both circulated, listening to conversations. Most students had little to say about the Depression and lots to say about their upcoming soccer game. In one group, a student thought the stock market had crashed and people were poor.

Next, Jerry invited students to write silently, in their journals, everything they recalled from their conversations and any new ideas they had. Again, we circulated, pausing to read what students were writing. It was obvious that students knew little about that period in history.

Prepared for this occurrence, Mr. Rich read a passage from Irene Hunt's *No Promises in the Wind* (Berkley, 1987) and one from *Bud, Not Buddy* by Christopher Paul Curtis (Scholastic, 2000; Delacorte, 1999). On a record player, he played the song, "Brother, Can You Spare a Dime?" and invited groups to discuss their feelings, and what they learned.

During our afternoon conferring time, Jerry said, "Did you feel the energy change?" I nodded. "Did you hear some of them say, 'I wonder what's gonna happen tomorrow?' Boy, they were engaged. All that stuff I read about background knowledge and learning worked today. And no one groaned when I asked them to write a list for homework of what they had learned about the Depression." Brimming with excitement, Jerry continued, "The principal said there's money to order these books, so I can get them for students to read."

Jerry's first, and thankfully positive, experience with preparing students for a study, enabled him to feel and observe the power of understanding research-tested learning theory and using it to make the decision to build students' prior knowledge about the Depression.

Invest Time and Activate Prior Knowledge

I use the word "invest" because that's exactly what you do when you engage students in experiences that reclaim what they already know. It's like investing in a stock that grows and brings you financial rewards. Fielding and Pearson wrote: "The more one already knows, the more one comprehends; and the more one comprehends, the more one learns new knowledge to enable comprehension of an even greater and broader array of topics and texts," (1994, *Educational Leadership)*. From their own reading and from classroom events, students can continually enlarge their knowledge base and improve their reading of a wide range of topics. That's why one of the most important tasks of content teachers is to provide rich experiences that will activate and enlarge what students know and provoke thinking.

Five Getting-Ready-to-Learn Strategies

Three of the five preparation strategies in this chapter work well whether you teach social studies, math, or science: Brainstorm and Categorize; Preview/Analyze/Connect, and Fast-Write. The Anticipation Guide, which creates tension between what students know and what they will learn, works best in social studies and science. Each strategy builds the background knowledge students need in order to comprehend new material.

The last strategy in this chapter is Setting Purposes because the most effective time to model how to set purposes for reading is after you prepare students to read and learn information. Often the purposes for studying a topic are readily apparent after students gain background knowledge. Moreover, students need background knowledge to set meaningful and relevant purposes for study.

Each one of these strategies reinforces responsive teaching because the strategy allows you to observe how much students know about a topic prior to learning. As you listen to students share ideas and/or read their journal writing, you can decide whether to move forward or invest time and build additional background knowledge.

STRATEGY LESSON:
Brainstorm and Categorize

How It Helps You

"What's the point of this?" Katie, an eighth grader, challenges Mr. Brown after he asks groups to think of headings for their brainstorming on causes of the Civil War. "We've got a great list, let's just read," Katie adds.

Without missing a beat, Mr. Brown flips the chart paper to an exercise that he modelled with them two days ago. Students see their brainstormed list for the Valentine's Day dance and the items organized under: *Food and Drinks, Music, Decorations, Time and Permission, Dress.*

"The categories do make the stuff easier to think about," concedes Jason.

"It was easier to give out jobs, too," says Rosa.

"You both have it," says Mr. Brown. "Categorizing helps us think about lots of information in an orderly way, and that makes it easier to use. With the Civil War, we'll look at different kinds of causes—social, economic, political—and how these relate to actions and decisions the North and South made."

Through brainstorming—a free flow of ideas and thoughts about a topic (i.e., plant cells) a key word (communism) or a concept (triangles)—students reclaim what they know and hear new ideas. Before a study, brainstorming sessions consist of what students think they know, and so not all ideas will be accurate. As long as ideas relate to the topic, they're fine; you can make adjustments as you continue the study.

When you ask students to categorize—to organize a random list of ideas under general headings—you require them to engage in higher-order thinking as they

Rebecca tells me everything she knows about fractions.

make and justify their decisions. Since categorizing items takes time, it's not necessary to do with all brainstormed ideas.

Purpose

To help students conceptualize and clarify data by creating categories for brainstormed information; to justify decisions logically

Materials

A topic, key word, or concept in social studies, science, or math; students' journals; chart paper, marker pens

Guidelines

1. Organize students into pairs or small groups.
2. Ask students to head their journals with name, date, and topic.

> **A third-grade class is studying owls**
>
> **Seventh graders are studying ratios and proportions.**

3. Allow four to five minutes for students to talk about what they think they know about the topic.
4. Set aside two to three minutes for students to write, in their journals, everything they recall about the topic and any new ideas they learned from peers. Students can write words and phrases without worrying about correct spelling and mechanics—it's content that's important here.
5. Record all of the students' ideas on chart paper.
6. Reread the list, then model how you categorize.

> **For owls, third-grade teacher Nancy Roche creates the category "What They Eat."**
>
> **For ratio and proportion, seventh-grade teacher Ginny Carnell writes "Ways to Write Ratios."**

7. Ask students to help you place items under the category.

> **Third graders suggest: mice, insects, snakes, voles**
>
> **Seventh graders offer: 7 to 15; 7:15; 7/15**

8. Invite pairs or groups to create their own categories. They should write these in their journals, then help one another organize items under headings.
9. Explain that some items will fall under more than one heading. Students can defend

their positions with persuasive reasons.

10. Collect headings and data. Write on chart paper.

> Third graders created these headings for owls: <u>Habitat</u>, <u>Food</u>, <u>Looks Like</u>, <u>Behavior</u>, <u>Uses</u>, <u>Beliefs</u>.
>
> Seventh graders thought of these headings for ratio and proportion: <u>Ways to Write Ratios</u>, <u>How Differ from Fractions</u>, <u>What They Compare</u>, <u>Solving Problems with Proportions</u> (see chart, right).

11. Adjust incorrect ideas as you study. Add new data.

Brainstorm and Categorize
Strategy Snapshot: Grade 5 Science

Topic: Avalanches

Time: Four 20- to 30-minute class periods. Spreading the lesson over several days enables students to reflect on and internalize the process and allows you to continue other work.

Materials: "Snowy Monster" from *Scholastic News,* January 10, 2000, or any short selection from a math, science, or social studies textbook or a magazine; students' journals, chart paper, markers.

Background Information: Mr. Chad, sixth-grade math and science teacher always searches for science articles that relate to students' studies. He stores helpful items in a file folder that he can dip into whenever he wants to develop and deepen students' understanding of a strategy. To offer students practice in brainstorming and categorizing during a study of weather and precipitation, Mr. Chad uses "Snowy Monsters," a one-page article with headings, a map, and a photograph. He purposely spreads the lesson over three days to build students' anticipation and to have time to continue with other projects.

During the first class, students brainstorm all they know about avalanches. Then students preview the one-page article by reading headings and captions, studying the map and the photograph.

- compare 2 things
- write as fraction
- write with word "to" or a colon
- compares part to whole
- compares part to another part
- percent problems
- not the same as fractions
- denominators of ratio differ from fractions
- compare unlike things
- proportion shows how 2 ratios are equal
- use with rate problems
- use with percent problems

Students adjust and add to ideas during the study.

Brainstorm and Categorize

On the second day, Mr. Chad takes 20 minutes to collect students' brainstorming about avalanches on chart paper. Students discuss their ideas, sharing what they know about avalanches.

deadly	destroy towns
soft snow	in mountains
kill people	bury people, houses
disaster	silent killer
lots in Alps	in U.S.
scientists study	safety rules
warning signs	in Alaska
powerful	bury trees
powdery snow	

On the third day, students work in groups to think about their brainstormed ideas about avalanches and then create headings. After listing their heading suggestions on the board, Mr. Chad asks students to record these in journals and help each other place items under the headings.

The fourth day Mr. Chad collects students' categories and items on chart paper:

Conditions	Destructive Forces	Words That Describe
soft snow	bury trees	silent killer
warning signs	bury people, houses	powerful
powdery snow	silent killer	deadly
mountains	kill people	

Where Occur	What's Being Done	
in Alaska	scientists study	
lots in Alps	safety rules	
in U.S.	warning signs	
mountains		

Here's how students justified placing "mountains" and "warning signs" under two categories.

Jimmy: Mountains are part of the conditions where avalanches happen because they happen in areas that have mountains and the conditions form on a mountain.

Marie: I put "warning" under Conditions because certain things happen that let you know an avalanche might form—it's heavy snow over light, powdery snow at the end of winter. It also goes under What's Being Done because avalanche hunters are studying warning signs and they sometimes cause an avalanche so it won't happen on its own.

MODEL WITH SHORT PIECES

To keep a strategy lesson brief (10 to 20 minutes), use a short piece that relates to your curriculum from a magazine or newspaper, or from a textbook or trade book. It's easier for students to absorb a demonstration when the text is finite. See page 299 for a list of magazines you can mine for concise selections.

STRATEGY LESSON:
Preview / Analyze / Connect

How It Helps You

"Why do we have to do this?" Nick, a fifth grader, asks this every time the class prepares to study a new topic in math, science, history, reading, or writing. By December, Nick's repeated lament irritated Mrs. Franco, his teacher, so much that she vented her frustration and mounting annoyance to me. "I want to shake him," she said. Yesterday, I asked Nick what he'd rather do—a huge mistake. After a long pause, he said, "Play soccer." We both laughed, and the tension broke.

I suggested to Mrs. Franco that she extend and enliven the preview to a 10- to 20-minute lesson and invite students to analyze information, and link ideas and data to their lives, to other experiences.

A few days later, Mrs. Franco stopped me at the top of the stairway. "Nick's group said that he made more connections between percents and our lives than any student," she said. "As the spokesperson for what his group discovered, Nick rattled off: 'For grades; when you have to budget money; and it's on food labels like the percent of fat, sugar, and stuff; and the interest you get on you money.'" Then she hurried down the stairs to her classroom.

By transforming the preview from a perfunctory exercise to an experience that asks students to think, analyze, and connect a topic in the textbook or other reading materials to their lives, you build students' curiosity and set the stage for putting facts to work throughout the study.

Purpose

To build background knowledge by looking at headings, captions and boldface words in a chapter, then analyze them and start making connections

Materials

A section from a textbook, magazine, or newspaper that has headings and visuals

Guidelines

You don't have to do all the activities listed. Choose those that are appropriate for the topic and your students.

1. Organize students into pairs or groups with 4 to 6 members.

2. Ask students to preview a section of a textbook or trade book by reading the following:
   - The chapter or section title
   - The bold face or colored headings
   - Bold face or colored words and the sentence each is in
   - Charts, diagrams, graphs
   - Pictures and captions
   - Sidebars—information in the margins
   - The first and last paragraphs of the selection

3. Have students silently think about ideas and connections they make from their preview, then share with a partner or group.

Mrs. Franco's fifth graders preview a one-page piece called "A Life-Saving Hug," an article about the Heimlich manoeuvre (Scholastic News, Feb. 21, 2000). Their discussion stirs great interest in learning more about this hug, and students can't wait to read the piece.

Here are some connections and comments students made:

- The heading print was so big that I knew this hug was really something that would save lives, but I wasn't sure how.
- The father looks like he's pleased with what his son did. The boy looks proud. It's not usual for a child to save a dad's life.
- The "How To" shows what to do if you're choking. My dad choked once and my mom did the Heimlich. Boy, that piece of chicken flew out fast.
- My mom said once that it [the Heimlich] can break your ribs.
- Maybe we could practice on each other and get good at it.

4. Foster connections if students aren't making any. Try prompts like these: Have you heard the term or idea before? When? Where? How does this affect or relate to your life? To your family and friends? Is this helpful or harmful? Explain. What connotations or feelings and thoughts do specific words trigger? How do these connotations relate to your reading?

5. Ask students to fold a journal page lengthwise and head one column "New" and the other "Known." Students then skim the piece and jot down facts and words that are new and ones they know; this information helps you know what to emphasize. After they read, students can work together on "getting" new information by using the text and each other. Words and ideas that remain confusing provide material for you to teach.

Denotative and Connotative Meanings

The denotative meaning of a word is its dictionary definition. Connotative meanings refer to associations the word brings to your mind. These connotations can be feelings, images, ideas, and similar words.

Tanequa explained that the word hug made her think of showing affection, loving, keeping warm, being happy and excited. "It's like the 'Heimlich Hug' saved a life but with love and care," she said.

Think aloud and show students your connotations for a word. For children in grades 3 to 5, connotative meanings will be a new idea, so take the time to build understanding and support them as they associate feelings and thoughts.

Preview/Analyze/Connect
Strategy Snapshot: Grade 6 Science and Grade 8 Math

Grade 6 Science Class

Topic: Characteristics of Plants

Time: one 30-minute lesson

Materials: Science textbook, *Life Science,* Glencoe (1997)

Background Information: Mrs. Bronson's sixth graders have been analyzing information and connecting what they've learned to their lives, to what they value, and to world issues.

Because the "Characteristics of Plants" section in their textbook had many new terms, Mrs. Bronson asked students to first organize words and facts in "New" and "Known" columns. Everyone had these words under "New": *bryophytes, vascular plant, non-vascular plant.*

To introduce students to these terms and build background knowledge before reading, Mrs. Bronson asked them to read the sentence that included the word (see pages 198–203). But her primary goal was to encourage analysis and connections, so she invited partners to practice those skills.

After students took several minutes to preview the five pages, Mrs. Bronson demonstrated making connections with this think-aloud. Notice she couches her connections in short sentences to duplicate the way her students think and reason, making her process more accessible:

We know that green plants make oxygen. We breathe oxygen in the air. People and animals need oxygen to live. Green plants and forests are important for our survival. The green trees and bushes give off lots of oxygen. We need to work to stop cutting down forests. Without oxygen, animals and people cannot live.

Mrs. Bronson invites partners to think-aloud, analyze and connect one fact from their preview. She places these prompts on the chalkboard to help students: **Can you connect anything to our needs and lives today? Are any plant parts useful to men and animals? Explain.**

Here is Maura and Michael's think-aloud:

MAURA: *A caption asked about destroying the rain forests and not having plants for new drugs.*

MICHAEL: *Remember last year Mrs. T. told us about plants in the rain forest. She said how they could dissolve a bad tooth or make you sleep.*

MAURA: *Yeah. So the rain forest is important for more than just the oxygen. There's plants that can help sick people. We need the rain forest.*

MICHAEL: *Also, birds nest in the trees. Insects eat plants. Animals do, too.*

The "Preview" closes with pairs sharing. Now students read with a richer background, a keener focus for clarifying connections and making new ones, and with a notion of the information's relevance.

Grade 8 Math

Topic: Reading and analyzing graphs

Time: one 15-minute lesson

Materials: *Middle Grades: Math Tools for Success,* Prentice Hall, 1996

Background Information: Ginny Carnell works diligently, from the start of the school year, to help eighth graders in her pre-algebra class analyze material and connect it to authentic life needs. "I find that showing them how math connects to their lives and how it can help them make decisions gets them more involved," she explains before I watch this lesson.

Ginny recaps the previewing process by writing the steps on a transparency. (Use the chalkboard or a chart if you don't have an overhead projector.) Because this is the second time her students have done a preview, Ginny models the process with the first page, then asks partners to preview the next three pages. She circulates around the room, responding to questions. Ginny notices many students are having difficulty making connections, so she prompts them by writing questions on a new transparency: *How can a graph help you make a decision? What can make a graph misleading? How does misleading information affect you? When might you use information in a graph?*

Ginny circulates again. First she stops to help Tamika and Rochelle, who don't see why the bar graphs on the busiest airports are misleading. "What do you notice about numbers listed for 'millions of passengers?'" Ginny poses.

"One starts at 55 and the other at 0," says Tamika. "Oh, I get it. It exaggerates the statistics and looks like Chicago's O'Hare is more than two times as busy as Hartsfield in Atlanta." Ginny praises the girls and moves to Jack and David, whose hands are raised.

"We can't figure out why the graphs on college enrollment look so different," says Jack. Ginny points them to the break symbol on one graph that eliminates 0 to 13 million.

"That makes it look like enrollment went up so much," says David. "The table and other graph show it went up in small amounts."

"A break symbol can change how you see data," says Jack. Ginny invites both pairs to share with the class what they now understand about break symbols and interpreting graphs.

"It's hard for them to think critically and look carefully, especially at the beginning of the year," Ginny tells me. "So, I give students all the support they need to catch on. They learn a lot about what we are going to study, and I'm also helping them draw conclusions and learn to look at graphed information with a critical eye."

STRATEGY LESSON:
Fast-Write

How It Helps You

Before eighth graders start a study of the Vietnam War for humanities, I ask students to complete a fast-write, a writing strategy in which students write about a topic for a few minutes to reclaim what they know.

Students' writing shows an emotional connection to the war peppered with images and some facts. More than half of the class refers to Robin Williams's movie, *Good Morning, Vietnam,* but none give details from the film. All students wrote that the war didn't have full U.S. support. Words and phrases like "hippies, burning draft cards, jeeps, villages, Ho Chi Minh Trail, gorilla [sic] warfare, and Forest Gump" were in most pieces.

A fast-write can quickly inform you of students' recall about a topic previously covered or one you think they should have some knowledge of. Particularly effective with students who are reluctant to share with peers, the fast-write is a safe "cognitive warm-up" that can be a springboard for discussions and provide you with data that inform instructional planning.

FAST-WRITES IN THIRD GRADE

I find that fast-writes work better if you start in the spring semester of third grade, when students have developed writing fluency and can freely express thoughts under timed conditions.

Teaching Reading in Social Studies, Science, and Math

Purpose

To discover what students know about a topic; to use continual writing to help students reclaim information

Materials

A topic you've studied; students' journals

Guidelines

1. Explain how to do a fast-write. I might say: "With a fast-write, you write about a topic for several minutes. Even if you're stuck, because no ideas are surfacing, keep writing. If no ideas come to mind, you can write 'I'm stuck,' or 'Nothing to write,' or repeat the last word you wrote until an idea surfaces."

2. Model a fast-write. On chart paper, I show students how a fast-write works, repeating words when ideas stop flowing.

3. Encourage students to ask questions about the modelled process. Eighth graders wonder if they can write in "phrases" and not worry about sentences. "That's fine," I tell them.

4. Call for volunteers to read their fast-writes and expand everyone's knowledge. If no one volunteers, collect papers and read them to determine the level of students' background knowledge.

5. Continue modelling and asking students to practice until they show you they can comfortably do a fast-write.

Vietnam

Sara A. Major   May 11

1960's, hippies w/ colored sunglasses and daisies. Wierd clothing, leather with fringes, and long haired guys. Very bad war, no one wanted to be drafted. Mr. Lathrop was drafted but didn't go because of a heart problem. He was happy he didn't go. Was fought over in Vietnam. Americans were trying to keep out Russia/Japan(?) stuck stuck stuck there was plenty of bombs and violence. We were there just to keep people out and offer a while people were mad about sending their kids over to die when nothing was happening. Protests, Bill Clinton is given grief for not going.

An eighth grader's fast-write shows how focused writing can reclaim memories.

Fast-Write

Fast-Write
Strategy Snapshot: Grade 8 Math and Grade 3 Science

Grade 8 Geometry

Topic: Linear Equations

Time: Eight minutes of one class; 10 to 15 minutes for the teacher to read and evaluate

Materials: A topic that you believe students might be familiar with, such as the solar system, multiplication, or the technical revolution; writing journals

Background Information: Tom Arthur, affectionately known as "Mr. A," teaches three math-talented eighth graders geometry. He wants to discover what they recall about systems of linear equations so he can develop a review that addresses students' needs and builds on their recall. "In less than five minutes," Tom told me, "the activity generated a simple and clear picture of the students' vocabulary knowledge and level of understanding."

After Tom read students' fast-writes, he was able to plan instruction for this review that would focus students practice and talk on:

- solution to an equation, and the method of solution
- linear combinations
- substitution
- graphic representations
- consistent, inconsistent intersection, union
- parallel and coincident

"As students practice," Tom wrote in planning notes, "they will explain their work to one another at the board, to me on their papers, and they will also discuss equations and problems that I model."

Grade 3 Science

Topic: Nutrition

Time: 10 minutes for the fast-write; 10 to 15 minutes for the teacher to read and evaluate

Materials: Writing journals or paper

Background Information: For several years, Nancy Roche has opened her study of nutrition by asking, "What do you know about nutrition and good eating habits?" Groups talk for five to ten minutes; then Nancy collects their ideas on chart paper. "I only get a handle on the five or six who talk," she confesses during our chat about this science theme. I show Nancy the fast-writes some eighth graders completed on Vietnam. "I've never done a fast-write with third graders," she says. "But I'm open."

A few days later, I meet with Nancy's third graders and explain what a fast-write is all about. Then I compose one on the water-cycle, modelling what I do when ideas stop flowing. Third graders pepper me with questions: *Will you always get another idea? How many ideas should I have? Is it okay if you don't know much? Can I stop if my hand's tired?*

After fielding questions, I invite groups to talk for a few minutes about nutrition and good eating habits. Then students complete their first fast-writes, which Nancy finds helpful because she knows what each student knows prior to the study. We both noticed how quiet and focused students were when thinking and remembering.

STUDENT RESOURCE FOR ALGEBRA

Algebra to Go, Great Source, Wilmington, MA, 2000

Fast-Write

> Ha the   May 16
>
> Nutrition is very important to a humin body. Nutrition is good eating habits. like eating fruit like apples bananas and and and pers. But you can all so eat bread cracers cracers cracers cracer. But spigetti is good for you too. Milk is a good drink and so is oning juse.

Third-grade fast-writes help their teacher see what each child knows about nutrition.

STRATEGY LESSON:
Anticipation Guide

How It Helps You

I launched our study of civil rights by asking my eighth graders to complete an anticipation guide before reading John Griffin's *Black Like Me* (Dutton Signet, 1960). An anticipation guide is a series of four to five statements created by the teacher to stir disagreement and discussion among students. Effective when students have some background knowledge, but not enough to develop valid opinions, the anticipation guide invites students to agree or disagree with the statements before and after learning.

I chose *Black Like Me* because every student could read this book, which I felt would provide them with an accurate picture of life in the South before the Civil Rights Movement. Tensions escalated in two groups, who disagreed on whether African Americans could be lynched without a trial. All but seven students argued that today, African Americans had equal education and job opportunities and could purchase a house anywhere, if they had the money. Students' beliefs changed my teaching plans, and I asked them to search for articles or notes from radio or television news that challenged the notion of equality for all.

With an anticipation guide, students' beliefs become visible and can support your instructional decisions (Duffelmeyer, 1984; Herber & Nelson, 1986; Readence, Bean, & Baldwin, 1998). The guide's statements create disagreement and build tension about issues that can only be clarified by information gained during the study. Discussion of students' responses to each statement builds some background knowledge and is a great motivator for reading to determine which statements are accurate.

Purpose

To improve comprehension by focusing students' attention on key concepts prior to reading; to motivate students to read to discover whether their opinions can be supported; to adjust opinions after a study

Materials

A topic that's slightly familiar to students

Guidelines

Teacher Preparation:

1. Identify the concepts you want students to understand.

2. Create four to five highly opinionated statements that can support or challenge students' current opinions and ideas about a topic.

3. Decide whether you only want to use this before learning or whether you want students to return to the anticipation guide after the study to reread and discuss the statements and adjust their responses (see page 116).

Guidelines for Students:

1. Read each statement below.

2. If you agree, put a check or "Yes" next to it. If you disagree, put an "X" or a "No" next to it.

3. Share your reactions with a partner or with your group.

4. Discuss reactions and reasons for them.

5. After discussing, write the main points you recall.

6. Return to the anticipation guide after the study; reread statements and mark your responses again.

7. On the back, write reasons for changes, if any, in your responses.

Students check their anticipation guides against the text.

ANTICIPATION GUIDE FOR BLACK LIKE ME BY JOHN GRIFFIN

Read each statement below. If you agree, put a check next to it. If you disagree, put an X next to it.

Share and discuss with your partner.

_X_ Posing as a black man in the South in the 1950's was an easy thing to do.

_X_ Getting food, drink, and bathrooms was easy for an African American before Civil Rights Legislation.

_X_ Hotels for African Americans were similar to hotels for whites.

_X_ African Americans could be lynched without a trial.

_X_ It was easy for African American to get an education before Civil Rights Legislation.

Briefly write about the high points you and your partner discussed.

Our group thought all the same things
- whites don't understand what it's like to be black
- blacks were able to eat just not as high quality
- blacks had to share bathrooms
- most stores were owned by whites

Luke's anticipation guide.

Anticipation Guide
Strategy Snapshot: Grade 5 Science

Topic: Tropical Rain Forest

Time: 15 minutes to complete the "Before" part of the guide; one 45-minute period to preview, analyze and discuss the article; 15 minutes to complete the "After" part of the guide.

Materials: anticipation guide; "Amazon Alert!" persuasive article, Level 4, *Write Time For Kids,* Time, Inc. 2000.

Background Information: To introduce a study of the tropical rain forest and build enthusiasm and background knowledge, Mrs. Bayliss invites her fifth graders to complete a "Before" and "After" anticipation guide. "I want them to revise their thinking and practice proving changes with specific details from the text," she says.

Students preview and analyze, then read and discuss the one-page "Amazon Alert!" article. Finally, they complete the "After" work.

While students revisit the article to find evidence for ideas and positions, Mrs. Bayliss circulates, supporting students who have difficulty locating proof by asking them to reread a specific paragraph or section.

Students share their position changes on statements and raise dozens of questions that Mrs. Bayliss records on chart paper. She's delighted at how the exercise has sparked students' interest and desire to investigate the topic.

ANTICIPATION GUIDE

BEFORE Agree/Disagree		AFTER Agree/Disagree
D X / A /	The rain forest is unimportant to mankind.	D / A /
	Many scientists feel that they will run out of time to study species before they become extinct.	
D X / A /	Wildlife can survive by finding other forests.	D X / A /
	The Amazon is important because it holds 1/5 of the world's fresh water supply.	
A /	One eighth of the Amazon rain forest has already been destroyed and this can affect everyone who lives on this planet.	A /

Predict what you believe this selection will be about:

I predict that this articale is abott rain forest and the amazon.

After Reading:
• Complete the "After" part of the anticipation guide.

• On the back of this paper, give reasons for any changes in your opinions that occurred after reading and discussing.

I learned a lot about the rain forests. We need it for fresh water, animals need it for homes, and also we need it for oxygen. It is also the worlds richest habitat.

A fifth grader completes an anticipation guide before studying the rain forest.

Setting Purposes

How It Helps You

After a three-minute preview of the physical science textbook section called "Describing Matter," Mr. Swann read and defined the words listed in the margin: *physical property, physical change, chemical change, chemical property,* and *law of conservation of mass.* Then he asked students to read the first section and take notes on important information.

As I walked up and down the rows in this seventh-grade class, I noticed a boy drumming his fingers on the desk, his eyes wandering everywhere but through the textbook pages. "Can I help?" I asked. He shrugged his shoulders. "Would you like to tell me why you're not reading?"

"How can I pick out stuff? I don't know what I'm looking for," he said and put his head on the desk, sending me the message to move on. This student was not alone. As I scanned students' notes, I noticed that most were simply copying entire sections.

During lunch, Mr. Swann and I debriefed. I suggested he reserve more time to prepare students for a new topic and conduct experiments that illustrate the differences between physical and chemical changes. "So students can focus on the essential information in the text," I offered, "help them set purposes for reading. If students know that their purpose for this first reading is to explain, in their own words, new vocabulary and give examples of each term, they can sift out key information."

Setting purposes helps take the mystery out of "What should I learn? What would I get out of this material?" It clarifies for students the information they need to understand and remember. It eases your teaching because students can work more efficiently on tasks, such as culling essential information (Dowhower, 1999; Harvey, 1998; Keene and Zimmermann, 1998; Readence, Moore, and Rickelman, 2000).

Purpose

To help students read for specific information; to teach students how to set their own purposes

Materials

A chapter or section in a textbook, trade book, or an experiment, such as testing solutions for acid or base or dissecting owl pellets

Guidelines

1. Set purposes before reading, observing, or conducting an experiment.

2. Once they understand the benefits of doing so, collaborate with students to set purposes. Show students how you set purposes by thinking-aloud. Here's what Nancy Roche tells third graders before they examine their owl pellets:

> The purpose of dissecting the pellet is to see what owls feed on. Work with your probe slowly and carefully, so you don't break any of the delicate bones and insect shells. Use your "Bone Sorting Chart" and try to match bones to those on the sheet.
>
> Let me show you how I open and dissect a pellet and match bones.

Students form a circle around Nancy at the table and watch, breathless and silent. Before each child receives a pellet, Nancy reviews the purpose and writes it on the chalkboard.

3. Show students ways they can set purposes on their own. Here are some prompts to share with students:

- Tell yourself the reasons for observing and make these your purpose.

  Example: I'm going to observe the guinea pig to determine its sleep/play pattern.

- Make understanding new vocabulary a purpose.

  Example: I'm going to learn about two new words in the chapter, "Matter" and "Temperature."

- Treat textbook headings as main ideas and find two to three details that explain each heading.

  Example: I'll use these headings to help me discover key ideas: "The Development of Trade," "A Superior New Ship Design," "A Powerful Kingdom."

- Think of the outcomes you hope to achieve when conducting an experiment and make those your purpose.

  Example: Does the shape of a container affect the volume of liquid?

- Explain the topic and give examples that help you understand it.

  Example: The topic is "Changes in State of Water." The purpose, then, is to list the changes in state of water and explain each.

More Guidelines for Teachers

- Use your preview to set purposes for what to learn.

  Example: Our preview showed the chapter was about Europeans searching for new trade routes. The purposes we set: discover why they wanted new trade routes, which explorers found these, and how trade changed the lives of Europeans.

- Use parts of your "getting-ready-to-read experiences" to set purposes.

  Example: We used "Brainstorm/Categorize" to set these purposes: discover how spiders are helpful and harmful.

- Use one or more processes for completing math computation or solving word problems.

  Example: Have students solve a percent problem in two ways, or ask students to explain how multiplication and division are related.

4. Move students to independence when collaborations reveal that students are ready.

TIP BOX

Use Think-Alouds and Model How to Set Purposes

Spend two to four weeks demonstrating how to set purposes by modelling and thinking aloud. Make your process visible to students. I did a think-aloud for setting purposes for sixth graders before they read about manners during the Renaissance. I based my words on a brainstormed list about manners that students generated in the past. I reread the list the class made of manners today and in the past. Some students remembered reading that people ate with their fingers and wiped their hands on dogs' backs in the Middle Ages. Then I thought—out loud— about the picture of the man eating with his fingers in the book. Next I inform students that our purpose for reading this section will be to see how manners were different in the Renaissance and to discover if any resembled ours today.

The think-aloud makes clear that students are to read for details about table manners during the Renaissance, then connect this information to present-day manners. It helps them sift out the information about clothing and music from that period—details they'll discuss on another day.

Once students have experienced the power of setting purposes and how it helps them focus their reading, offer some guidelines that show students how to set their own purposes before reading and learning.

Setting Purposes
Strategy Snapshot: Grade 3 Science

Topic: Dissecting owl pellets

Time: Five to ten minutes to set purposes; 50 minutes for dissecting and writing self-evaluations

Materials: owl pellets

Background Information: For two months, third graders have been researching owls, learning how to take notes for reports, and watching videos. While students are writing their reports, Nancy Roche reserves a class for students to dissect their own owl pellets.

"It's important that students understand that they can also set purposes for things that aren't reading-centered," says Nancy. "I was constantly setting purposes for completing note cards on different topics and for their reading. But purposes are part of solving math problems, observing trees or ants, and doing experiments."

Matthew and Emilee, third graders, dissect their owl pellets.

During the last fifteen minutes of class, Nancy and I help students place their pellet remains in a plastic bag so they can continue to study them at home. Then we invite students to write about their feelings toward dissecting the pellets and what they learned. The pieces below illustrate students' enthusiasm and how much they learned. Nancy and I loved that many "felt like real scientists."

> Owl Pellety Dissections
> Grace 17   April 2
>
> I felt a little queasy when I got my pellet. I though it was pretty sick opening stuff that came out of owls somache.
>
> I learned that owls eat alot of diffrent things. I learned that owls stomache works like a macine. Their stomach plucks the fur and takes out the bones. I learned that owls eat pretty much the same things every day.
>
> I liked doing this because you got to see how how the owls ate each day.

Third graders self-evaluate their experience of dissecting owl pellets.

> Owl Pellet Disections
> #8 Grant   April 2
>
> When I got my pellet I felt excited because I thought it would be neat to se a bone from a mouse or somthing. What I learnd was that the owl sucks out all the meet and spits out the bones. I liked doing this.

Pause and Reflect on:
Preparing Students to Learn

Time spent building background knowledge prior to learning is a sound investment and an essential part of teaching; it enlarges students' knowledge base and supports students' long term growth as readers and learners.

The experiences you offer students before they learn relate directly to how much students retain and understand from reading, observing, writing, and experimenting. When you increase students' preparation time and deepen their comprehension, students have a better chance to learn and retain new material and vocabulary.

⚶ Chapter 5 ⚶

Strategies to Use
During Learning

*Effective reading to me means having sufficient control over oral
language and the processes and skills, understandings and knowledge
of written language to be able to interact with written texts,
comprehend what the author of the text(s) intended...and unpack
the agendas of those who wrote them.*   —Brian Cambourne

My daughter, Anina, teaches English and World History to 35 sixth graders in New York City. About a month into her third year, Anina telephoned me and told me that several students read faster than she does, but they can't retell what they've read.

"It's as if some students eyeball each page and think that's reading," she said. We discussed having Anina model how to read a textbook chapter slowly and thoughtfully, pausing after two to three paragraphs to retell and evaluate her recall of information, rereading if she remembers only a little. "I know I'll have to do this many times throughout the year," Anina said. And initially, some students became angry, insisting "That's the way we always do it."

"It's tough to change established patterns and perceptions," I told her. "But it's important to keep modelling how reading rates change with the purpose of reading tasks. Show them how you read slowly when you have lots of new information to learn. Think aloud and explain how pausing to retell helps you check recall. Also model how you read quickly and even skim parts with a fashion magazine or a mystery novel. We'll talk about paired reading and questioning when I visit."

During the second week in October, I spent the day in my daughter's class. "Finished," sixth grade Susan blurted out, a note of victory in her voice. She scanned the room. Thirty-one classmates were still reading the four-page section in their social studies textbook.

Anina bent down next to Susan's desk. "Can you tell me something about how the Egyptians built the pyramids?" [Long pause.]

"Ummm. I think they used stone. I read the words, I did, I did, I can read all of them," Susan said. Her voice escalated in volume and pitch. For Susan, finishing first means she's a good reader. She does not equate understanding and remembering information with reading.

"I'm sure you did," Anina said patiently. "But you need to reread and slow down and stop to retell. It's important to remember what you read." Susan sighed deeply and opened her book. Her body language revealed frustration. "Let's share the reading," Anina suggested. Shoulders drooping, head down, Susan reluctantly followed her teacher to the back of the room where they sat together, read and practiced retelling.

Like Susan, many students develop the belief that fast equals good. Sometimes adolescents use this speedy reading behavior to cover up the fact that a text is too difficult because they can't read many of the words. Fast reading to finish first can also develop among students who have a history of completing in-class reading tasks last. Feelings of inadequacy and lowered self-esteem can result from holding up the lesson, from peer put-downs, and from a teacher repeatedly asking, "Are you finished yet?" To compensate, students skip over sections of text or don't complete the reading and make the appearance of finishing more important than comprehending and learning.

Students like Susan need teachers to model metacognitive strategies and then practice them with short chunks of text. If we want these students to be able, as Cambourne notes, to "unpack the agendas" of the texts they read, to analyze for bias, stereotyping, exaggerating and omission of facts, (see pages 311–315), then developing strategies that foster understanding and recall of material is a prerequisite.

Metacognition: Defining the Term

Metacognition is the term for the research and theory that examines "thinking about thinking" (Garner, 1987). When I'm participating in a workshop about assessing and evaluating reading and I start thinking about fixing dinner, my ability to pinpoint that my mind is wandering is an example of metacognition. If I review my test-taking strengths and decide that I'd prefer a short-answer test to an essay test on cell division, I'm using metacognition to assess my test-taking strengths.

Researchers identify three categories of metacognition: personal test-taking strengths; awareness of mind-wandering (Flavell, 1981); and uses of learning strategies (Garner, 1992). Information gathered from thinking about reading and learning is what self-monitoring is all about. Once students know how strategies work and why they support learning, they'll be able to access strategies that can improve comprehension and increase recall (Gillet and Temple, 2000; Fountas and Pinnell, 2001; Vaughan and Estes, 1986).

You'll explore three strategy lessons in this chapter that foster self-monitoring: *Using Context Clues to Figure Out New Words; Paired Reading and Questioning;* and *Read/Pause/Retell.* Each strategy focuses students on thinking about whether they understand what they are reading and learning. As you adapt and present these lessons, let students know that you use the same strategies when learning new material or reading a challenging text. Model how you cope with tough words and confusing sentences from texts you are reading. When you teach self-monitoring, you provide students with tools that enable them to solve reading problems throughout life.

True independence occurs when students can determine what they do and don't understand, then access fix-it strategies that will enable them to comprehend and recall. In this chapter, you'll also explore three fix-it strategies: *Think-Aloud; Close Reading;* and *Rereading.* In addition, it's helpful to discuss reading rate with your students as they need to understand that reading rates change with the purposes of reading tasks.

Guided Practice of During-Learning Strategies

Guided practice is a short session of 5 to 15 minutes that allows you to support students as they try to use a strategy. After you present a strategy lesson and field students' questions, invite students to practice with a short passage from the textbook you're using or from a magazine article that relates to the topic (see page 299).

Because during-reading strategies can boost students' level of comprehension and recall, it's important for content teachers to set aside class time for student practice. And because class time is so valuable to content teachers with required curricula, here are some suggestions to help foster meaningful guided-practice sessions and make the most of that precious time:

1. Isolate and model a during-reading strategy, and make it visible for students.

2. Have students practice the strategy during class time. Make a point to have guided-practice sessions involve a topic from or related to the curriculum.

In schools that schedule classes for 45 minutes, four to five times a week, finding time for guided practice as well as covering required content is particularly challenging. I suggest that you schedule brief (10–15 minutes), targeted practice sessions consistently throughout the week.

Kathleen Hobbs decided that developing students' metacognitive powers was a top priority. She firmly believes that students who self-monitor and apply fix-it strategies will learn more. Kathleen developed the following schedule for her science class that meets for four, 45-minute periods a week. In her own words, "I like leaving a week between introducing and practicing the strategy, so there's time for students to process the first phase."

Day	Week 1	Week 3
Monday	strategy lesson think-aloud	guided practice: 10 min.
Tuesday	review strategy lesson field questions: 15 min.	no guided practice
Wednesday	guided practice: 15 min.	guided practice: 10 min.
Friday	guided practice: 10 min.	guided practice: 10 min.

Hunter Haggerty, a middle school math teacher, prefers to immerse eighth graders in guided practice. His schedule revolves around two week blocks that occur after introducing a strategy. Hunter's eighth graders have five, forty-five minute math classes a week.

Day	Week 1	Week 2
Monday	strategy lesson:15 min. problem-solving guidelines	guided practice: 10 min.
Tuesday	model process again field questions students share process 15 min.	partner work: 10 min.
Wednesday	guided practice: 10 min.	review process: 10 min.
Thursday	guided practice: 10 min.	guided practice: 10 min.
Friday	field questions: 10 min.	quiz: 10-15 min.

According to Hunter, providing the time for guided practice immediately after the strategy lesson helps students unravel kinks, clarify misunderstandings, and answer questions. And it affords Hunter multiple opportunities to circulate, spot-check students' work, and answer questions that can clarify the process.

A student once asked, "Do I have to write my plan for solving, even though I know it in my head?"

"Well, if you know it, writing is easy," he replied. "If you can't write it, you're probably unsure and need to reread the problem and think about what you have to solve."

Organizing Guided Practice: Grade 4 History

Since teachers in self-contained classes have more flexibility with managing their time, it's easier for them to reserve chunks of time for guided practice. "My students need more than ten minutes for practice—sometimes just organizing them takes five-plus minutes," says Nan Richards.

Nan likes to present a strategy lesson, such as Read/Pause/Retell, one day, gather students feedback, and answer their questions (see pages 134–138). The next day, Nan reviews the lesson, which she wrote on large chart paper, and invites students to share any experiences they've had with the strategy. One student said that she always stopped at the end of a chapter to do a rerun of what happened. "Now I use the term rerun," Nan says. "It really sums up that retelling process."

On a third day, Nan engages students in fifteen to twenty minutes of guided practice and continues practicing each day until most students can apply the strategy. "I can always take a small group for review and additional practice while others read or write independently," she adds. "I also find that I can whittle the guided practice to fifteen, sometimes even ten minutes after four to five sessions."

> ### Guided Practice Snapshot
> ### Grade 3: Partner Read/Pause/Retell

Topic: Owls

Time: 20 minutes a day for five days

Materials: Trade books from the library

Background Information: To teach students to read, retell, and jot down notes in their own words, Nancy first models the strategy with Mary Hofstra, Powhatan's reading resource teacher. The pair model the strategy on three consecutive days. Then Nancy invites third-grade partners to practice reading several sentences or a paragraph and retell. During guided practice, partners read the same text, then evaluate the richness of one another's retellings. "I know they're ready to work independently," Nancy says, "when I notice the retellings are more detailed. Their notes improve, too." This strategy is ideal for research; it also supports students' independent reading and assigned textbook reading.

Knowing When Students Can Use a Strategy Independently

It can take six to eight weeks for students to absorb, process and use a strategy such as Close Reading or Read/Pause/Retell independently. The amount of time the students need varies with grade levels and whether students have had previous experiences with practicing and applying a strategy. Continue guided practice until just a small group (2 to 5 students) remains who don't "get it." Support those students who continue to need extra help while others complete reading and writing assignments.

When to Put a Strategy Aside

Sometimes, no one or only a handful of students understand a strategy you've demonstrated. If most struggle, consider moving on and returning to this strategy later in the year. Students can get discouraged if practice continues and they make little progress. Often, introducing and practicing a strategy several times, then switching gears and focusing on another strategy is beneficial. Time allows the subconscious mind to process new ideas, to repair confusions, and to make connections to known information. One fifth grader's comments illustrate this point. The model his partner provided helped this student sort out negative feelings. Three months later, he had gained confidence in his ability to learn.

> The first time we tried *Close Reading*, I could hardly listen. It was hard for me to explain details. I thought it was stupid to do, even after practicing with a partner (she did the work). Three months later, we did *Close Reading* again. I could do it and it made sense. It's weird how I got it now.

Here are some behaviors and work that can help you decide whether students are ready to move on to another strategy.

- Questions about the strategy have diminished because students understand how it works.
- Students apply the strategy to other reading or experiences.
- Students can explain, in writing or by talking, how the strategy works and ways it can improve reading and learning.
- Written work illustrates the strategy is being used.
- Quizzes and tests demonstrate the strategy is supporting learning.
- Participation in whole- and small-group discussions reveals students' knowledge of and ability to use a strategy.

Give Students a Self-Monitoring Reading Strategy

The more we foster independent growth, the more our students will gain. To help students monitor their reading, teach them how to use INSERT, the acronym for Interactive Notation System for Effective Reading and Thinking, developed by Vaughan and Estes (1986).

INSERT Notations

I agree = ✓

I disagree = ✗

That's new = +

I don't understand = ?

WOW! That's terrific! = ★!

That's important = ★

Plan several 8- to 10-minute guided-practice sessions where students read a paragraph from a textbook using INSERT. Have students mark lightly in pencil, then erase after they finish. Invite pairs to compare their responses and help one another access fix-it strategies (see pages 142–151).

STRATEGY LESSON:
Using Context Clues to Figure Out New Words

How It Helps You

"The last thing I want to do when I'm reading a great book is look up a word I don't know in the dictionary." These words, spoken by Lisa, a fourth grader, sum up my feelings and the feelings of students everywhere.

I recall teachers telling me to "look it up in the dictionary," when I asked for help with a word's meaning. My immediate reaction was to tell them "No way." What I usually did, and what most students do, is skip over the word. Interrupting reading with a trip to the dictionary can disconnect readers from the text. It's also frustrating when you're in the middle of a great part. The dictionary is an important tool that I invite students to use once they have some knowledge of a word, but teaching students how to use the context clues—phrases and sentences in the text—enables learners to figure out tough words while reading.

When you teach students about context clues, you provide them with a lifelong strategy. Once students become experts at using clues embedded in the text, they gain independence in reading, improve comprehension, and enlarge their knowledge of words' multiple meanings. Keep in mind that it's also important to give students strategies that help them solve word problems when there are no context clues (see pages 133–134).

Purpose

To develop students' ability to use clues in the text, photographs, charts, diagrams, and captions to figure out the meanings of unfamiliar words

Materials

Overhead transparency and projector or chart paper; sample sentences from a textbook, nonfiction trade book, magazine, or newspaper article

Guidelines

1. Print three to four difficult sentences from students' reading on the transparency or the chart paper. You might have to include sentences that came before or after the sample sentences (See sample, right.)

2. Uncover samples one at a time. I read a selection to seventh graders from a *Science World* article, "Can Alaska Heal?" First I read the sentence with *decompose,* telling students that this word confused me. Then I back up and read the preceding sentence.

3. Think aloud and model how you use clues in the text to

SAMPLE SENTENCE

Since oil seeps deep into gravel and rock, workers brought in bulldozers to churn up hidden oil globs, then applied chemicals to break apart oil molecules. But ultimately the natural flushing action of waves— in which sunlight and oxygen naturally *decomposes* oil particles—proved more efficient than all the mops, sponges, power hoses, and well-meaning human effort (p. 12, *Science World,* March 20, 2000, vol. 56, #12).

figure out a word's meaning. Here's what I modelled for my seventh graders:

> I'm not sure what "decomposes" means. I don't see a clue in this sentence. The sentence before says chemicals were used to break apart oil molecules. That's what the waves and sun and oxygen did. So decompose must mean break apart.

4. Continue the process with a second word.

5. Invite students to study a third sample and then write the context clues that enabled them to determine the word's meaning.

6. Ask volunteers to share the process they used to decipher the word's meaning.

7. Continue practicing with texts students are using.

8. Let students who have internalized the strategy work independently.

9. Support students who need additional reinforcement by having them work with you or a peer expert.

Using Context Clues to Figure Out New Words
Strategy Snapshot: Student-Led Eighth-Grade Lesson

Topic: Civil rights

Preparation Time: 15 minutes—students printed their sentences on transparencies with washable colored markers

Presentation Time: 30 minutes

Materials: overhead transparencies and projector or chart paper; trade books and magazines students are reading

Background Information: Throughout the year, students share how they apply the strategy to their reading. Our study of civil rights was framed in a reading workshop, where pairs or individuals read books they chose—titles that related to our theme.

Since it was already April, the students had observed me model this strategy and they had practiced it often; I invited them to model the process. I've included Molly's think-aloud, for it illustrates the level of problem solving I hope all students will achieve.

Students' Examples for Eighth-Grade Strategy Lesson

Jennifer Johnston, a white Charlotte resident, worries that ending busing could spell the beginning of <u>resegregation</u> in Charlotte and other cities. Johnston was bused to predominantly African-American West Charlotte High in the 1980's. She is now in charge of the Swann Fellowship, a Charlotte organization dedicated to integration. —From *Scholastic News,* vol. 68, # 17, p. 5.

Molly's think-aloud for resegregation:

I know that busing ended segregation—all white and all black schools. So if busing stopped, you'd have resegregation—going back to segregation. I also know that "re" means to go back. This girl's in charge of integration, which is the opposite of segregation. So I'm right—resegregation means going back to separation.

When I ask students to make their thought processes visible, it offers me the opportunity to observe how well they apply the strategy to their reading. Moreover, as students share, everyone observes how a peer adapts the strategy and learns from peers that backing up or reading ahead often helps decode the meanings of words.

What to Do When Context Clues Aren't Enough

Educators agree that using context clues is an important vocabulary-building strategy. As readers repeatedly meet the same words, in different contexts, they refine and enlarge their understanding of a word's multiple meanings (Ryder and Graves; 1998; Graves and Graves, 2000; Nagy, 1988; Vacca and Vacca, 2000).

However, there will be times when the passages or texts have few or no context clues, and discovering the meanings of these words becomes a frustrating experience. Teach students what to do if context clues aren't there.

Strategy 1: Preteach Concepts and Vocabulary

- Introduce unfamiliar words and/or concepts to students *before* they encounter them in the text (Chapter 11). Do this by composing an original sentence rich in context clues and asking students to explain the word; that way, even though the text may not provide context clues, you have pre-taught the vocabulary using (and reinforcing) the context clues strategy.
- Create a collaborative word web or concept web by inviting students to tell you what

they already know (Alvermann and Phelps, 1998; Vacca and Vacca 2000). As the study continues, students can add to and adjust items on the web. Josh Mosser and I want students to think about the term *Middle Ages* by considering these categories: religion, social system, feudal system, war and sieges, vassals, chivalry. During the eight weeks the students study this historical period, Josh takes a few minutes, three to four times a week, to collect ideas for the web. Students gain deep insights into a topic or concept when they build and review the web.

Strategy 2: Strengthen Students' Word Knowledge in Your Subject

- Teach students the meanings of prefixes, suffixes and roots or word parts. Middle school teachers can ask the English teacher on their team to support them by teaching word parts. Teachers in grades three to five can integrate word-building lessons during the day.

Knowing word parts can quickly multiply the number of new words students can start to understand. Your students become detectives, using the clues the word parts provide to figure out meanings of words they've never met. If they know that the Latin root *equi-* means equal, they can begin to unlock the meaning of an entire family of related words. Many of the words related to "equi–" invite them to learn more about additional words and roots by referring to the dictionary.

A Family of Words Related to the Root equi-

equal	equilateral	equidistant	equator
equation	equiform	equidiurnal	equilibrium
equipotential	equimolecular	equimultiple	equirotal

STRATEGY LESSON:
Read/Pause/Retell/Reread or Read On

How It Helps You
"It takes too much time to stop and retell," complains Eddie, a sixth grader. "Then I have to read it again," he whines. "It's too much work."

Teaching Reading in Social Studies, Science, and Math

Eddie is failing history, science, and English. Reading and retaining details is a struggle for him. The reading specialist and I take turns helping Eddie obtain a repertoire of reading strategies. This scenario repeats itself during the first six weeks. Each time, I model and think aloud how rereading helps me recall details. Finally, Eddie gives the strategy a try. "It helped—some," he begrudgingly admits. "But it means work."

School for Eddie and many other high-risk students is something they "have to do." Their poor performance, low self-esteem, and zero confidence often result in disruptive behavior or what many teachers describe as "having attitude." Deep down, these students don't want to be difficult; they wear a badge that dares the teacher to get them involved with learning by calling attention to the fact that they need and want help.

To help students, set aside 10 minutes, three to four times each week so students can practice reading and retelling with small chunks of text. Repeated practice enables them to internalize the strategy and experience how it can support recall and their ability to understand complex passages. These practice sessions also build students' self-confidence as they experience that the strategy does help them recall and understand new material.

Purpose

To help students self-monitor their comprehension and recall; to show students how to improve sketchy recall

Materials

A passage from a textbook, nonfiction trade book, magazine or newspaper article, or a math word problem; overhead transparency and projector or chart paper

Guidelines

1. Print the passage or math problem on the blank transparency or chart. Here's a math problem I share in seventh grade:

> Dave has a 36-inch board and a 48-inch board. Dave wants to cut each board into the same number of 7-inch pieces. What is the greatest number of pieces into which he can cut the boards?

2. Read the math problem or passage to students. Think aloud and express your feelings. For the math problem, I say:

> I'm confused. My head seems to spin the first time I read a math problem.

3. Recap everything you remember from the first reading without looking at the passage. Here's my math recap:

> **The only thing I remember is two boards with different measurements, and something about pieces, too.**

4. Reread the passage out loud to students, then silently read it to yourself.

5. Retell again, and don't look at the text. Retelling for math problem after three readings:

> **There are 2 boards. One is 36 inches; the other is 48 inches. Each board is to be cut into the same number of 7-inch pieces. So I have to find the greatest number of pieces that can be cut from both boards.**

Point out how much more you remembered by rereading the passage. Explain that sometimes you have to reread a difficult passage three times. That's fine, especially when

---

Read/Pause/Retell with a Social Studies Selection

1. Here's a passage from *Give Me Liberty!* by Russell Freedman (Holiday House, 2000) that I share with fourth graders:

> *Women did not take to the streets, but they made their views known by banding together in societies called the Daughters of Liberty. The colonists had pledged to boycott English goods. They would refuse to buy anything made in England, especially cloth, a mainstay of the British economy. The Daughters of Liberty gathered in churches, courthouses, and meeting halls to spin and weave their own cloth. In place of fine British wools and brocades, sturdy homespun cloth became the patriotic fashion (p. 16).*

2. For the passage from *Give Me Liberty!* I say:

> *Wow! There's a lot to remember here. I don't remember much.*

3. Here's my recap:

> *There were Daughters of Liberty. They made cloth.*

4. Reread the passage out loud to students, then silently read it to yourself.

5. Here's my retelling of the *Give Me Liberty!* passage after two readings:

> *The colonists said they would not buy English goods. This is a boycott. They would not buy things that helped the British make money. So the Daughters of Liberty met in churches and courthouses to spin and weave their own cloth so they didn't have to buy cloth from England. Homespun, not very fancy, became the cloth the women in the colonies wore.*

Third graders read and retell with a partner.

you achieve your goal—retaining many details. Emphasize that if you don't recall the information in a math problem, it's impossible to make a plan to solve it.

6. Tell students that if you recall enough information, then you can continue to read.

7. Organize students into pairs and invite them to practice the strategy using materials that relate to your curriculum.

8. Continue short practice sessions until you're sure that students understand the strategy and are comfortable using it.

9. Remind students to apply the strategy when reading in class or at home, especially if the material is new or contains many facts packed into a short section.

Read/Pause/Retell/Reread or Read On Strategy Snapshot: Grade 6 Exploration

Topic: The Age of Exploration

Time: 10 to 15 minutes for each practice session

Materials: "Bartholomew Diaz" in *Around the World in a Hundred Years: From Henry the Navigator to Magellan* by Jean Fritz (Putnam & Grosset, 1994)

Background Information: By inviting partners to work together, Dick Bell implemented a variation of the read/pause/retell strategy. Working in pairs added legitimate social interactions to the strategy, and his sixth graders loved socializing. Dick also believed that partners would drive one another to reread if retellings were sketchy, whereas individuals might delude themselves into believing that they could read on.

First, Dick and I model the process for students. You can also model with a student who is a proficient reader. Decide on two passages to be read: text passages can be a paragraph, half or whole page, or a few sentences. Here are the guidelines Dick and I establish for partners. Post these on chart paper or the chalkboard:

1. Both read one paragraph of the text.
2. One student retells without looking.
3. The partner listens carefully and monitors the retelling by looking at the passage.
4. The listener decides whether his or her partner needs to reread and retell or read on.
5. Partners take turns until each one has practiced with a paragraph.
6. Students continue reading texts, using the strategy to monitor recall and comprehension.

Here's what Johanna and Kirstin said when the class debriefed:

Johanna: Kirstin helped me and explained that I didn't remember enough to continue reading. At first, I was mad. She's my friend. She should say it was okay. I thought "I'll make her reread even if she doesn't need to."

Kirstin: Johanna said to me how she felt. I told her that it was hard to tell her to reread. I was trying to help. And when she did reread she got tons of stuff.

Johanna: Mr. Bell said we should be honest. That's how we'd get better. This made me see that I needed more practice. I didn't make Joanna reread, and I felt good about getting over it [wanting to get back at Joanna].

Like Kirstin and Johanna, many students find the balance between helping one another and maintaining a friendship confusing at first. Aware that students often see the two as mutually exclusive, Dick restated his feelings about "covering up" for a friend before guided practice and after our demonstration. "Keep the goal in your mind," he explained. "The goal is to practice a strategy that can help you, not test your friendship."

STRATEGY LESSON:
Paired Reading and Questions

How It Helps You

When a textbook chapter or section is information-heavy or difficult to understand because it uses many new words, students tune out. An adaptation of Topping's Paired

Reading (1987) and Manzo's ReQuest Procedure (1968), the paired-reading and questioning strategy fosters a close examination of one sentence at a time and asks students to focus on and process all details by posing and answering questions. Working together to self-monitor and construct meaning from a difficult, information-laden text benefits the entire class and reinforces close readings (see pages 145–150).

"I never asked questions for every sentence until I did this strategy." That's how fifth grader Jamal started his self-evaluation of this strategy. His final thoughts showed how well Jamal had come to understand the benefits of closely questioning the text in order to comprehend: "I ask questions and I'm into the book. It [the strategy] is fun to do with a partner. It makes me think about every word and sentence."

Purpose

To develop the habit of posing sentence-by-sentence questions in order to self-monitor comprehension and to pinpoint unfamiliar words

Materials

Passage from a textbook, magazine article, information trade book, or newspaper; math word problems

Guidelines

1. Ask a proficient reader to be the questioner. I take the role of answering questions during this modelling.

2. Select a passage from a book, article, or a math word problem. My student partner and I use a paragraph from the *Science World* article, "Can Alaska Heal?" (page 12). We agree to switch roles after each sentence. Here's the first sentence from the paragraph:

Before the spill, harbor seals were already in decline due to habitat

USE TRADE BOOKS

If the text is far beyond students' ability to read, then look for trade books (in your school and/or community library) on the same topic that students can read. Instead of frustrating students with a textbook that is too difficult for them to read, many teachers use multiple texts, trade books on different reading levels that deal with the same topic (see pages 336–345).

Paired Reading and Questions

loss, but their population has greatly diminished even further.

3. We read the first sentence silently. Here are the questions and answers for the first sentence.

Questioner: Why were harbor seals declining before the spill? What happened to the seals after the spill? What does "diminished" mean?

Responder: I reread the sentence for each question to be accurate: Their habitat—where they lived was getting smaller. After the spill the seal population got still smaller. I'm not sure what "diminished" means, but I'll guess it means the number of seals got smaller because that's what happened after the oil spill.

Questioner: Jot that down, and we'll check it out after we're done.

4. Continue the modelling so each has takes a turn with the two roles.

5. Establish behavior guidelines such as talking in a soft voice and reading silently when pairs complete their work (Tierney and Readence, 2000).

6. Call for student feedback and observations. Eighth graders made these comments:

> You reread the sentence a lot; You admitted you weren't sure of a word and wrote it down to look up later; You both were serious; You questioned every part of the sentence.

7. Model many times, until you feel students are ready to try the strategy with each other.

8. Organize students into pairs who work well together and can both read the material.

9. Explain what students should do when they are finished, since pairs will complete their assigned sections at different times.

10. Have students follow the procedure outlined in numbers 3, 4, and 5. Note these steps on the chalkboard or chart paper.

11. Debrief after the first two practices so students can share their feelings, any adjustments they made, and point out the strategy's benefits.

Paired Reading and Questions
Strategy Snapshot: Grade 7

Topic: Solving math problems; specifically, how to collect data from a problem, state what has to be proven, and create a plan for solving it.

Time: 15 minutes for teacher-student modelling; 15–20 minutes for each guided practice session

Materials: *Pre-Algebra: A Problem-Solving Approach,* Merrill, 1996.

Background Information: Seventh graders had difficulty using information in a problem to create a solution plan. I urged Mrs. Carnell, their teacher, to model how the paired-reading and questioning strategy could develop these problem-solving skills. The questioning process slowed down students' reading and thinking and returned them to the problem's text to answers the questions and thus find a way to solve it.

The teacher gave each student one word problem from the textbook. Students took turns being questioner and responder. They had to develop a plan for solving the problem (see margin box). Here is Devon's and Jose's conversation.

DEVON: *How many jobs does Mrs. Sanchez have?*
JOSE: *Two jobs.*
   What does the first job pay?
DEVON: *Fifty dollars more than the second job.*
   What does the second job pay?
JOSE: *It doesn't say.*
   What are her weekly earnings?
DEVON: *$220. We got to show what the second job pays.*
JOSE: *We're working with variables so it must be x or any letter.*
DEVON: *And the first job is $50 + x. Now we can solve. Write what you think, and I'll write, too, and we'll compare.*

Both boys wrote $x + x + 50 = 220$. The sentence-by-sentence reading, questioning, then rereading and answering focused the pair on the need to express the earnings using a variable. Continued practice can foster students' ability to use the strategy independently.

SAMPLE MATH PROBLEM

Mrs. Sanchez has two jobs. The first job pays her $50 more per week than the second. Her total earning are $220 per week. How much does she earn from each job?

SOLUTION TO EQUATION

$2x + 50 = 220$
$2x + 50 - 50 = 220 - 50$
$2x/2 = 170/2$
$2x = 170$
$x = 85$
$85 + 50 = 135$

Some Additional Fix-It Strategies: During-Reading Repair Tools

When your car breaks down, you take it to the garage to see what's wrong and then have it repaired. If you're unsure about how to bake that chocolate-almond torte, you invite a friend who's an experienced cook to walk you through the process. It's the same with reading. Students who can't make sense out of a sentence or passage, or who find a topic perplexing because the text has many new words and concepts, need strategies that help them construct meaning from unfamiliar information and vocabulary.

First, students need to cultivate self-awareness, or metacognition, so they can identify those "clunks" (see page 41) that signal "I don't get it" when they read a rate, time, or distance math problem, or a section in science about gasoline engines. They will also need some "fix-it" strategies to help them solve their reading problems and thus prevent them from developing the following unproductive behaviors and feelings:

- Skipping over key words
- Avoiding the reading of chunks of text
- Giving up and not reading assignments
- Copying a classmate's work
- Feeling inadequate and dumb
- Becoming disruptive during class
- Cutting classes and school

Introduce and practice one fix-it strategy at a time. Practice allows student to pose questions and to boost their comprehension of important topics and vocabulary. Invite students to talk about ways the strategy helped them cope with a tough passage or math problem. What you're doing is asking students to become metacognitive, to think in their heads and aloud, about the strategies and processes they employ to transform *clunks* into *clicks of comprehension*.

Think Aloud to Deepen Understanding of Meaning

Thinking aloud is a comprehension strategy that enables readers to make sense out of confusing passages. It can also foster self-evaluation of strategies practiced and applied as readers pinpoint what they do and do not comprehend. When a sentence or short passage confuses, thinking aloud can also help readers construct meaning. During the process, as readers hear their reasoning and explanations, they can experience the clicks of comprehension that signal information has been processed and understood. In their study, Baumann et al. (1993) found that the group of children taught to think aloud employed more fix-it strategies (like question/answer; reread, retell; and read on then double back) in their monologues than the group exposed to the Directed Reading-Thinking Activity (Stauffer, 1976).

Though there is little research data on the long-term benefits of think-alouds (Tierney and Readence, 2000), teachers and researchers such as Lytle (1982), Davey (1983), Baumann et al. (1993), and Wilhelm (2001) offer classroom evidence that suggests thinking aloud helps students read and think more strategically. I have found that the think-aloud is effective when teachers show students how to use it to clarify a tough passage or to problem solve in math. Think-alouds can be monologues, where the students talk out loud alone, or dialogues, where partners talk out loud.

Teach Students How to Think Aloud

Baumann et al. suggest that students benefit from a series of lessons showing why the think-aloud strategy can support comprehension, what goes into a think-aloud, and how it works. Use the suggestions that follow to model several think-alouds for your students, illustrating the purposes and importance.

1. On chart paper, write questions that identify the reading problems students encounter —problems that a think-aloud will help.

- Does this phrase, passage, sentence make sense?
- How do I say that word?
- What does that word mean?
- Do I recall what I just read?
- How can I find the main idea?
- How can I figure out the implied meanings?
- How do I solve that math problem?
- What should I look for during that experiment?

2. Explain that a think-aloud invites you to tell everything that's in your mind as you read a passage—even struggling, negative thoughts.

Here's my think-aloud for a section in a science textbook about natural polymers. My think-aloud also points to the importance of jotting down new words in a notebook, since writing supports recall.

> This part makes my head hurt. I don't remember what a <u>polymer</u> is, but I understand that it can be unravelled to get silk from the silkworm. I looked back two pages and it says that plastic is a <u>polymer-based</u> material. And then it says that <u>polymers</u> were in the section before this, but I don't remember much about them. Now I have to reread that part. It's frustrating going back and forth, and I don't have any notes on that word. [I read section out loud.] Now I know a polymer is a huge molecule formed from thousands of smaller organic molecules. I'm writing this down so I remember and can study from my notes.

3. Present think-alouds that address each of the reading problems in #1. Fifth-grade students had completed a test on adding and subtracting fractions with unlike denominators; all but one student had difficulty with this type of problem: 7 1/8 - 4 3/4. I put a prevalent, incorrect solution on the chalkboard and shared my thoughts in this think-aloud.

> The least common denominator is eighths. I had to change 4 3/4 to 4 and 6/8 so the problem could read 7 1/8 - 4 6/8. Next I had to borrow one whole from 7 and make it 6. The one whole is 8/8 and I wrote 6 8/8 - 4 6/8. I borrowed 8/8 and something went wrong. I didn't add the 1/8 I had to the 8/8. What I should have is 6 9/8 - 4 6/8. Every time I borrowed, I forgot to add in the numerator of the mixed number that was there. Now I can write this in my double-entry and redo the problem.

Encouraging students to think-aloud to discover mistakes can reshape their process.

4. Organize students into pairs and have partners think aloud using a tough passage in a textbook, trade book, or magazine or newspaper article.

Pairs working together offer different perspectives on a piece and provide alternate thinking processes for each other. It also makes the think-aloud more palatable for middle school students who, unlike younger children, worry about self-image and peers' perceptions. "If I sit at my desk and think aloud, my friends will think I'm nuts," a seventh grader wrote while evaluating the process his teacher modelled.

What follows is a paired think-aloud between sixth graders who read directions for a science experiment together, paraphrased directions in their own words, said what they needed to do, then compiled a time-order list in their notebook. Before partners worked independently, Mr. Legge, their teacher, approved their notes.

> DIRECTIONS: You are going to design an experiment to test the ability of 15 students in grades 5, 7, or 8 to recognize the odors of different foods, colognes, and household products. You can pick a list of students in one grade or a list that mixes grades. Choose 2 items from each of the three categories. Develop a data table for recording responses. The table should note the gender of each stu-

dent taking the test. Develop a hypothesis for the experiment. After testing your hypothesis, analyze the data. Did the data support your hypothesis? Can you offer an explanation.

DEVON: *Let's do one grade.*

JAKE: *Let's figure out what we have to do.* [both reread]
We have to pick 2 items from each list on the chart.

DEVON: *Let's do grade 5 only.*

JAKE: *Okay. Should we write a hypothesis first or set up the table?*

DEVON: *Let's do the hypothesis. Then the table can help it.*

JAKE: *How about girls will smell the stuff better than boys.*

DEVON: *Man, that's sexist.*

JAKE: *Yeah. But they're around all that stuff.*

DEVON: *We need to make a data table. Let's have 2—one for boys and one for girls.*

JAKE: *The last part comes after we set up the experiment. We need a good blindfold.*

DEVON: *Let's each bring in stuff from all 3 categories so we have enough for 15 tests.*

JAKE: *We'll have to ask Mrs. Haston [grade 5 teacher] when we can do this.*

DEVON: *It will have to be in a science time.* [Both boys tell Mr. Legge that setting up a time
for the experiment should be in the directions.]

"Sixth graders have trouble with multiple directions. They often read quickly and make
many errors in their work," said Mr. Legge. "Asking pairs to think aloud, and then having
me approve their notes, teaches students how important it is to slowly sift through directions and make sure they understand them, and know where to start and how to proceed."

5. Reserve time for students to practice thinking aloud to figure out the meaning of a
new word, to understand new information, to find mistakes in math problems, to determine what a question in history or science asks them to do.

6. Once students show that thinking aloud improves their comprehension, invite them to
think aloud independently and silently with a close reading.

Close Read to Slow Down and Think Deeply

A close reading asks the learner to look back at a passage or page of a text and reread it
to deepen and/or clarify understanding. Though the purpose of close readings differs for

math, literature, and graphics, the process starts with students analyzing words, phrases, and visuals.

With a close reading, students become cameras and silently zoom in on words, phrases, sentences, paragraphs, graphs, illustrations, to figure out what the author means or what the math problem invites them to discover. Many turn to the dictionary to explore word meanings.

Close Reading of Poetry

Poetry is a great way to introduce close readings of literature, for poems are rich in connotative and implied meanings and in figurative language. Readers naturally stop to savor each word and experience the images and emotions. Model the process for the class using poems that connect to the topic you're studying. Encourage interaction and an exchange of ideas by having students close read poems in pairs or small groups, then invite them to:

- Read their poems aloud
- Discover the meanings of unfamiliar words by using the dictionary
- Explore the connotative meanings of words
- Explain the meanings of figurative language
- Look for loaded words, words that signal meaning, words that connect to the title or other words.

Each group of eighth graders in the humanities class receives a different poem that relates to our study of prejudice. Poems are on overhead transparencies so students can share their close readings with everyone. Groups collaborate for two 20-minute periods using the above guidelines. I schedule two presentations a day; doing them all at once dilutes the power of each presentation—and bores eighth graders. Here's part of a transcription of my notes for the group that close read "History of My People" by Walter Dean Myers *(Soul Looks Back in Wonder,* Dial, 1993).

Part of One Group's Presentation

"History of My People"

Molly: *We had to look up* griot *and* Niger. *A griot is an African storyteller and the Niger is a river in central Africa.*

Ryan: *Some words have capital letters like Ancestors and Black that Myers did on purpose. It makes you think about their meanings more. Like Ancestors connect to history in the title. It* makes you think of what it was like for Blacks when they were captured as slaves.

Lia: *He writes "Black dreams swell." The metaphor is water, the Niger River in Africa swells too. There's "blood-tide"— that's also water and makes me see the blood of Africans tossed into ocean—ones that got sick or beaten or like in* Slave Dancer *(by Paula Fox) were thrown overboard.*

Eric: *History here was blood and pain— "blues-moan" but they turned pain into great music.*

History of My People

by Walter Dean Myers

My eyes touch, my fingers trace

The griot chants, clicks, songs of the Ancestors

The warrior words stretched taut across the soul

Drum words whispering the name of God

They say that beyond the blood-tide cries

    there is continuance

Triumph and continuance

A reaching back and a forward surge

A place where Black dreams swell consciousness

Even as the Niger swells old seasons into new life

What these students are learning is that every word counts when doing a close reading. Lia made a connection to *Slave Dancer*, a book she had read in seventh grade as part of a Civil War study. I like to introduce close readings with short poems and help students experience the value of pausing, like a detective, to read the clues and comprehend the meaning.

Close Reading of Math Problems

Close reading is an ideal strategy for helping students gather information from math word problems to figure out a way to solve the problem. Instead of skipping over key information because of anxieties about math and/or reading and making sense of the words, a close reading can help students figure out a solution. The purpose of a close reading in math is to figure out what the problem asks, what information is needed to solve it, and planning how to go about finding the solution. Here are the guidelines I offer fifth graders:

- Read the problem two or three times.
- State what the problem asks you to solve.
- Select the data that will help you solve the problem.
- Decide if there is a formula you can apply.
- Do you need to set up an equation?

- Draw a picture to help you see the problem and data.
- Substitute small, whole numbers, if necessary, and see if your solution works that way.
- Write what you understand about the question in words.
- Ask: Does my answer make sense?

Fifth graders apply some or all of these guidelines to area problems. Rebecca makes a drawing of each problem that asks her to find the area of a triangle. Problems with negative numbers confuse Rebecca, so she draws and uses a number line to solve.

A number line helps Rebecca add and subtract negative and positive numbers.

Here is a problem that confused one student because it contained fractions. Substituting small, whole numbers "got me to see what I had to do to solve it because we just learned them [fractions]."

Problem:

Tim picked strawberries for 5 1/2 hours on Monday, 2 3/4 hours on Tuesday, and 1 3/4 hours on Friday. Tim earned $2.00 an hour. If Tim's friend Jim earned $27.00 for picking strawberries, who earned more?

Prevent skimming or skipping over words that students find difficult by teaching them to close read perplexing parts. Posting guidelines and practicing in class can transform students into careful readers.

Close reading helped Tim understand what he had to find in order to solve the problem.

Close Reading of Graphics

Most middle-school students glance at a graph, diagram, or picture, while reading. Rarely do

Teaching Reading in Social Studies, Science, and Math

they pause or return to a visual to read labels, headings, or brief explanations. Help students understand that graphs, charts, and diagrams are important because they present information in the text in a different way or provide additional information that relates to the topic. Reading the visual carefully often provides the clues that enable students to figure out the main idea or understand a passage. Give students this six-step plan for reading a graphic element:

1. Look at the graphic and read the title. Think about the title's meaning and what it tells you about the graphic.
2. Read all of the text in the graphic.
3. Think about the information. Ask yourself how it relates to the chapter or article.
4. Ask yourself "What's important?"
5. Make sure you understand the words.
6. Connect this important information to your personal life and experiences and/or issues in your community and the world.

Seventh graders in Ray Legge's science class are studying the greenhouse effect. Before he gives students the article about greenhouse gases from Scholastic's *Science World* magazine (March 20, 2000, vol 56, #12), he reviews the steps to reading a visual, then invites partners to read it using the steps as a guide.

Here's how Caitlin and Tommy follow the six steps to reading the graphic.

Caitlin: The title goes with the diagram. It's about burying the gases.

Tommy: CO_2 is gonna be buried under the ocean with pumping stations.

Caitlin: What's an aquifer?

Tommy: Doesn't say here. [Scans the article.] It's in italics. It's a place under the

A visual students used to learn more about greenhouse gases.

ground where water's stored.

Caitlin: I think it's a place to pump in CO_2.

Tommy: It's a way to stop global warming. It's been in the newspapers and on TV news. Scientists say that the temperatures get warmer and ice caps are melting.

Caitlin: But it says [in the caption] that this burying is years away.

Tommy: We need another way to lower the CO_2 in the air.

Partner conversations all reveal students reading the diagram carefully. Following the steps many times during guided practice acts like a bridge moving students to using the process when they read texts for class and those they select to read independently.

Rereading to Boost Understanding

Sometimes, simply rereading a sentence, paragraph, or page can put learners back on the comprehension track. Often while I'm reading, my mind wanders to cooking dinner or picking up a prescription for a sick child. When I'm preoccupied, I read words, but do not process them to make meaning and recall details. Students experience the same lapses in focus. They're thinking about a soccer game, a weekend visit to a friend, or inline skating after school. And anytime a student hits a "clunk" and doesn't or cannot apply a strategy for comprehension, that interruption can lead to a loss of focus.

Perhaps one or two words on a page are new and there are no context clues that can support rereading. This is the time to ask a classmate, partner, or the teacher to help. Rereading the section armed with vocabulary knowledge can deepen comprehension.

Nathan, a fifth grader, enjoys reading and rereading.

Teaching Reading in Social Studies, Science, and Math

There are three other reasons for not comprehending material, and for which reread-ing may not suffice as a fix-it strategy:

1. The student has little background knowledge or interest in the material.
2. The text has too many unfamiliar words.
3. The text is filled with long, complex sentences.

When this is the case, try instead to:

1. Enlarge students' background knowledge and then continue the study.
2. Read the passage aloud, sit side by side and take turns reading. Best of all, find a more readable piece on the same topic.
3. Do a close reading and model how you look for loaded words, words and phrases that relate to the topic, and how you divide the long sentences into chunks, trying to gath-er meaning from each part, then putting ideas together. Avoid having students read texts whose syntax is beyond their literacy development.

I find that most students can tell me the benefits of rereading. However, in every grade, when I introduce rereading as a fix-it strategy, I hear students say, "Only dumb kids reread." They have internalized the universal student myth that equates high performance and being smart with "getting it the first time." What's disturbing is that many students have accepted the fact that they won't understand what they read. "You want my friends to think I'm dumb," an eighth grader said to me. "No way."

However, when students are metacognitive, as fast as a light blinks, they can deter-mine whether they need to reread or continue. After four guided practice sessions using the history textbook, here's what a fifth grader who hates "reading school books" said to his group about rereading:

"I didn't want to do it; I thought it was dumb. But doing it in class – since everyone was doing it—I gave it a try. After two rereadings, I could almost remember everything in a section. The problem is it will take more time."

Help students understand that rereading also occurs when part of a book or article or poem is so great that you feel compelled to repeat the experience. I model this with read alouds, rereading a poem or part of a text. "I enjoy it more and hear things I didn't the first time," eighth grader Kate says.

And that's the goal: enjoyment and improved understanding.

Pause and Reflect on:
Self-Monitoring and Fix-It Strategies

"Mrs. Robb! Mrs. Robb!" Sixth grader Jesse shouted my name and brandished a paper as he zigzagged through a hallway of Johnson Williams Middle School, where students chatted noisily as they walked to their next class. "It worked," Jesse said as he fell into step alongside me. "I did all that retell and reread stuff for the science assignment and I got 100% on a pop quiz. Me. Jesse. My first 100 percent on any quiz this year."

For Jesse, getting to this point represented a struggle to try new ways of learning and a struggle to give up beliefs about himself. Part of a group of fifteen readers who met with me and Cindy Hughes three times a week before the school day began, Jesse, like many of his classmates, resisted learning about and practicing reading strategies. But 10-minute one-on-one practice sessions with Jesse created the opportunity to build a trusting relationship and help Jesse risk trying strategies and studying. I use the word "risk" because at this stage, Jesse felt achieving and studying were pointless for him. The working-hard-and-getting-good-grades scenario defied every myth Jesse had adopted. "I'm part of the dumb group and won't ever do well," he told me just before Thanksgiving break. Low grades and being in the "low group" had convinced Jesse and many of his classmates that school success was not for them.

Providing self-monitoring and fix-it strategies, building trust, and developing self-confidence through successful reading experiences can change the negative, self-destructive view of school and learning that the Jesses in this world have embraced. Keep at the forefront of your mind that it takes a long time to change entrenched patterns and beliefs. Jesse's epiphany occurred in May, months after we began working together. He worked diligently during seventh and eighth grade in the extra-help and required classes. By the end of eighth grade Jesse developed several self-monitoring and fix-it strategies. "What I really learned," he said about a week before graduation, "was that you do get the grades if you work hard."

✑ Chapter 6 ✑

Strategies to Use
After Learning

The aim of education should be to teach the child to think,
not what to think. —John Dewey

I t's the second day I have spent in a junior high school in the South Bronx where my daughter, Anina, teaches seventh graders history and English.

After a strategy lesson on taking notes, Anina divides her class of 35 into pairs and invites them to talk about a paragraph in their history text for one minute, then take notes in their journals. One minute is all these students can sustain; they've had little experience talking about their reading and longer conversations tend to derail. Anina's approach is new to them, and they resist it.

"No way," groans Angel. "Why do we have to write about it? We read it and talked about it. Isn't that enough?" echoed Jude and Ricardo.

Patiently, Anina explains how taking notes can help them remember the information. "Try it. See if it helps," she urges. They're not swayed.

As I watch, I think about the quizzes Anina graded last night. Two students answered eight out of ten questions correctly. The rest scored fifty percent or lower.

"Why are you trying so hard, Ms. Robb?" Shaquetta asks.

"Yeah," says Enrique. "No big deal. We fail lots of tests." I watch, breathless, hoping Anina will see this resistance for what it is: a veiled plea for help. They're not ready to work independently, even in pairs; they need more support from their teacher.

"Let me do the writing," Anina says, and I smile inwardly. Quickly, she tapes a piece of chart paper to the chalkboard. Several students offer details, and Anina records these on the chart, carefully noting students' names next to their words.

A small beginning, but an important one for these adolescents who have not yet developed reading, talking, and writing strategies for improving comprehension skills. And it represents a significant milestone for Anina, who in a perfect moment of responsive teaching, responded to her students' negativity by shifting the lesson to collaborative talk assisted by her.

I've found that collaborative conversations are a surer starting ground than independent writing for high-risk students whose school experiences have been predominantly negative and discussion deprived. In her 1996 study of eighth graders, Alvermann pointed out that many students felt "talk-deprived," which made reading for meaning difficult for them.

The Need for Reflection

As Anina discovered, teaching students how to talk and work with partners and in small groups takes time and much modelling of productive behaviors (Robb, 1993). But offering students experiences that allow them to process new information and build new understandings is vital. Vaughan and Estes (1986) call this work "contemplation" or "reasoned reflections that enable understandings to be synthesized," (p. 156). If our students are to apply what they've learned to writing, oral presentations, and authentic projects, as well as connect these new understandings to issues in their lives, then they need time in class to ponder, share, construct, and connect (Alvermann and Phelps, 1998; Gillet and Temple, 2000; Keene and Zimmermann, 1997; Tierney and Readence, 2000; Vacca and Vacca, 2000). Without this crucial after-learning time, students resort to memorizing information at the expense of understanding.

In this chapter, we'll explore ways to help students experience this important step in learning that enables them to claim new knowledge as their own.

The five after-learning strategies are:

- Skimming
- Using a graphic organizer
- Connect and apply
- Paraphrasing
- Visualizing

These strategies help students to:

- Locate information
- Study
- Clarify
- Retain new information
- Understand how the topic is relevant to their lives

Moreover, using after-learning strategies encourages students to think with the facts and discourages rote memorization where information is learned for a quiz or test and is then quickly forgotten because connections to prior knowledge and experiences don't exist (Gillet and Temple, 2000; Pressley, 2000; Vaughan and Estes, 1986).

STRATEGY LESSON:
Skimming a Text

How It Helps You

A sixth grader tells me, "When the teachers says, 'Skim the chapter to find the answers to these questions,' I don't know what to do. I write what I remember or leave it blank." Her words convey the trouble that starts when teachers ask students to use a strategy, such as skimming, without first determining whether they understand it. Remember to define and explain the strategy you are using and model it if necessary.

Teaching students how to skim by using certain text elements helps them employ the strategy with precision and purpose. These text features include:

- Section headings in a textbook chapter
- Chapter titles in nonfiction trade books
- Illustrations, photographs, graphs, diagrams, maps, math examples
- Captions
- Boldface terms or concepts
- Repeated words
- Boxes and sidebars
- Key words in questions
- The index.

Purpose

To show students how to locate essential information that can help them answer a question, fill out a graphic organizer, and study for tests

Materials

A textbook chapter or nonfiction trade book students have read.

Guidelines

1. First, think-aloud to show students how to skim to locate information. Explain that the goal is to discover the characteristics of the Renaissance man and woman and then list them:

> In this example, the topic is the Renaissance. I begin thinking aloud: "I think that information was near the end of the chapter, so I'll look there first. Yes, it's on the last two pages, under bold face headings that say: 'The Renaissance Man' and 'The Renaissance Woman.' I'll reread the section about men and list details. Then I'll read the second section about women again."

2. Gather feedback and questions about your process from students. Encourage them to share their take on skimming.

3. Invite students to practice finding information that's under a boldface heading, in a graph, diagram, or in a caption.

Harry Holloway asks seventh graders to skim the middle of chapter four in their math text to locate and study the two problem-solving examples that will be on their test. He points them to the middle section to reduce frustration levels that can build when leafing through a lengthy chapter. William finds "sequences" and Sage finds "look for patterns." Jenna points out the process of explore, plan, solve, and examine. "You need to follow these steps," she says, "to solve the problem."

Mr. Holloway thinks aloud and shows how he studies for the word problem test: "I'll study the sample problems, including the plan that Jenna mentioned. Then I'll do several odd-numbered problems because the book gives answers to these and I can check my work. All of us should list the problems we can't solve and we'll review those tomorrow."

Guidelines 4 – 6 Can Be Completed on Another Day

4. Model how to use key words in a question to locate information. Here's a question I used to think-aloud with a fifth grade class: What is the feudal pyramid?

There are two key words in this question: feudal and pyramid. I remember seeing a triangle-shape model of this in the chapter, but I'm not sure if it was in the beginning, middle, or end. To save time, I'll skim the index and see what's listed under feudal. Here it is. With essential words, I know the index can help me quickly locate information.

5. Repeat Guideline number 3.

6. Continue modelling and practicing until students demonstrate they can successfully skim to locate information.

History   September 18

Noah

Pages 235-237

1. Who was king of Mali at it's highest power? pp 236

2.) What year did Song hai get powerful? pp 237

3.) What years did Song hai not lose a battle? pp 237

4.) How many pounds of gold can camels carry? pp 237

5.) How did the gold value drop in Cairo? pp 237

At the start of the year, history teacher Dick Bell motivates students to use skimming by asking them to create discussion questions that review the facts. Partners then trade questions, locate and note the page that contained the answer and skim the material to plan for a think-pair-share (see pages 266–269).

Skimming a Text
Strategy Snapshot: Grade 4

Topic: Studying for a test on "America: A Developing Country"

Time: three 45-minute class periods

Materials: textbook chapter

Background Information: Fourth grade at Powhatan is the year students learn how to skim and take notes. They also use these strategies to plan their essays on tests. In October, teacher Debi Gustin asked me for advice after her students couldn't develop their ideas on a recent test essay. "I modelled how I collect ideas and then write," Debi told me, "but students just dove in. All of the essays were a list of some facts, and most struggled to write half a page."

I suggested that students practice writing short essays in class *before* being asked to complete one on a test. This way Debi would be available to answer questions and support students. Here's the process I suggested Debi offer students:

- Read the essay question and think about the specific details needed to answer it.
- Select key words from the question that will allow you to skim the text to locate information.
- Jot down on index cards all the data collected from skimming the text.
- Frame a topic sentence. (For those students who struggle with creating a topic sentence, suggest that they restate the question as a declarative sentence. For example, if the question is, *"Why did the Stamp and Townshend Acts anger the colonists?"* then a possible restatement is: *The Stamp and Townshend Acts angered the colonists because...)*

```
William                Essay
Cotton Gin = lawyer Eli Whitney
before Gin = 80,000 bales cotton produced
after Gin = 525,000 bales cotton produced

Spinning Mills = Englishman Samuel Slater
England had secret machine for sewing cotton
before Revolution  cotton sent there. Memorized
machine came to america met Moses Brown and
built the 1st swater powered mill in Rhode Island
1790.

Erie canal - Governor Dewitt Clinton  canal
New York
Albany to Buffalo and lake Erie. 1817  workers
```

A fourth grader's notes for writing an essay.

- Use the details on the index cards to write the essay. Elaborate the details and make sure the examples are specific and support the question.
- Write a wrap-up or concluding sentence that restates the topic sentence in a different way.

Students practiced this process in class and revised their work. At the start, most insisted, "I don't need to take notes, I know it." I recommended to Debi that notes become a percentage of the grade so all students would be motivated to practice the strategy before passing judgment on it. Naturally, attitudes towards collecting and writing notes before completing an essay changed as students experienced the benefits.

I also urged Debi to give students the essay question one or two days before the test, allow them to prepare notes independently at school, and use these to write during the test. William, like his peers, began the year by writing about one-third of a page. "I wasn't sure what to do," he said. When students prepared notes, essays illustrated their learning. Here is an essay from the last history test students took—the progress is evident.

History
William Essay

Three ways to show that America was developing would probably be the inventions of the cotton gin, spinning mills, and the Erie Canal. The cotton gin was invented by a lawyer named Eli Whitney. In the South plantation owners made their slaves pick the cotton cause cotton has thorns in it and can really scratch up your hands so, the plantation owners made their slaves pick the cotton and only 80,000 bales of cotton was made a year then Eli Whitney invented the cotton gin then 525,000 bales of cotton were made a year.
Before the Revolution we sold our cotton to England cause they had the only sewing mills. And they also had a secret way of making

Fourth graders can write detailed essays as long as they prepare by taking notes.

BENEFITS OF SKIMMING A TEST

Teach students that before they start a test, it's helpful to skim it, as they would any other text, to gain a feeling for what the test will be about and the kinds of questions it includes. Skimming helps students:

- Become familiar with directions.
- See the range of questions: short answers, true/false, multiple choice, essay questions, or math computation and/or word problems.
- Familiarize themselves with readings they will complete.
- Plan time so they can complete all the questions they know first. Then, if time permits, work on the tougher ones.

Pre-Test Study Tips to Share with Students

Show students how to study for tests in your subject. In grades 3 to 5, practice studying in class all year long. In grades 6 and above, after practicing test-prep strategies three to four times, gradually release the process to students. If your middle school students have not learned test-taking skills, then set aside more class time for practice.

Offer students time-management suggestions so they learn to study effectively over three to four days before the test. Science teacher Ray Legge constructs a review study sheet with students. He encourages them to complete specific sections each night and on the next day, reviews answers in class.

Dick Bell challenges groups of history students to make a list of review questions. He collates them, types them up, and hands them out. Several days prior to the test, pairs help each other locate and study answers. Then Dick has students check questions that

he might choose for the test.

Math Test Study Tips

- Make sure you understand which formulas will be on the test. Practice problems that use formulas.
- Study examples in your textbook of the kinds of problems you will have on the test. Do some of these to make sure the process is clear.
- Study your class notes that relate to the test topic.
- Review quizzes to ensure you understand errors. Redo incorrect problems.
- Make sure you understand the language of the word problems you've studied in the chapter.
- Find out if there will be any cumulative review of math from previous chapters; review and practice this information.
- Do several practice problems from the

STRATEGY LESSON:
Graphic Organizers

How It Helps You

Graphic organizers allow students to create a visual word-image of essential ideas, details, or concepts from their reading. To build this word-image successfully, students first select chapter.

- Ask the teacher to re-explain anything you find difficult or confusing.
- Ask: "Do I understand the concepts in this chapter or section?" If not, then seek help and clarification from your teacher.
- Complete problems you haven't attempted to see whether you can successfully apply the concepts.

Social Studies Test Study Tips

- Learn the names of places and people and dates the teacher has emphasized.
- Study the boldface or colored words in the chapter.
- Review and study your class and reading notes.
- List 8 to 10 points you think might be on the test and study them.
- Answer the end-of-chapter questions; this is good preparation.
- Study maps and graphics in the chapter.
- Make sure you can reproduce a map and locate places, and that you understand the data in the graphics.

Science Test Study Tips

- Make sure you understand. Then learn definitions of boldface or colored terms.
- Study information the teacher has emphasized in class.
- Review your class and reading notes.
- Be able to reproduce and label diagrams, such as those for plant or animal cells or the food chain.
- Study the sequence of information by making visuals of the steps in a process, such as metamorphosis or photosynthesis.
- Review any experiments completed for this chapter or topic.
- Make a list of 8 to 10 questions that might be on the test; study these.
- Review and practice reading and interpreting the charts and graphs.
- Answer the end-of-the-chapter questions as part of your review.

several main ideas or categories from the reading; these become headings for the graphic organizer. Next, students skim their text and select details that describe and/or explain each heading (Alvermann and Phelps, 1998; Buehl, 2001; Burke, 2000; Vacca and Vacca, 2000; Vaughan and Estes, 1986).

Students give high ratings to organizing information into graphic organizers because:

- Once I write, I remember things. *David, Grade 6*
- It makes me think about what I read. *Chris, Grade 8*

- It's fun because I can draw stuff and write. *Allison, Grade 3*
- It makes studying for tests easier. *Jose, Grade 7*

   Not only are graphic organizers an effective note-taking strategy, they also provide a framework for organizing information and translating facts into critical thinking. This strategy lesson focuses on two graphic organizers: the web and T-chart, which are kin to a double-entry journal (see examples on pages 163–166). I've selected these because they are versatile and foster thinking about information.

Purpose

To organize information visually and develop categories; to show how organizing and writing supports recall and retention

Materials

A section or a chapter in a textbook, a section of an informational trade book, or a magazine article that students have read and discussed

Guidelines

Part 1: Model Using a Web

1. Introduce the web as a graphic organizer.

2. Model for students how to find the topic for the organizer. In a web, place the topic in the center box.

3. Show students how you decide on categories or topic headings for a web. Skim the text; use boldface headings as guides. This helps students pinpoint the main ideas and collect related details.

> Fifth-grade math teacher, Lisa Johnson, develops these categories for a web about triangles: Category, Properties of All, Names and Properties of Acute, Right, Equilateral, Isosceles, Uses Of.

4. Limit the number of headings or categories to seven.

5. Skim each section to fill in details using a single word or

short phrases.

6. Show students how a graphic organizer can reveal relationships and show connections.

> Lisa's fifth graders collaborate to complete the web on triangles. Using the web, students observe:
>
> * Though the properties are the same, the shape of each changes.
> * Right triangles are everywhere — building corners, ceiling and floor corners, doors, stairs, plastic crates, chairs.
> * Tortilla chips come in triangles.
> * Pyramids' faces have a triangular shape.
> * Our tangrams have triangles.
> * Cut a square or rectangle on the diagonal and you get a triangle.

7. Draw a Five W's web on chart paper. Put the title of an article or the topic in the center of the web. This web also makes a great organizer for students who are writing a news story or a short article.

The Five W's Web

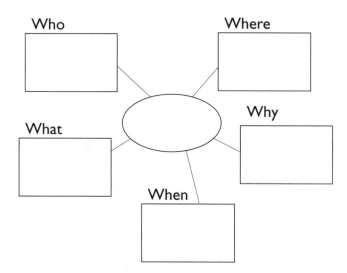

IDEAL FOR T-CHART (OR DOUBLE-ENTRY JOURNAL)

◆ Hypothesis or Opinion/Proof (see page 165)

◆ Defining Words (see pages 216–217)

◆ Cause/Effect (see pages 292–293)

◆ Compare/Contrast (see page 176)

◆ Inferring (see pages 312–317)

◆ Quote/Reader's Thoughts (see page 239)

◆ Sequencing Picture and Notes (see pages 185–186)

Graphic Organizers

Three times, I collaborate with a group of struggling seventh-grade readers to construct a Five W's web. Convinced students can work alone, I invite the group to use an article about wrestling in **ACTION** (Scholastic, Vol. 23, No., 11, pages, 4-5).

The strategy helps students organize and select key details from a text, a task that has been challenging for this group.

Erin   April 27

Main Idea   Details

2 New Olympic   ① tae kwon do
Sports get gold   get gold if you give a
                                           punch or a kick
                                        ② it started in Korea 100s of
                                           years ago. very popular
                                        ③ triathelon can get
                                           gold medal

A t-chart with main idea and supporting details

Kate   March 15
          5W's WEB

Who   WHAT
The Rock   - wrestling is a
a wrassler   danger to kids
has big ego -   - kids are
loves hisself   try to do the moves
                                       of pro wrestlers
                                     - 1 mill fans of
                                       wrestling are R or less

WHEN   WHERE
Watch with an   on tv
adult to talk   in a stadium
about it -
the vilence

WHY
- pros are entertainers
- pros train hard
- kids get hurt - brake neck, bones
- The Rock says don't try what I do

The Five W's graphic helps students select and organize details.

8. Encourage students to use the graphic organizer to study for a test and/or to write about a topic.

Part II: Model Using a T-Chart
(Note: Can be completed on another day.)

1. Model how to organize the main idea and details of an article or book section in a t-chart. Help students understand that the main idea may be found in a section heading in a textbook or article, the first or last sentence in a paragraph, or implied by the details and examples in a paragraph. Place the main idea on the left-hand side; note supporting details on the right-hand side.

Fifth graders use short articles in <u>Scholastic News</u> to find the main idea and related details.

On page 164 one student's t-chart of main idea/details based on "Olympic Firsts," (Vol. 62, No. 22., p. 3).

2.   Model how to form an opinion or hypothesis (see below) about a topic and then provide support. Establish how much support you want students to offer (two to three supporting details is what I suggest).

Eighth graders have completed reading James Clavell's <u>The Children's Story</u> (Delacorte, 1981). Students and I collaborate to develop a hypothesis and test its validity. I collect their ideas on chart paper, which I tack to a bulletin board as a resource students can refer to when working in pairs or independently.

GRAPHIC ORGANIZERS AND WRITING

Since information in graphic organizers is structured and detailed, students can use them as writing plans to summarize or to explain a concept (see pages 178–184).

<u>The Children's Story</u> by James Clavell

Hypothesis	Proof
Memorizing without understanding is dangerous.	* Children memorized the "Pledge of Allegiance" and did not understand it. This enabled them to cut up the flag. They had no idea what the flag symbolized. * Memorizing in school prevented the kids from questioning what others said and did. That made it easy for the new teacher to take over the class. * The kids' minds were brainwashed in 25 minutes because they accepted authority. Johnny's dad had to be sent away for months to get rid of bad thoughts.

Graphic Organizers

Graphic Organizers
Strategy Snapshot: Grade 8 Social Studies

Topic: The concept of prejudice

Time: One 45-minute class

Materials: Informational chapter books, biographies, historical novels, videos, newspaper articles

Background Information: John Lathrop and I created a humanities class that combined history and English, so eighth graders could study the Civil Rights Movement and deepen their understanding of prejudice in our nation. We used *To Kill a Mockingbird* by Harper Lee (Warner, 1982) and *Roll of Thunder, Hear My Cry* by Mildred Taylor (Viking, 1976) as the core texts that all students read and discussed. Over 12 weeks, students also chose books related to the theme to read on their own.

During the study's last week, I invited students to create a web that would show them how much they had come to understand prejudice. Students suggested four headings—*stereotypes, causes, feelings, examples*—for organizing their ideas. If a student suggested a heading that didn't work, I said, "That's a good try. Let me help you clarify your idea" or "Let me help you think of another heading." The point is to honor the attempt and then gently provide support.

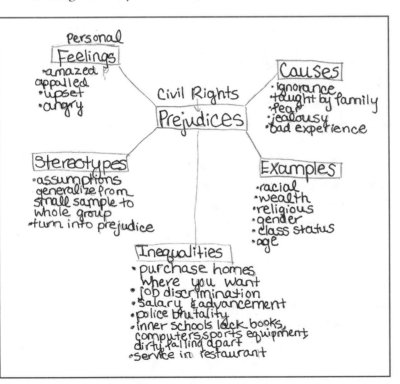

Celeste, an eighth grader, creates a web to illustrate what she knows about prejudice.

STRATEGY LESSON:
Connect and Apply

How It Helps You

"Why are we learning this stuff?" is a question teachers repeatedly hear. When I went to school, the teacher's answer was usually "Because you have to." As teachers, we ought to have a better answer. Better yet, we must strive to teach in a manner in which the question never gets asked, because the relevance of what we teach is clear to our students.

We must use information in textbooks, experiments, films, nonfiction trade books, articles, etc., to make connections to students' lives. As students link their own lives to texts, other people, and the world, they translate information into new and meaningful understandings, and at the same time gain insights into the relevance of their studies (Harvey, 2000; Keene and Zimmerman, 1997; Robb, 2000).

Once students understand a topic's relevance, they are more likely to invest energy because relevance is intrinsically motivating. Once students develop a passion for studying a topic, it can even lead to community service and social action (Keene and Zimmerman, 1998; Santa,1997; Wigfield, 1997; Robb, 2000).

A case in point: An eighth grader at Powhatan school, Steve Monroe, organized a team of his peers to work in soup kitchens after his class connected the plight of people during the Depression with today's homeless population.

Purpose

To help students see the relevance of their learning to their own lives, to other texts, to family, friends and community, and to world issues

Materials

A chapter in a textbook, nonfiction trade book, magazine or newspaper article

Guidelines

I have divided this section into appropriate guidelines for the types of connections students can make so they can practice and understand each kind. However, you'll find that students often blend two or more, which illustrates the diversity of integrated thinking.

Making Personal Connections

1. Offer prompts and questions that enable students to connect information to their own lives (see margin boxes and examples in strategy lessons).

2. Show how you make personal connections as you read aloud. Sandy Bayliss reads parts of Jim Murphy's *Blizzard!* (Scholastic, 2000) for third graders' study of storms. After reading, "Obviously, the snow was too deep for an engine [train] to simply push its way through," she pauses to think aloud and model her personal connection:

> I remember when I was your age and my mom and dad and I were on a train to northern Vermont. It snowed the whole way. Finally, the snow on the tracks was so deep that the train stopped. I wasn't worried at all because my mom took out a thermos of hot chocolate and a box of homemade oatmeal cookies. I sipped the warm chocolate and munched on cookies and watched the snow until men cleared the tracks. When I was older, mom told me that she was worried we wouldn't move for days.

To prompt her students to make their own personal connections, Sandy asks: "Have you ever been stuck in a snowstorm?" Immediately, dozens of hands go up, and the children share stories about staying all night in a bus station or a friend's house or sinking into the snow and worrying that they couldn't get out. "That's why the colonists had a rope from their barns to the house," says Melissa. "We learned that in history. They used the rope to get back and forth safely to feed the animals in blizzards and deep snow." It's these conversations among students that give learning information depth, color, and relevance.

Connecting the Text to Daily Life

Third graders in Sandy Bayliss's class study ways to prevent wasting resources such as water, energy, trees, and metal. To introduce the theme, Sandy uses an article from *Scholastic News* (vol. 57, No. 23, page 2).

1. Have students read and discuss the article.

2. Pose a question or make a statement that compels students to connect the information to their daily lives and extend their thinking beyond the text.

3. Sandy wrote "Energy, Water, Recycle" on chart paper and invited partners to discuss this statement: *"Shortages of energy, water, metal, plastic, and paper can change your lives."* Many of the ideas Sandy collected had to do with students' own experiences or from parents' conversations they had heard:

Energy	**Water**	**Recycle**
• no gas for cars	• limit number of baths or showers	• fewer pages in newspapers and magazines
• can't travel a lot	• no swimming pools	• fewer issues to read
• might lose power and have no lights	• no watering gardens	• books on computer to save paper and trees
• no more air conditioning	• drink bottled water	• no more canned food to save metals
• small cars run by batteries	• limit when you can wash clothes	• have reusable glass bottles for milk, juice, and soda
• computers use electricity; maybe shouldn't have them in schools		

"I like to think of things," Maria, a third grader, announced after Sandy read the completed chart.

"Why?" asked Sandy.

"'Cause it makes my brain work," said Maria. Like Maria, most learners relish the challenge to construct understandings they would not discover if learning consisted of reading and answering factual questions.

Connecting the Text to Other Texts

1. Show students how you connect ideas to other texts and experiences. Not only do I model this with textbook information, but also when I'm reading aloud poems or

parts of nonfiction texts, a biography, magazine article, or historical novel.

Eighth grade is studying World War II, and during history, they read John Hersey's *Hiroshima* (Random House, 1989). I have a teaching partnership with John Lathrop, the history teacher, and I weave literature into students' history studies (see Chapter 11). Here's how I use a read-aloud to model connections to other texts:

Book: *Peace Crane* by Sheila Hamanaka (Morrow Junior Books, 1995).

Passage: I stop after the passage below and think aloud:

> *My teacher says Sadako*
> *folded a thousand paper cranes,*
> *each one a wish for peace.*

Robb's Think-Aloud:

Yesterday, I read aloud <u>Hiroshima No Pika</u> (by Toshi Maruki, Lothrop, Lee, & Shepard, 1980). Sadako's name in <u>Peace Crane</u> brought me to the horror of that day and the horror of the aftermath that's here today in deformed births and crippled men and women who survived the bombing. I thought of the last page that tells of August 6 when people send lanterns with names of loved ones who died adrift on the seven rivers that run through Hiroshima. I thought of the last words of the book: "It can't happen again if no one drops the bomb."

Then I pose a question to involve students: "What have you read or seen that sheds more light on Hiroshima and the aftermath of dropping the bomb?"

Silence. I wait. Then Katherine says. "In fifth grade, a group of us read *Sadako and the Thousand Paper Cranes* (Eleanor Coerr, Dell, 1977). It made us understand the long-term effects of radiation. Sadako was young and innocent. But she died."

Students work on making connections using their reading.

Nicole, says, "In science we saw a film about the atomic and hydrogen bombs. It's scary how the destruction lasts for generations. We have enough bombs—Russia, too—to destroy the world."

"I thought of Gary Paulsen's *The Foxman*" (Puffin, 1977), said James. "It's about this guy whose face got blown to bits and mutilated in World War II. He becomes a hermit and hides his hideous face behind a mask. It's not only nuclear bombs that make war horrible."

2.   Continue thinking aloud and posing a question (see margin box) that fosters connections and develops students' ability to see common themes and ideas among texts. Guided practice can lead students to connect to other texts during discussions and on their own.

Connecting to the Environment

1.   Follow the modelling and think-aloud process outlined above.

2.   Pose a question that stimulates students to think about how information translates into their surroundings and experiences.

> Geometry was part of my fifth-grade math curriculum. Students never tired of constructing quadrilaterals and triangles on geoboards or of posting plane geometric figures on bulletin boards. For several years, that's as far as I went with this study. After observing a science teacher help students connect a study of erosion to their surroundings, I realized that putting facts to work was the enjoyable part of learning. Here's the question I posed to fifth graders: "Can you show evidence of geometry in your environment?" That day groups brainstormed, and I collected their ideas on chart paper. Then I suggested that students walk around their neighborhood or main street and also think about places they have visited, and we added more details. Here's part of the list:

SOME QUESTIONS THAT FOSTER CONNECTIONS TO OTHER TEXTS

◆ Do the authors' share a purpose?

◆ Were characters in similar situations? Compare how each handled the situation.

◆ Did you find similar themes? Settings? Problems?

◆ Were problems resolved in the same way?

◆ How were social, family, and economic issues alike? How were they different?

◆ How did characters' problems in the movie or video relate to the book?

◆ Did the magazine article offer new information about the topic in your book?

◆ How did each text improve your understanding of the motivation or decision making?

Geometric Figure	Examples
* parallel lines	* highways, train tracks, streets, bridges
* rectangles	* doors, pool, skyscrapers, bed, parts of chairs, desk's top, movie, TV screens, books, notebooks, bathtub
* cylinders	* silo, lighthouse, canister,
* circles	* igloos, yurts, school library, pools, UVA's rotunda, Jefferson Memorial, mirrors,

Through this experience students recognized how important geometry and math were to buildings, furniture, roads, and bridges. Dana, who had recently returned from a visit to The Museum of Modern Art pointed out that Picasso and Braque painted the human body in terms of geometric shapes.

In science, seventh graders read the textbook section "Conserving Resources." Their teacher, Kathleen Hobbs asks: "How can conserving resources make a difference in people's lives?"

Bobby points out, "You can save 17 trees every time a metric ton of paper is recycled." Zack says, "My mom has everyone in the family making a compost pile. Even leaves I rake in October become compost for mom's flower and vegetable gardens. Nothing goes to waste in my family."

"My dad makes us shut the water while we brush our teeth, and when he and my brother shave, they shut the water off until it's time to wash up. You use 16 liters of water if you let it run and only 2 liters if you shut it off," says Sara.

Connecting the Text to the Community and the World

1.   Get students into the "connecting mode" by posing a question that invites them to apply what they've learned to issues that still need our attention. For example, the questions that follow ask students to link their learning with the problems we all wrestle with today: Are there other ways of solving our energy problems besides placing oil rigs in national forests? How does stereotyping affect minorities? How will cutting down forests change life for animals, insects, plants, and people?

2.   In a think-aloud, model how you make connections to community and world issues. By permitting students to enter your thought process, you show them how you connect information and ideas from social studies, science and math to present-day issues.

Third graders have read and talked about "Trick-or-Treat for UNICEF" from *Scholastic News*. The question I pose is: "Are there problems with malnutrition and healthcare in our community?" Here's my think-aloud:

> Our community has a food bank for families that are out of work and can't buy healthful food. We also have soup kitchens and churches that serve lunch to poor people, especially on holidays like Thanksgiving. Our schools have large numbers of children on free lunch and breakfast, so there is obviously much need. But I wonder if preschoolers and parents get the nutrition they need. Health care is a problem. Poor families can't afford vaccinations and visits to the doctor. Even the clinic can't serve everyone. Last year there was an outbreak of measles among children who weren't vaccinated. We need to give to UNICEF to help children all over the world, but we also need to make sure we are helping poor people in our community.

Third graders ask questions and share their observations to clarify the process they have observed. Dominique says, "My friend's mom is losing her teeth 'cause she doesn't have money to go to a dentist." Randy says, "My brother goes to Washington, D.C. to work in a soup kitchen every weekend. He says people are hungry and have no work or place to live." Think-alouds usually result in students sharing experiences and ideas that shed even more light on an issue.

3. Model many times until you feel students' feedback demonstrates they understand how to be "poised to connect" as they read or reflect on their reading.

4. Organize students into pairs or small groups and ask them to connect the material they've studied with current issues and problems in their community and the world.

> ## Connect and Apply
> ## Strategy Snapshot: Grade 5 Math

Topic: "If you had one million dollars, how would you spend it?"

Time: Six class periods (45 minutes each), plus time spent at home

Materials: Math textbook as a resource for graphs, charts, finding fractions, decimal percent equivalents

Background Information: Fifth-grade teacher, Josh Mosser, continually plans experiences that foster making connections to students' lives. To illustrate how knowing fractions, decimals, and percents could help them in a real situation, Josh planned the "One Million Dollar Project."

Some students had difficulty spending their huge budget. Others, like Ciara, used a fantasy about owning a horse farm as the basis for budgeting and completing a pie graph and chart that showed the translated fractions to decimals to percentages.

Once students can make connections and have a solid understanding of two or three strategies in each part of the learning framework, groups can create plans to teach themselves, classmates, and other grades.

Parts of Ciara's project.

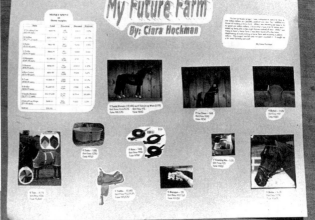

▨ Building Materials
▨ Land
▨ Farm Equipment
▨ Horse Supplies
▨ 8 Horses
▨ Trainer
▨ 2 Farm Hands
▨ Food
▨ Vet/Farrier
▨ Utilities
▨ Insurance

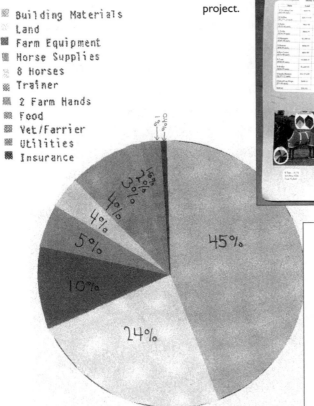

On this particular project, I was instructed to spend as close to one million dollars as I possibly could on one idea. So, I fulfilled my dream of building a horse farm. While I was storming up ideas to try to spend one million dollars, I found that it was a lot of money and I ended up being able to buy eight horses instead of four. While I was trying to build a horse farm, I may have dozed off a few times daydreaming of really owning a horse farm and receiving a million dollars. This project was fun and I'm glad I received it. It taught me a lot about farming and math.

By Ciara Hockman

MONEY SPENT on My Future Farm

Category	Total	Fraction	Decimal	Percent
Land (40 acres)	$240,000	240,000/1,000,000	0.240000	24%
Building Materials (house, barn, fence)	$450,000	450,000/1,000,000	0.450000	45%
8 Horses	$40,000	40,000/1,000,000	0.040000	4%
Farm Equipment	$100,000	100,000/1,000,000	0.100000	10%
Food (Initial Setup)	$20,000	20,000/1,000,000	0.020000	2%
Horse Supplies	$50,000	50,000/1,000,000	0.050000	5%
Vet/Farrier	$16,000	16,000/1,000,000	0.016000	1.6%
2 Farm Hands	$30,000	30,000/1,000,000	0.030000	3%
Trainer	$40,000	40,000/1,000,000	0.040000	4%
Utilities	$10,000	10,000/1,000,000	0.010000	1%
Insurance	$4,000	4,000/1,000,000	0.004000	.4%
TOTAL	$1,000,000			

Students Connect What They Know About Strategic Learning to Their Own Learning Process

Inviting pairs or small groups to create lesson plans for learning or teaching a section in a textbook or trade book is an effective way to measure how well students understand the learning strategies they've practiced in the three-part framework. In a speech at the Brigham Young Reading Conference in Provo, Utah, on June 14, 2001, Carol Santa pointed out how this exercise deepens students' knowledge of their learning process and the strategies they've practiced, and how it motivates them to do a top-notch job of constructivist teaching.

Here's what students do after you assign pairs or groups different sections of a chapter or different chapters:

1. Read your section carefully.
2. Discuss the contents and list what key ideas need to be understood.
3. Suggest strategies that can be used before, during, and after learning.
4. Choose one strategy for each part of the learning framework that will help you and others actively learn this information.
5. Prepare a process plan that you will submit to the teacher.
6. Work with the teacher to establish deadline dates.

An Eighth-Grade Example: Teaching Others About Shakespeare

For three weeks in March, John Lothrop and I combine English and history classes. Our eighth graders research Shakespeare's life, the Globe Theater, and everyday life in the Elizabethan period. They also watch and discuss clips from several films of Shakespeare's plays.

The students' "audiences" for creating projects and learning experiences were younger children. At the start of the study, groups drew, from a box, the grade level they would teach, which meant that they had to adjust information and experiences to the ages of their audiences. Groups discussed their plans for engaging younger students with me. To guide students, we asked them to create before, during, and after learning experiences. Here are the highlights of one meeting, when Kate, Daniel, Michael, and Cameron shared their plans for teaching fourth grade:

KATE: *First we'll ask them what they know about Shakespeare. If they don't know enough, we'll read parts of what we took off the Internet.*

DANIEL: *I'll be dressed in costume and will show a chart of the kinds of clothes that the rich, poor, and middle classes wore. I'll quickly discuss the chart; then I'll ask if they see clothing today that comes from Elizabethan times.*

MICHAEL: *I'll write an original song about men taking women's parts and sing it with my guitar. They'll learn about acting then with a song. (See margin, opposite page, for song lyrics)*

KATE AND CAMERON: *We have a handout of the Globe theater—it's a picture that's labeled. We'll get groups to study it and ask us questions. Then we'll have them complete a Venn diagram that compares the Globe Theater with movie theaters (see below).*

ALL: *We're bringing in some typical Elizabethan foods. While they eat, we'll discuss what they learned and collect any questions they have. We can help them answer questions and leave some picture books in their classroom so they can investigate some.*

Kate and Cameron invited fourth graders to complete a Venn diagram that compared movie theaters with Shakespeare's Globe Theatre (see below). Michael used what he learned to compose and sing an original song about Shakespeare's actors. Daniel and Ryan, wearing costumes, used their outfits and an illustrated chart of Elizabethan clothing to teach fourth graders about dress from the poorest to the wealthiest citizens. Fourth graders gave high ratings to this experience.

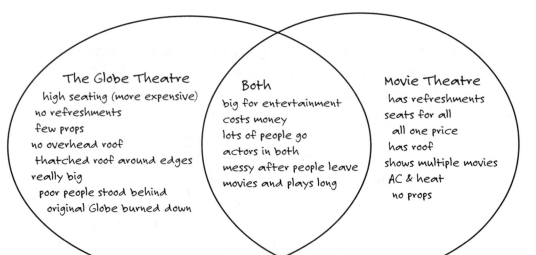

The Globe Theatre
high seating (more expensive)
no refreshments
few props
no overhead roof
thatched roof around edges
really big
poor people stood behind
original Globe burned down

Both
big for entertainment
costs money
lots of people go
actors in both
messy after people leave
movies and plays long

Movie Theatre
has refreshments
seats for all
all one price
has roof
shows multiple movies
AC & heat
no props

Teaching Reading in Social Studies, Science, and Math

Other groups choose a historical novel or biography about the Holocaust. Students select books at their independent reading levels. Before they read their novels, groups submit a "process plan" that outlines how they will incorporate strategies from the three-part framework. Here's the plan three students designed for Anita Lobel's *No Pretty Pictures* (Morrow, 1998) and the plan a group of four designed for Johanna Reiss's *The Upstairs Room* (Harper Keypoint, 1972).

No Pretty Pictures

Before Learning:
- Read the inside of the jacket, the back cover, and the first two pages. Discuss.

During Reading
- Divide the book in four parts. Jot down the words you didn't get and the page. After each part group retells to see if they recall. Help each other get hard words.

After Reading
- Dramatize a powerful part of the story for the class. Answer questions students ask.

The Upstairs Room

Before Learning:
- Brainstorm all the ideas you get when you read the title. Relate to what you know about Holocaust.

During Reading
- Divide book into five parts. After each part, make a list in journal of the main events. Compare with group and discuss. Jot down hard words and page number in journal. Help each other.

After Reading
- Interview the main characters in front of the class. Answer any questions class has.

MICHAEL'S SONG: "GUYS AS GIRLS"

Back in the day
No girls in plays
It was outlawed
For girl dialogues
In the theater
Some poor guy became
    a her.

Refrain:
Say it ain't so,
    I don't wanna go
Onto the stage,
    dressed up as a girl.
Lipstick, bad wig
Fit nicely on his lid,
Get your dress, put it on
You make a good blond

Keep my head down
Don't see my frown
I didn't want to be
This she.

Students' plans reveal the kinds of learning experiences they have had in all subjects. In addition to literature, you can divide a science or history chapter among groups and have them design a plan for learning.

In math, students can create process plans during a review of material. This is an effective way for students to study and reteach one another; it also enables the teacher to determine students' level of understanding prior to a test.

You can make the process a self-evaluation tool by inviting students to write about how each strategy or experience supported their learning. This raises students' self-awareness of how strategic reading and writing improve comprehension and recall.

STRATEGY LESSON:
Paraphrasing

How It Helps You

Nancy Hershey and I look through sixth graders' definitions of vocabulary from a history chapter. Nancy has assigned this activity to see how well her students understand the material, expecting students would paraphrase or infer meaning from their reading. Twenty-five out of twenty-eight students, however, simply copy definitions word-for-word from the text or the glossary. What's going on? To me, their work indicates one or a combination of these possible interpretations:

• They don't have a process for paraphrasing.
• They've never practiced how to put ideas into their own words.
• They don't know the information well enough to put ideas in their own words.
• They copied definitions in other grades and it was fine.

Students' ability to paraphrase lets you know whether they truly understand material they're studying. Copying from a text, without citing the source, is plagiarism.

Paraphrasing, akin to retelling, is a strategy that's best learned with a teacher's guidance. It is a great note-taking strategy, since students translate text passages into their own words. Notes can be simple rephrasing, or they can be in a web, double-entry journal, or heading/details (see pages 164–166). Paraphrasing works extremely well in social studies and science. It's also great for explaining a process in math.

Purpose

To teach students how to write ideas and definitions in their own words; to show how paraphrasing supports note taking and recall

Materials

Part of a chapter from a textbook; a section from an informational trade book, or a magazine or newspaper article

Guidelines

1. Start modelling paraphrasing with a visual, such as a chart, diagram, map or illustration. You can also use addition, subtraction, multiplication, or division, since students can paraphrase how to compute based on the sample problem. Because most visuals have few words, students have to grasp the meaning of the visual in order to explain it in their own words.

2. Ask the student to read the chart's title and any other print.

3. Next have the student study what data the chart reveals.

4. Finally, ask the student to pull all of the gathered information together and paraphrase what was learned.

5. If a student exhibits difficulty at any point in the process, offer support by prompting. If prompts don't work, try modelling.

Here's how third grader, Zeta, paraphrases what she grasps from the "Electoral College Map" in *Scholastic News* (Vol. 57, No. 9, page 3).

> This map shows how people in the U.S. voted for president. Most of the states voted for Bush. They are in red, and you can see they cover all parts [of the U.S.]. The blue shows the states Gore won — not too many. And Florida and Oregon could not decide for either [Bush or Gore].

6. Have students practice about 10 minutes, twice a week, until they show that they can paraphrase.

7. Move students from oral to written paraphrasing by having them write what they have said in a journal.

8. In a think-aloud, demonstrate how you paraphrase the definition of a bold face word in a textbook. Here's my think-aloud for a sixth grade science class.

I read aloud: "A **variation** is the appearance of an inherited trait that makes an individual different from other members of the same species," (p. 156, *Life Science,* Glencoe,

1997). I reread the word and the definition many times, until I can make sense of it. Then I tell myself the key ideas I want to include when I paraphrase:

- inherited trait
- different from others
- same species

I close the book, keeping my hand on the page, and try to explain the word. Here's what I say: *When an individual has an inherited trait that makes it different from others in its species, that trait is called a* **variation**.

Now I write these words on the chalkboard and check them against the key ideas I wanted to include.

9. Set aside time to practice paraphrasing material students already comprehend. Continue until students' written work reveals they can apply the strategy.

> ## Paraphrasing with a Double-Entry Journal
> ## Strategy Snapshot: Grade 4 Science

Topic: Systems in the human body

Time: 30 to 40 minutes

Materials: Notes students have taken; information trade books and textbooks with diagrams

Background Information: I introduced the double-entry journal to fourth graders towards the end of their study of the systems in our bodies. This was the students' first experience with this strategy, and their teacher, Debi Gustin, agreed that it would be an excellent assessment piece. Here are the guidelines we set:

- Fold a piece of composition paper in half, lengthwise.
- Place your name and date at the top of the paper.
- On the left-hand side of the paper, draw and label a part of the system you're studying that you found interesting or would like to spotlight. (Debi and I vetoed tracing as we wanted students to practice making an accurate, freehand drawing.)
- Explain your illustration, using your own words, on the right-hand side.

Fourth graders loved the double-entry strategy, and each student completed two enthusiastically. Mckenzie's words mirrored everyone's feelings: "I only had to look back [in the book] to draw my picture. Taking notes and talking about them in groups helped me really know it."

Teaching Reading in Social Studies, Science, and Math

Grade 5: Paraphrasing to Correct Math

Topic: Correcting math test problems

Time: 15 to 30 minutes, depending on the number and complexity of the problems.

Materials: A math test; class work; homework

Background Information:

Heather Campbell and I have been discussing math, a new subject for her this year. A dedicated teacher who always works to

A fifth grader shows what she has learned about knee and shin joints in a double-entry journal.

respond to students' needs, Heather asks, "How can I help my students find and correct their math errors without overwhelming them?"

"You should have students revise parts of their math class work, homework, or a test," I advise. "If they can pinpoint the errors in their reasoning and computation, if they can redo or fix the work, they will gain the understanding necessary to clarify their process."

Start by inviting your students to correct one or two problems (more than that could become frustrating). Work one-on-one, or in groups of two to three, with those students who are making many errors and continually show they don't understand. Place your process on center-stage by modelling how you reread, rethink, and redo math problems.

I recommend that students use the double-entry journal structure to revise math problems. Have students prepare their paper with these steps.

- Copy the problem with its errors on the left-hand side.
- Reread the problem. Rethink your process to discover your error.
- Explain, using words, your error on the right-hand side.
- Redo the problem on the left-hand side.
- Tell what you did to solve it on the right-hand side.

Post steps and a sample double-entry on chart paper so students have a resource while they redo a problem.

Heather bubbled as she shared students' work with me. "The children got so excited when they found their own mistakes. And having them do just one was just right. No one felt the task was impossible, and I had time to help my weaker students." Inviting students to revisit, rethink, and redo can also support students' learning in science and social studies.

A double-entry journal helps this fifth grader correct her math.

Paraphrasing to Review a Chapter
Strategy Snapshot: Grade 6 History

Topic: Buddhism

Time: One 45-minute class period

Materials: History textbook

Background Information: In sixth- and seventh-grade history classes, Dick Bell takes 10 to 15 minutes of his four class periods to teach students several paraphrasing strategies. "I introduce the 'Chapter Review' to students when I am planning a quiz or test," says Dick.

Partners help one another, but each student completes his or her own review sheet. Since they have spent several classes reading and discussing the information and taking notes, students can rely on their journals and what they've learned to complete the review sheet. And the notes are in their own words. Students revisit their textbook only when they are unsure of an answer; then they reread, discuss, close the book, and write their notes on the sheet.

A seventh grader's chapter review helps her recall key data. It makes a great study sheet.

Following is a reproducible samples of a Chapter Review sheet for history or science. This format can be adapted to math as well by asking for sample problems and formulas, etc.

Teaching Reading in Social Studies, Science, and Math

Chapter Review

Name _____ Date _____

Chapter Title _____ Pages _____

Here is a list of the most important things I learned:

Key vocabulary and definitions I want to remember:

Draw and label diagrams or maps or math problems I should remember:

Connections I made:

Points the teacher made in class:

Possible questions that might appear on the test:

Paraphrasing: Putting Paraphrased Notes to Work
Strategy Snapshot: Grade 7

Robin Northrup and I sift through the notes her eighth grade students took on short articles they had read from the kit, *Write TIME for Kids,* Level 4 (Time, Inc. 2000). "They are so sketchy," Robin says. "The next day, even the students couldn't use them to recall what they had read." The process Robin and I developed stresses the importance of taking notes that can be used for studying. The goal for students was to create a web of detailed notes that another student, *who has not read the article,* could use to successfully compose a paragraph. **The Process:** Robin modelled the entire process and called for student input before asking students to work independently.

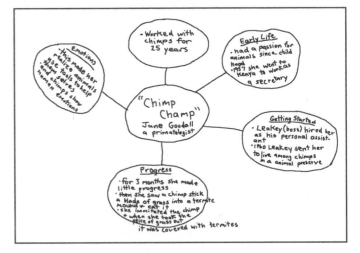

Ginna's web contains detailed notes.

• Read a short article two or three times.

"Chimp Champ"

Ted

   In the article "Chimp Champ" it talks about a primatologist, Jane Goodalls, shteragle to discover something about the Chimp. Jane had a passion for animals since her childhood. So Jane became a primatologist. In 1957 she went to Kenya to work as a secretary for a man called Leakey. In 1960 Leakey saw Jane's passion for animals and sent her to an animal preserve in remote Gombe, to study chimps. She made little progress untill she saw a chimp stick a blade of grass in a termite hill, so she tryed it and when it came out termites all over the blade of grass. So she descovered that chimps used tools and had emotions like humans, she when on working with chimps for 25 years.

Ted writes a paragraph using Ginna's notes.

• Place the title and author of the article in the center circle of your web.

• Around the web's center, draw spokes that end in circles.

• Write notes that relate to one idea in each circle.

• Check notes against the article to make sure you've included main details.

• Give your notes to a partner who will write a paragraph using the notes.

Teaching Reading in Social Studies, Science, and Math

Visualizing

How It Helps You

In content area subjects, visualizing can help students recall a sequence of information, solve and/or graph a math problem, test their comprehension of new vocabulary, or draw and label diagrams, graphs, and experiments in science, and maps in social studies.

When you encourage visualization, you develop students' ability to picture information. Mental images help students replay, reflect on, and comprehend information.

Purpose

To offer students practice with making mental pictures; to show students the connections between visualizing, remembering, and understanding

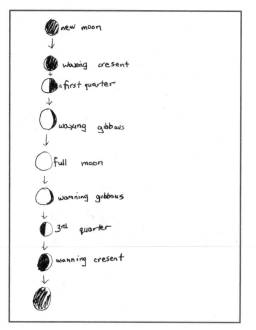

David Glaize, a seventh grader, draws and labels the phases of the moon to recall the correct order and the names of each phase.

Materials

Information in a textbook; a math problem, a construction, an experiment; vocabulary

In Harry Holloway's math class, when students design their kites, they draw and label pictures before constructing them.

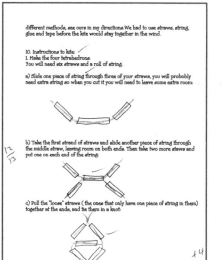

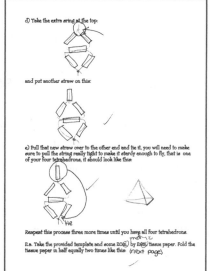

Guidelines

1. Invite students to visualize information as you read aloud sections from nonfiction trade books, poems, or magazine articles.

2. Have students draw information in a sequence and use their drawings to discuss the information with a partner, group, or the class.

3. Ask students to use drawings to help them understand math problems or a science process.

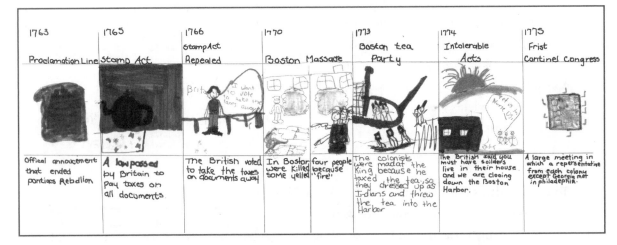

Heather Campbell's fifth graders comprehend the events leading up to the American Revolution by illustrating their time line.

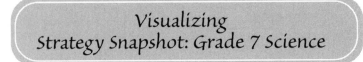

Visualizing
Strategy Snapshot: Grade 7 Science

Topic: *Pangaea:* the name Alfred Wegener gave to the large mass of land made up of all continents. Wegener believed that the continents were once a single, large land mass that eventually broke apart.

Time: One 45-minute period

Materials: Science textbook

Background Information: During two classes, students read and discussed Wegener's theory and related terms. Now, their teacher, Kathleen Hobbs, models how she visualiz-

Teaching Reading in Social Studies, Science, and Math

Rachel, a seventh grader, understands Pangaea by illustrating related terms.

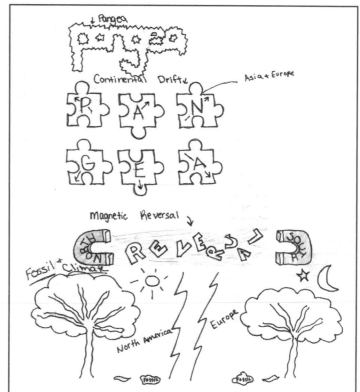

es *Pangaea*. She then asks students to illustrate and label these new terms: *seafloor spreading, fossil, climate,* and *continental drift.*

For 30 minutes, students remain focused, and Kathleen circulates, stopping to answer questions and offer praise. Students enjoy the challenge of translating ideas into pictures. "Once I figured out how I would illustrate it [new term], I really understood it," said Rachel.

STRATEGY LESSON:
Summarize and Synthesize Through Journal Writing

How It Helps You

When students write summaries, they must have an understanding of the main idea and then select details that support it. Summarizing asks students to synthesize what they've read by putting information into their own words. Students' summaries can be used as springboards for discussions and offer another opportunity to clarify meaning.

Purpose

To see what students have learned about a concept, topic, article, chapter, or book; to use writing to generate explanation

Materials

Short article; a section of a chapter or article; a chapter from a trade book

Guidelines

Note: First model the process using the steps below. Then collaborate with students, inviting them to help you complete a summary. In *Grades 3 and 4,* collaborate many times, until you feel that students can write a summary independently. In *Grades 5 to 8,* collaborate two to three times; then decide if students can try the process without your support. If not, continue modelling and collaborating with the entire class or small groups of students who need extra help.

1. Read the piece two to three times.

    Fifth graders read "Russia's New Leader" in <u>Scholastic News,</u> 68 (24).

2. Think about the main points in the piece.

    I remind students that their purpose is to summarize information about Vladimir Putin.

3. List four to five main points on a piece of paper.

    Here's the list these fifth graders offered:
    *   **Russians vote in Putin as new President.**
    *   **People hope Putin will keep making Russia's economy strong.**
    *   **Putin will fight bribery and other corruption in gov't—this costs Russia $20 billion a year.**
    *   **He has promised to keep Russia democratic even if he was a KGB agent.**

4. Write your topic or lead sentence. This should include the title and main idea or point of the article.

    The students composed this topic sentence: The article, "Russia's New Leader" points out the problems faced by Vladimir Putin, Russia's new President.

5. Reread your list of main points. Put them in chronological order if you are summarizing a story. You can do this by numbering the points on your list. Otherwise, put your main points in a logical order.

6. Turn each main point into a complete sentence.

7. Write a wrap-up sentence or conclusion that ties all your points together. You can restate the main idea in a different way.

Transition Words for Summarizing and Synthesizing

As you teach your students how to summarize, it is also important to give them vocabulary tools that will assist them in their writing. I suggest you post the following words on chart paper. As you model, show students how these words create smooth transitions from one idea to the next.

Words that show time:

About	during	until	yesterday	finally
after	first	meanwhile	next	then
at	second	today	soon	as soon as
before	third	later	tomorrow	when

Words that can emphasize a point you are making:

again	in fact	for this reason	for these reasons

Words that can help you add details:

again	and	for instance	also	besides
next	along with	another	for example	such as
finally				

Words that help you conclude or wrap up:

as a result	finally	therefore	last

Thumbnail Summaries of Four After-Learning Experiences

Again, once you are sure your students have learned a strategy, you can reinforce that learning with a multitude of after-learning experiences such as these.

Brochures: Kathleen Hobbs invites seventh graders to prepare a travel brochure for "A Journey Through the Solar System." Students review brochures from a local travel agency and discuss their contents and formats. Then Kathleen gives them a guideline sheet, and students take notes, plan an itinerary, and design a brochure.

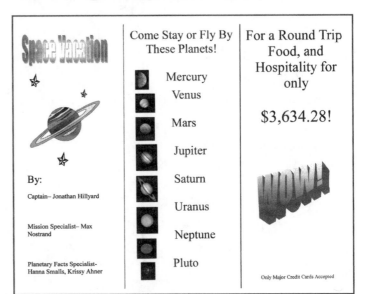

Jonathan's brochure for a trip to the planets.

Constructions: Construction projects score high ratings because, as one student designing a tetrahedron kite said, "It makes you use all you know. I can't wait to see if my design will fly." Tom Arthur invites his eighth-grade algebra students to design and build a bridge. Groups of fourth graders construct models of the solar system. Josh Mosser helps fifth graders design and construct a Medieval

Itinerary

July 1, 2004 depart Earth on Interplanetary Shuttle.

September 14, 2004 (76 days) arrive on Mercury. Stay for five days.

November 1, 2004 (42 days) orbit Venus for five days. Due to a very thick cloud system we will not be able to land.

March 28, 2005 (142 days) land on Mars and stay for five days.

May 9, 2006 (1.1 years) observe Jupiter's "Great Red Spot". Keep orbiting when done observing. Stay for five days.

November 13, 2007 (1.5 years) arrive on Saturn's rings. Stay for five days.

March 9, 2010 (3.3 years) arrive on Uranus. Stay for five days.

November 28, 2013 (3.7 years) orbit Neptune. Due do a severe storm system we are going to be unable to land. Stay for five days.

February 15, 2017 (3.2 years) orbit Pluto. Covered with ice, unable to land. Stay for five days.

March 29, 2030 (13.1 years) return to Earth!

Jonathan plans the trip's itinerary.

Teaching Reading in Social Studies, Science, and Math

Seventh graders Hanne and Bobby construct their kite.

castle and the village outside the castle's walls.

In Harry Holloway's seventh-grade class, designing and building a tetrahedron kite is a yearly project. It takes students five 45-minute classes to work through the ten-question exercise Harry assigns them (See Appendix, p. 375). "I've designed the questions to help them plan and think through the project, but I also want them to have an experience with technical writing," says Harry. Students complete a first draft, and Harry provides feedback that helps students rethink and revise their work. After students complete their final drafts, they build kites and wait for a windy day to fly them.

Simulations: Reenactments of events and situations in the past or present can deepen students' understanding of a concept, such as slavery, or how to react in an emergency, such as a volcanic eruption or a hurricane.

History teacher Dick Bell believes that simulations stimulate students to think deeply and converse about issues they might gloss over or merely pay lip-service to. His seventh graders take on

A seventh grader hones his technical writing skills through a kite project.

Tetrahedral Kite Project

By Clarke Crenshaw

1.   A tetrahedron is a pyramid whose four are sides all equilateral triangles. The kites we are building are called tetrahedral kites because we made four little tetrahedrons and we put them together to make a bigger tetrahedron.

2.   A definition of a box kite is a tailless kite consisting of 2 rectangular boxes with open ends. They are connected together with a space in the middle. Other kinds of box kites are winged box kites and ones without wings.

3.   The surface area of one of our small tetrahedrons is 720 square cm. We measured the height of the tetrahedron and got 18 cm. Then we measured the base and we got 20 cm. Then we multiplied 18 by 20 and got 360. To get the area of one face we would have to divide 360 by 2. This gave us 180. A tetrahedron has four faces so in order to get the surface area we would multiply 180 by 4 and this will give us 720 square cm for our surface area.

To get the volume of a small tetrahedron we used the formula 1/3 times the area of the base times the height. In the problem above we have already the role of *slaves* and *masters;* slaves have to do their masters' bidding. Those portraying slaves wash the chalkboards, pick paper up from the floor, sharpen pencils, etc. Then students debrief, sharing how a slave might have felt having to do everything a master ordered, as well as the power and control masters had.

Kathleen Hobbs uses a simulation from the Internet and has seventh graders plan an evacuation for an impending volcanic eruption. She asks students to complete a "Reflection Sheet" to evaluate what they learned from the experience. The students all agreed that the exercise helped them move from "Yeah, no big deal," to "really understanding the dangers and options."

Reflections on Evacuation

1. What were your thoughts and feelings about this activity?

It was neat because you had to think about what to do in a situation with different options. Although someone in my group does not resolve easily

2. What, if anything, did you find difficult about the evacuation?

That there were many camps and many routes to choose, but it was pretty easy w/ the facts

3. How did this simulation compare to a real life situation?

This actually could of happened

4. How did your group resolve conflict?

We left camp B, and followed the X river

5. What kinds of behaviors are important in an emergency situation?

- Stay calmed
- find the quickest and easiest route out
- figure out something to do quickly

6. What issues prevented, or threatened to prevent, your groups getting out in the time allowed?

Mudslides avalanches   ASH

A seventh grader evaluates her simulation.

Drama: During the process of preparing a drama, students converse, read and reread, compromise, and make decisions that transform the facts in a text into a narrative. The drama exemplifies students' understanding of new information. Dramas can be informal, where small groups meet to sketch out the plot, understand the characters, then improvise their lines.

Nancy Roche's third graders read chapters on George Washington, Thomas Jefferson, Patrick Henry, and George Mason from *Virginia's History and Geography* (Charles Scribner & Sons, 1965). For two class periods, groups discuss their characters and decide what parts of the chapter they want to dramatize.

Four groups verbally outline plays in three to four brief acts, then rehearsing lines. They also make props from paper, such as The Bill of Rights and Lord Dunmore's letter announcing he was leaving Virginia and never returning. Some wear signs that name their characters. Their teacher supplies shawls, women's caps, three-cornered hats, feather pens, candles, and scrolls to add realism to the plays.

After watching the plays, I ask third graders to tell me what they liked about this experience. The points they make illustrate that dramas develop children's comprehension of new information, and their social interactions, decision making and compromising abilities as well.

- You can't come up with lines that others believe if you don't know it. So you have to learn the history and you get to have fun. —*Elizabeth*

- I got to make friends with people I usually don't play with. —*Conner*

- I got to feel like the people we acted. Doing it means you understand it. —*Hattie*

- I liked watching all the other plays. I learned from them. —*David*

- I think it was good we all had to make up the scripts. We argued about points, but then we compromised. —*Finn*

- Doing it felt like a long recess. —*Jay*

In math, science, and history, dramas can include impromptu skits, simulations of an historical period, such as the Depression or Westward Expansion, radio plays that recreate an event as if it were occurring today, or dramatic monologues (see pages 330–331) based on biography, nonfiction, and historical fiction. Students can also base dramas on the behaviors of animal and plant cells.

Elizabeth and Justine recreate Paul Revere's ride.

෨ Pause and Reflect on: ෨
The Importance of Post-Reading Experiences

The reflective experiences you offer students during the third part of the learning framework deepen the connections between new information and what students already know. As a teacher, I realize that's it's impossible to spend large amounts of contemplative time on every topic, chapter, and theme, but you can pick and choose, reserving more reflective time for topics you and the students consider important.

I keep in mind what a fifth grader said after his group performed a play about justice in ancient Rome: "You learn about history and you work with others. It's better than tests, 'cause you become the person and try to think and walk and speak like him." He's so right; learning is doing.

✿ Chapter 7 ✿

Building Students' Vocabulary

It is hard to imagine tools more useful than words. Without them, talkers, philosophers, actors, and writers, would simply be out of business.

— Karla Kuskin

I t's February. I'm working with a group of middle school students who read several years below grade level. We've just begun a reading workshop, where every student reads books at his or her independent level. During independent reading, I can confer for 5 to 10 minutes with students who need extra scaffolding. My meeting with Kawan pushes me to consider an issue he and his classmates face—an issue that continues to diminish Kawan's self-esteem and nourish his negative feelings towards school. Here's part of our conversation:

ROBB: *How's the reading going?*

KAWAN: *I'm liking* Stone Fox *(J.R. Gardiner, HarperTrophy, 2000), but I still can't read my history and science book.*

ROBB: *Have you spoken to your teachers?*

KAWAN: *Yeah. The history's better now cause I know a lot about the Civil War. David reads the science to me. But I can't learn all those new words in the chapter. They go out of my head. I try to memorize them for the quizzes we get. I'm failing [science].*

Even students reading on grade level express feelings of frustration similar to Kawan's. An average of 15 to 25 new words bombard students weekly if you total the boldface vocabulary in social studies, science, and math. Disfluent readers who also lack the background knowledge that would enable them to figure out many new words in their textbooks, have an especially tough time. They lack the strategies to figure out the meanings of words while reading (Alvermann and Phelps, 1998; Gillet and Temple, 2000; Nagy, 1988; Readence, Moore and Rickelman, 2000; Vacca and Vacca, 2000).

Researchers agree that textbooks are the core instructional tool in grades 4 to 8 in content area subjects (Freeman and Person, 1998). A study of science and social studies texts by Harmon, Hedrick, and Fox (2000) indicates that textbook authors need to reconsider how they present vocabulary instruction. Including a list of new words at the start of a chapter, then defining these in the text and glossary is not enough for students to make a huge leap from new label to using terms to comprehend new concepts. What's missing, according to Harmon et al. (2000), are instructional guidelines that suggest experiences that can build students' word knowledge before, during, and after reading.

Building word knowledge isn't the same as memorizing definitions, however. As students like Kawan can attest, asking students to retain the meanings of long lists of words doesn't mean the students are comprehending the textbook.

Instead, building students' word knowledge means offering vocabulary study in each part of the learning framework (see pages 37–49). During this three-phase process, stu-

Teaching Reading in Social Studies, Science, and Math

dents connect new terms and concepts to related ideas they understand. In addition, students also have multiple opportunities to use words while talking, reading, and writing before, during, and after each chapter or topic studied (Allen, 1999; Alvermann and Phelps, 1998; Gillet and Temple, 2000; Harmon et al., 2000; Nagy, 1988; Robb, 1999; Vacca and Vacca, 2000; Vaughan and Estes, 1986).

In this chapter, we'll explore:

- Ways to help students think of words as tools that enable them to unlock meaning from any text.
- Writing experiences that enable students to use words to connect ideas, build new understandings about a topic, and integrate new words into their thinking process (Murray, 1984; Robb, 2000a; Self, 1987; Hansen, 1987 and 2001).

Which Words Do I Teach?

The teachers I work with during professional study meetings often ask me, "How do I know which words to pre-teach? Which words do I emphasize?" I think all teachers wrestle with these questions, and the answers to them are not as easy as "going by the book"; simply teaching the vocabulary spotlighted in the textbook won't necessarily build understanding of a topic. To plan effective vocabulary instruction, a teacher must first make a judgment about the group of words highlighted in a chapter. Here are questions I use to sift through the list and support my decision-making process:

- Is the word essential for an understanding of a main concept in the chapter?
- Are there enough clues in the text and visuals for students to start building their knowledge about this word without my support?
- Is the word repeated often, and do the repetitions deepen students' understanding?
- Do I sense that students have some prior knowledge about this word or concept that will help them understand it?
- Can I keep the number of pre-teaching words to three to four for grades 3, 4, and 5, and four to five for grades 6, 7, and 8?
- Is there a word in the chapter that's not highlighted but that I know my students will struggle with?

- Should I maintain students' focus on these words during and after reading? If the word is new or students have a small amount of prior knowledge, then the answer here is "Yes."

Let me model my thought process as I consider a chapter from a grade 7 science textbook. There are five sections in this chapter titled "Igneous Rocks;" each section introduces two to six words that students should learn prior to reading. The words in section one are *rock* and *rock cycle*. I'm confident that students have background knowledge and experiences with the word *rock*. However, *rock cycle* is a concept that students will need to understand in order to grasp all the information about how rocks form.

I devise a strategic teaching plan that builds on what students know about *cycles*.

- Because they have studied the water cycle in grade 3 and life cycles in grade 6, I want students to start with what they already know about the term *cycle*.

- Then I invite students to study the *rock cycle* diagram in the textbook and think-pair-share. Study means read the captions and labels, and paraphrase the information during the think-pair-share (see pages 266–269).

Section two, on the other hand, introduces six words: *igneous rock, lava, intrusive, extrusive, basaltic,* and *granitic.* Students all know a great deal about *lava* and its destructive power. However, when I try to collect information from them on the other words, it's obvious they know little to nothing about each one. I must now decide on a strategy, and I choose "Predict and Clarify" (see below) because it invites students to predict the meaning of words, then refine and adjust their knowledge of a word before, during and after reading.

The "Predict and Clarify" strategy drives students back to the text three times to reread and enlarge their explanation. Returning to the text is desirable, since it enables students to make firmer connections to new words prior to and after reading and discussing. It also deepens students' knowledge of the words, information, and concepts in the chapter.

STRATEGY LESSON:
Predict and Clarify

Purpose
To predict the meaning of words after previewing the text; to refine and clarify the words' meaning before, during, and after reading

Teaching Reading in Social Studies, Science, and Math

Materials

Textbook; four to five pre-selected words; chart paper, markers

When to Use

An ideal strategy to introduce and extend students' knowledge of unfamiliar words and concepts. As students read, reread, discuss, and write, they extend their understandings of new words throughout the three-part framework.

Guidelines

First Day:

1. Print on chart paper these headings in three columns: WORDS, PREDICTIONS, and WHAT I HAVE LEARNED.

2. Under WORDS, list three to five words students need to know to understand the concepts in a chapter or section of a textbook or trade book. Leave several lines between words.

> Before introducing third graders to a chapter on "Native Americans," Nancy Roche writes these words on the chart: <u>longhouse, tribe, wigwam, legend</u>.

3. Preview the selection by reading the boldface headings, words, and captions that accompany pictures, charts, diagrams, and graphs.

4. Have students *predict* the meaning of each word. If the preview does not help, then have students guess. The point of this strategy is to move students, over time, from a prediction to a refined explanation.

> For <u>longhouse</u>, Nancy Roche says: "I think it might be a house that's long."

5. Locate the first word in the text, and read aloud the sentence that contains the word.

> Nancy Roche reads: "These longhouses, as they were called, were used by some Native Americans as homes."

6. Think out loud, explaining what the sentence tells you about the word's meaning and the clues you used.

> Here's Nancy's think-aloud: "The sentence tells me that longhouses were homes for some Native Americans."

7. Record your ideas under WHAT I HAVE LEARNED.

> Nancy writes: "Native American homes."

8. Read aloud the entire section containing the word. Think out loud, sharing with students any extra information you discovered.

Here's what Nancy said: "I had to read two sections to get the full meaning of <u>longhouses</u>. The first section says they're built in groups and low. The second section said that animal skins, rope-like grass and tree bark covered a frame of bent young trees. There was a hole in the roof so smoke from the fire could escape. Sometimes it's helpful to read ahead to make sure you have all the details."

9. Write these ideas under the WHAT I HAVE LEARNED column.

10. After students ask questions about the strategy lesson, have them predict and start refining the meaning of the remaining words using the process you modeled.

Second Day:

1. Have students read the chapter or section and discuss.

2. Ask students to add details under the WHAT I HAVE LEARNED column.

Third graders added these details: "Longhouses were built near the shore or in clearings in the woods. They were part of a village."

At the close of the study ask students to refine their definitions using all the knowledge gained during the study. Then, be sure to invite students to use some of the words in discussions and in their writing.

Guidelines for Having Students Use the Predict-and-Clarify Strategy Independently

Organize students into pairs or groups of three to four. Give each student a copy of the *Predict and Clarify Sheet* (see page 203). Have students record 3 to 5 pre-selected words on the sheet and then instruct them to do the following:

1. Skim the pages and read boldface headings, words, captions and words for every visual.
Learning benefit: As students skim, they become familiar with the contents of the section or chapter.

2. Discuss the preview with your partner or group and predict the meaning of each word.
Learning benefit: Sharing enables students to learn from one another and expand their knowledge of the word and the chapter's content.

3. Locate a boldface word and read the sentence that contains it.
Learning benefit: Students meet the word in context and start figuring out its meaning using available clues.

4. Read the sentence that contains the word as well as sentences that come before and after the word.

Learning benefit: Students enlarge their understanding of the word prior to reading the entire text.

5. Discuss what you've learned with your partner or group. Add details under WHAT I HAVE LEARNED.

Learning benefit: Students share ideas and expand their understandings. Talk and writing improves recall.

6. Read the entire section and discuss it. Add details under WHAT I HAVE LEARNED, and if necessary, adjust early ideas.

Learning benefit: Students can connect the word to the entire selection. They reread their notes, add details, and fine-tune their explanations.

7. Have students write sentences when they've completed the study. Sentences should reflect an understanding of the word's meaning.

Learning benefit: Students have an opportunity to translate what they have learned into an original piece of work. Once students can use the word correctly, they have begun to own the word.

As you read on in this section, you'll explore several vocabulary strategies that can help your students move from not knowing a word or having little prior knowledge of it, to:

- knowing a word in one context;
- understanding several meanings of a word;
- understanding the word while reading it in different contexts;
- being able to correctly use a word in different situations while writing and speaking (Allen, 1999; Alvermann and Phelps, 1998; Gillet and Temple, 2000; Nagy, 1988; Vacca and Vacca, 2000).

Teachers can help students move toward the deepest level of word knowledge by providing experiences that repeatedly allow them to hear and work with the word in a variety of ways before, during, and after learning. According to Nagy (1988) students need to recall a word's meaning quickly so as

Note: If pairs or groups each have different words, have them share what they've learned with the class. Schedule presentations over two to four days so students have time to reflect and absorb the new words.

Learning benefit: Students share the responsibility of investigating words and develop their listening and note taking skills while tuning into classmates' presentations.

Predict and Clarify

not to disconnect from the text while reading. To achieve this automaticity, Nagy explains, it's important for students "to have had sufficient practice to make its [the word's] meaning quickly and easily accessible" (p. 23).

Two fifth graders discuss their clarifications of words from their history text.

Pre-Teaching Vocabulary and Getting Ready to Read

This section explores three strategies that introduce students to new words and concepts: *The Discussion Chart, List-Group-Label,* and the *Word Map.* When you provide strategies that enlarge students' understandings of key words before reading, completing math problems or science experiments, you offer them the support that can improve their comprehension and recall (Nagy, 1988; Readence, Moore, and Rickelman, 2000; Robb, 1999).

Predict and Clarify

Name _____ Date _____

Words	**Predictions**	**What I Learned**

Sentences: Use each word in a sentence that shows you understand its meaning.

STRATEGY LESSON:
The Discussion Chart

Purpose

To stimulate class discussions about vocabulary that relates to a topic; to discover what students know and/or remember about the new terms

Materials

Chart paper, marker pens, Post-its or index cards

When to Use

This strategy supports responsive teaching as it quickly helps you determine how much prior knowledge students have about a topic. If students' discussions about the words reveal that they know a great deal about them and the topic, then quickly review the known material and move on to other topics.

Sometimes, using the "Discussion Chart" reveals that a group or the entire class has little or no knowledge of the words. If this occurs, take time to build students' prior knowledge and vocabulary before starting the chapter or unit. Without word knowledge and background information, comprehension falters.

Build students' prior knowledge by connecting words to what students already know. Do this by showing a video, reading parts of informational trade books, looking at photographs, or completing some hands-on activities. When I used a Discussion Chart to discover what fifth graders knew about fractions, I learned that all the terms, except *numerator* and *denominator* were new (see chart below). And, in fact, their explanations of these terms were rather limited: "numerator is top number, denominator is bottom number." To familiarize students with the terms in the Discussion Chart below, I engaged them in several hands-on experiences with math manipulatives, drawing examples of the terms before plunging into the study.

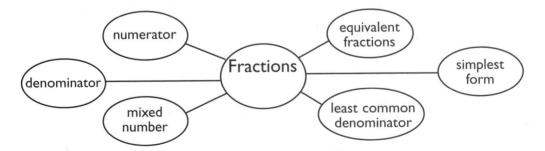

Teaching Reading in Social Studies, Science, and Math

Guidelines

1. Record the lesson on large chart paper, so you and students can revisit it during and after the study. Each time you invite discussion of a term, observe whether students' insights, explanations, and examples deepen. As students apply new terms to their math work, understandings should enlarge and be easier to explain in a think-aloud.

> At the start of the fraction chapter, Dana explained equivalent fractions this way: "It's like the same, like if you get half of a cupcake or you get 2/4 of it, it's the same you're eating."
>
> By the end of this introduction to fractions, Dana was able to move from a concrete example to abstract thinking: "You name the same amount with equivalent fractions. You can add, subtract and compare them. The value doesn't change but the number of parts changes. Like 2/3 and 4/6 — it's the same value: one is in 3 parts, the other in 6 parts. But size could be different. Like if you have 2/3 of a cupcake and 2/3 of a layer cake. "

2. Write the topic in the center of the chart.

3. Write five to six words that illustrate key concepts about the topic. Place these around the word in the center so each one branches out.

> In an eighth-grade science class studying simple machines, Mr. Locke developed a Discussion Chart, placing <u>levers</u> in the center: <u>fulcrum</u>, <u>effort arm</u>, <u>resistance arm</u>, <u>Ideal Mechanical Advantage</u>.

4. Conceal the words with large Post-its or index cards, taping just the top of the index card to the chart.

5. Start the strategy lesson by flipping one card, reading the word, and thinking aloud, relating to students what you recall about the term.

> Eighth graders had heard the word "lever." Jim said that a car jack was a kind of lever. "You can pick up real heavy things with levers," said Paul.

6. Explain to students that's it's okay if they know nothing about a word, since the purpose of the strategy is to discover how much information they have.

7. Flip up the remaining cards one at a time, and ask students to talk about each word.

> Eighth graders agreed that the rest of the terms were new, though as Jennifer said, "I guess they all relate to levers, but I'm not sure how."

8. Decide whether the text has solid context clues that can move students forward with the topic or if you need to build students' vocabulary and background knowledge. The time you reserve at this point to enlarge what students know can improve their comprehension of the material.

> Before asking students to read parts of this chapter, Mr. Legge introduced students to the new

terms by using scissors, a wheelbarrow, and a hockey stick to explain the three classes of levers. These demonstrations helped students understand that the fulcrum, effort, and resistance change position in different classes of levers.

STRATEGY LESSON:
List-Group-Label

Purpose
To activate students' content knowledge through word association and organization; to ask students to generate, then organize a large vocabulary list (20 to 25 words) related to a topic or chapter

Materials
Chart paper, markers, a textbook chapter, trade book, or magazine article

When to Use
The strategy, developed by Taba (1967) was originally used to improve students' vocabulary in science and social studies. It also works well in math. *List-Group-Label* is effective when students have some prior knowledge of a topic since they have to create a list of words that they associate with a topic and then add more associations as they respond to the list. Words can be organized in lists or in a web (see page 166).

Guidelines
1. Make sure students have had experiences with the topic.
> In fifth grade, students studied some geometry. The sixth grade textbook chapter on geometry is longer and more detailed, with an in-depth look at triangles and quadrilaterals. Based on this information, sixth-grade teacher, Mr. Holloway, decides to introduce the topic with the "List-Group-Label" strategy.
>
> Seventh graders were introduced to the Civil War in fourth grade. Many students are Civil War buffs who collect bullets, flags, hats, and attend reenactments of battles. Dick Bell, their teacher, evaluates students' prior knowledge with a "Discussion Chart." Satisfied that students know enough about this topic, he, too, chooses the "List-Group-Label" strategy.

2. Invite students to browse through the textbook chapter, a magazine article, or trade books related to your topic.

3. Organize students into pairs or small groups.

4. Ask students to talk about the topic for 2 to 4 minutes and think of words associated with it.

5. Have students write all the words they can recall in their journals.

6. Collect words from students and record on chart paper. Middle school students can add words from the chart that aren't in their journals.

Here's the list of words related to quadrilaterals and triangles that sixth graders compiled.

4 sides	angles	scalene	square
protractor	ruler	right angles	rhombus
equilateral	rectangle	trapezoid	side
vertex	base	area	perimeter
acute	equiangular	obtuse	straight angle
inches	centimeters	corner	diagonal
right triangle	isosceles		

What follows is the list of Civil War words seventh graders generated.

North	Union	South	Confederate
secede	slave states	plantations	agricultural
manufacture	battles	Lee	Grant
Sherman	burning Atlanta	free states	slave trade
underground railroad	Gettysburg	Lincoln	Bull Run
casualties	weapons	death toll	Jim Crow laws
Uncle Tom	slave quarters	overseers	battlefields
marches	training armies		

7. Model how you group a set of words under one heading.

> **Here's what Dick Bell does: Slavery Issues: agricultural, slave trade, underground railroad, Uncle Tom, slave quarters, overseers, Jim Crow laws.**

8. Ask pairs or groups to organize words from the list under common headings.

> **Here's the heading and words one group of sixth graders organized. Kinds of Triangles: equilateral, isosceles, acute, right, scalene, obtuse.**

9. Ask students to explain the reasoning behind the grouping and labelling. This step is crucial for it holds students accountable for headings that don't relate to the topic, such as: "words that end in a consonant" or "words that are plural."

You can also use List-Group-Label after learning, but the reasons for using it then are different (Readence et al., 2000). Students can add words they acquired during the study to specific headings. The list and labels provide students with the main points and concepts they need to review before a test a quiz.

Fifth graders help one another use new words from their Revolutionary War study.

STRATEGY LESSON:
Word Map

Purpose
To study a word or concept by looking at related elements; to help students internalize the three mapping questions and move to independence

Materials
Chart paper, markers, chapter from a textbook, article from a magazine, or nonfiction trade book

When to Use
If students have some prior knowledge about a key word or concept, then "word mapping"—creating a visual representation of a word's meaning—is an effective strategy.

Developed by Schwartz and Raphael (1985), the strategy is based on the belief that before students can define a word, they must develop a "concept of definition." Because students give examples of the word and describe its features, the strategy moves students from knowing a word in one context to exploring layers of meaning in different contexts. Word mapping works best with nouns, but you can also use the strategy with many action verbs.

As students read and discuss, have them add details to the word map. Doing this enlarges their understanding of meaning and raises the chances of students' incorporating the word into their reading, speaking, thinking, and writing vocabulary.

Guidelines

1. Set up the three parts of the word map on chart paper: What is it? What is it like? What are some examples?

Word Map

Word _____

What is it?   What is it like?

What are some examples?

---

2. Write the general class of the word or concept to be studied under "What is it?" Use a word or short phrase.

    The concept third graders reflect on is "shelter."

3. Ask students to give an example or an alternate name for the word/concept.

    Students offer "house" as an alternate word for "shelter."

4. Have students help you list the important properties or features under, "What's it like?" Here's the list third graders compile:

    - protects you
    - place to stay
    - keeps you warm, dry
    - other people live in it
    - eat and sleep there
    - can be made of different things—wood, brick, cement, etc.
    - can be big or small
    - has your room
    - has lots of rooms—kitchen, bathroom, living room
    - has a porch or terrace

5. Invite students to offer examples.

Word mapping invites students to categorize what they know about a word or concept.

Teaching Reading in Social Studies, Science, and Math

Third graders give these examples: birdhouse, nest, apartment house, cottage, private house, condominium, tree, tree house, playhouse

6. Ask students to think-pair-share and discuss which features go with each example.

Building Vocabulary Power During Reading

When I was in middle school, I quickly learned to skip over a word I didn't understand. If I asked my teacher for assistance, she'd say, "Look it up in the dictionary." I'm sure this is a common experience among all learners. Just imagine, setting aside a book you're engaged with to take a dictionary off a bookshelf, fumble through pages, find the word, read six definitions, and not know which applies. Undoubtedly, such a detour would disconnect you from the text. Looking up a word *during* reading isn't ideal, but neither is instantly skipping the word, as I did in middle school.

Instead, I want my students to use all available context clues to figure out a word's meaning (see pages 130–133). I also want them to know what to do when there are no obvious context clues (see pages 133–134). You can improve students' ability to use context to figure out tough words by teaching them how authors embed meaning in texts. With these clues, students become detectives who can decipher the meanings of words while reading. For example, look at this passage and the underlined word from *Lyddie* by Katherine Paterson:

(1) "She [Lyddie] saw the overseer's *impeccable* wife with the end of a towel in either hand briskly polishing her husband's head, just above the ears, then carefully combing back the few strands of grayish hair from one ear to the other." (pages 97–98)

Robb's Think-Aloud for Figuring Out Meaning With Context Clues
In this example, the actions of the overseer's wife explains the meaning of <u>impeccable</u>. The wife, who is impeccable, takes great pains to clean her husband's head after a day's work at the mill. It's possible to use what the wife does to figure out that <u>impeccable</u> means someone who values cleanliness.

Help Students Become Context Clue Experts

Authors are generally kind to readers; often, when they use long, difficult words, they provide clues that allow readers to figure out the word's meaning. Helping your students become familiar with the different types of context clues will serve them well when they are reading for pleasure, learning information, or taking standardized tests.

CONTEXT CLUE

A Clear Definition or Synonym

When a writer feels that a word is difficult to understand, he or she may give a synonym or a definition of a tough word. To assist the reader, this explanation is in simpler terms. A definition or synonym follows a comma, a dash, or words such as: *or, is called, that is, in other words.*

This type of clue will appear most frequently in your science, history, and mathematics textbooks.

> **Example:**
>
> A *chemical bond* is a force that holds together the atoms in a substance (page 301, *Physical Science* by Smith, Ballinger, and Thompson, Merrill, 1993).

> **Example:**
>
> *Nirvana* is the end of desire. It is a condition of complete emptiness where the soul finds perfect peace (page 253, *Experiencing World History,* by King and Lewinski, AGS, 1991).

CONTEXT CLUE

Concrete Examples

Writers provide examples that illustrate and make clear a difficult concept or idea. The example may be found in the same sentence as the new word or in sentences that come before or after the word, and it can help you figure out the meaning of a new word or concept. Sometimes, authors include words that signal an example is coming: *such as, including, for instance, to illustrate, are examples of, other examples,* and *for example.*

> **Example:**
>
> Penicillin, an antibiotic, is an important product of this fungus. *Other examples* of imperfect fungi are species that cause ringworm and athlete's foot (page 244, *Life Science,* by Daniel, Ortleb, and Biggs, Glencoe, 1997).

CONTEXT CLUE

Contrast Clues

To make clear the meaning of a challenging word or concept, authors will sometimes include the opposite meaning or a situation that illustrates the opposite meaning.

> **Example:**
>
> …I took occasion to remark on the difference in general betwixt a people used to laboring moderately for their living, training up their children in *frugality* and business, and those who live on the labor of slaves, (page 32, *The American Revolutionaries* by Milton Meltzer, 1987).

CONTEXT CLUE

Words or Phrases that Modify an Unfamiliar Word

Sometimes modifiers, such as adjectives, adverbs, or relative clauses, contain clues to a word's meaning. A relative clause, for example, begins with *who, which, that, whose,* or *whom* and often explains or extends an idea or word in the main part of a sentence.

> **Example:**
>
> In many cities she visited during her travels in Europe, Anderson found a small number of black American *expatriates* <u>who</u> had chosen to live and work in Europe because of the freedom and opportunities they enjoyed (pages 55-56, "Marian Anderson" in *One More River to Cross: The Stories of Twelve Black Americans* by Jim Haskins, Scholastic, 1992).

CONTEXT CLUE

Conjunctions Connect Relationships and Ideas

Coordinating and subordinating conjunctions show relationships between words and allow readers to link unknown ideas to known ones. *And, but, or, nor, for,* and *yet* are coordinating conjunctions. Common subordinating conjunctions are *since, even though, if, just as, when, whenever, until, although,* and *because.*

> **Example:**
>
> Some small Italian states were called *duchies.* Their rulers were afraid of *unification* because they would lose their power (page 529, *Experiencing World History,* by King and Lewinski, AGS, 1991).

My Prompting:

Sometimes I try to forge connections and understanding by prompting students' thinking with questions. First I ask: What do you know about states that can help you explain "duchy"? Then I ask: Why would unification cause duchies to lose power?

CONTEXT CLUE

Repetition of a Word

Often, writers repeat a difficult word in familiar and new situations. This way you can construct an unfamiliar word's meaning by using what you already know.

Example:

America is a nation of immigrants. Immigrants are people who come to a new land to make their home. All Americans and Native Americans are related to immigrants or are immigrants themselves. (From *Coming to America: The Story of Immigration* by Betsy Maestro, Scholastic, 1996, unpaged)

CONTEXT CLUE

Unstated or Implied Meanings

Many times, it's possible to determine a word's meaning by using the situation the word appears in or by drawing on your own knowledge or experience that the situation triggers.

Example:

Most Italian Jews were *assimilated* and well-educated middle-class people. Their families had lived in Italy for generations. Indeed, before the birth of Christ, some 8,000 Jews were settled on the banks of the Tiber River (page 117, *RESCUE: The Story of How the Gentiles Saved the Jews in the Holocaust* by Milton Meltzer, HarperTrophy, 1988).

My Think-Aloud:

It's easy to figure out the meaning of <u>assimilated</u> by inferring that since the Jews had been in Italy for thousands of years, they were part of Italy and had adopted Italian culture.

Continue the Word-Building Process After Reading

Learning words is similar to developing meaningful and lasting relationships. People you've

Prompts for Figuring Out Unfamiliar Words

Use the prompts that follow to build your students' word-solving strategies, help them explore meanings, and figure out how to pronounce a word. Post these as a list in the classroom or photocopy and have students staple it in their journals for easy reference.

Point out that textbooks always define boldface and/or italicized words. This does not occur in trade books or most magazine and newspaper articles.

To use context clues to figure out meanings:
- Reread the sentence.
- Read two or three sentences that come before the one that stumped you to find meaning clues.
- Find the base or root word and think of its meaning.
- Have you seen or heard that word in another situation or book? What do you recall?
- Think of what you've already read and see if that provides some meaning clues.

To help you notice errors and pronounce words:
- Did that sound right?
- Find the part that was not right.
- Take a good look at the beginning, middle, and end of the word.
- Does what you say match the letters you see?
- Can you think of another word it looks like?
- Can you say the word in chunks or syllables?
- Does the word have a prefix? Say it.
- Does the word have a suffix? Say it.
- Can you say what's left of the word?

seen only infrequently remain acquaintances; you rarely develop insights or exchange confidences when you have just a few encounters a year. Friendships develop from frequent meetings, sharing feelings and stories, and long and short telephone chats. It's the same with words and concepts. Read and hear a word two to three times, and your knowledge of its meaning is superficial. Read, hear, and use a word or concept countless times before, during, and after a study, and you're on your way to developing a lifelong relationship with it.

In this section, I've selected two journaling strategies that use writing to extend vocabulary building after students have learned about a topic. Besides the two that follow, you may want to use "Concept Mapping," a strategy that supports students' development of a "concept of definition" in the three parts of the learning framework (see pages 37–49) as well as visualizing words (see pages 186–187).

Build Word Power with Journal Responses

Before inviting students to try a journal response show them how you head the page and complete the response. Once they observe what the entries should look like and are clear about your expectations, the quality of students' responses can improve greatly. Here are some suggestions of what to include in your demonstrations:

• How to set up the heading: name, date, topic/title
• How to write responses: lists, phrases, complete sentences, diagrams
• Reference chart: hang the chart in your room so students can refer to it as they write.

Encourage students to ask questions after you complete your demonstration. If students' questions reveal they need more practice, continue collaborating with them.

STRATEGY LESSON:
Concept/Explanation Through Journaling

How It Helps You
After studying a new and complex concept, asking students to explain the concept using words—or drawings and words—enables you to gain insight into each students' level of understanding. If the concept, such as *variables* or *nationalism*, is a building block for understanding other concepts, such as quantities fluctuating or internationalism, then writing is an effective way for you to evaluate what every student has learned before moving forward.

Purpose

To help students deepen their knowledge of a concept

Materials

A concept that's been studied; students' journals

Guidelines

1. Have students head a page in their journals.

2. Invite students to think-pair-share about a concept (see pages 266–269).

Nancy Roche's third graders think-pair-share about the water cycle.
Ginny Carnell's eighth graders think-pair-share then brainstorm a list of symbols they use in math.

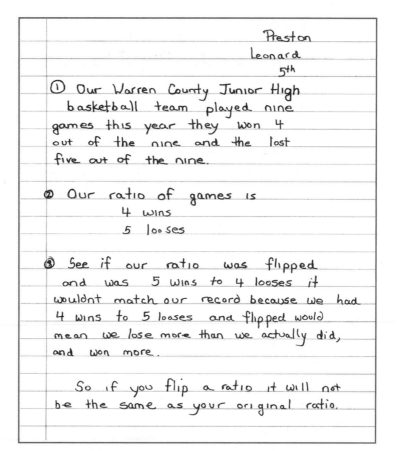

Preston
Leonard
5th

① Our Warren County Junior High basketball team played nine games this year they won 4 out of the nine and the lost five out of the nine.

② Our ratio of games is
 4 wins
 5 looses

③ See if our ratio was flipped and was 5 wins to 4 looses it wouldnt match our record because we had 4 wins to 5 looses and flipped would mean we lose more than we actually did, and won more.

So if you flip a ratio it will not be the same as your original ratio.

An eighth grader shows what he understands about ratio.

3. Ask students to write what they have learned about a concept. Students can use words or pictures and words.

Ginny Carnell invites students make up a ratio problem and explain what happens to the numbers in a ratio when they are reversed. To test students' knowledge of math symbols, Ginny asks them to use words to explain their list of symbols.

4. Call on for four or five volunteers to share their journal entries with the class.

5. Support those who need additional concept-building by working one-on-one or in groups of two to three.

Word Collecting Through Journaling

How It Helps You

Building vocabulary strength is like pumping iron or training for football or track and field events. By consistently training for and practicing a sport, students improve and develop their breathing, muscle strength, tactics, and concentration—allowing them to compete at a higher level. It's the same with learning vocabulary.

If you encourage students to practice and use the plan described here, you'll help them learn words that didn't "stick" and thus improve students' knowledge of a topic. At the same time, you'll offer students a personal learning strategy that can help them throughout their education.

Purpose

To help students learn words they don't understand well; to develop a lifelong word-learning strategy

Materials

Journals, pencils, 3 to 4 words that students need to revisit

Guidelines

1. Have students reserve a section in their journals of about ten pages for words they still need to learn.

2. Ask students to skim their vocabulary quizzes, boldface words in the chapter, and fast-writes to find and record up to four words they don't understand.

3. Have students reread the section in their textbook that contains the word, a concept map the class created, the glossary's explanation, and any class notes.

4. Invite students to paraphrase the word's meaning in their journals and include examples.

5. Organize students into pairs. Have pairs share their notes for each word. Partners offer additional details, connections, and examples that can deepen students' understandings. Here a transcript, from my notes, of a conversation between two eighth graders about buoyant force:

JOSH: *I can't keep the definition of buoyant force in my head.*

TIM: *Think of yourself floating on your back in a pool.*

JOSH: *I'm doing it.*

TIM: *The pool's water pushes up on your body—that's a buoyant force.*

JOSH: *So how does that connect to floating or sinking?*

TIM: *When you're in the pool, your body pushes water aside. If the weight of the water pushed aside is equal to the buoyant force, you float. If it's greater, you sink. Now say it back.*

Tim repeats all but why something sinks. Josh reviews it, this time drawing a diagram. Tim is closer to understanding. Writing notes and copying Josh's diagram all support his learning. Partner shares, like this one, build on students' ability to help one another.

6. Have students jot down, in journals, any additional ideas they collected by discussing the word with a partner.

Help Students Move New Words into Their Long-Term Memory

Explain to students that study and use are the two actions that can make a new word or concept part of their thinking, speaking, reading, and writing vocabulary. Post the suggestions that follow in your classroom and show students how you apply the guidelines to restudy a word.

Make the Most of Those Spare Minutes

1. Set aside short bursts of time (4 to 8 minutes) two to four days each week.

2. Read the word. Try to recall the definition and example.

3. Check your journal notes to see if your recall was on target. If it was, go to the next word.

4. Reread the definition and example two or three times if you were unable to recall the   correct meaning.

5. Star or circle words that need extra study so you can restudy these on another day.

HOW TO START OWNING THOSE NEW WORDS

The more learners include a new word in their thinking, speaking, and writing, the better chance they have of making the word part of their daily vocabulary. Post these suggestions in class and reread them with students frequently.

1. Try to use the new word when you answer in class and when you speak to friends and family.

2. Include the new word when you write answers to questions at school, and when you plan and write paragraphs and essays.

3. Think about the word's meaning when you meet it again in your reading. Ask yourself, "Did I learn something new about this word's meaning?" Then tell yourself what you learned.

4. Try to connect the new word to your life or important issue in the news. For example, you might connect the word *decimal* with a baseball player's average.

Pause and Reflect on: Building Students' Vocabulary

No matter how intensive your vocabulary building program is, there will always be more words for students to learn than can be taught by you. Vocabulary instruction continually invites you to make decisions about which words to teach and which words students can start to comprehend with context clues (Nagy, 1988). You can be selective when pre-teaching and planning strategy lessons by reflecting on and periodically reviewing and asking yourself:

• Do I pre-teach words that are central to the concept or topic?
• Am I spending time on words that students partially know, since it takes less time to enlarge their knowledge of how these words work?
• Do I offer students word-learning strategies they can use independently?
• Am I using key words in my speech?
• Do I model, when appropriate, how words work in sentences?
• Am I encouraging students to read widely in my subject? Reading improves vocabulary power as learners repeatedly meet the same word in similar or different contexts.

∾ Chapter 8 ∾

Scaffolding Instruction: Support Students as They Learn

You never really understand a person until you consider things from his point of view — until you climb into his skin and walk around in it.

—Atticus Finch from <u>To Kill a Mockingbird</u> by Harper Lee

I keep Atticus's advice in mind when contemplating the needs of students who arrive at school with diverse backgrounds, experiences, and knowledge. Walking in another's shoes (becoming the person and trying to think like him, to paraphrase one fifth grader) is at the core of responsive teaching; it can deepen our understanding of students' frustrations, anxieties, hopes, and victories (Rudell and Unrau, 1997). By watching students read and practice strategies, by interpreting their body language, by listening to their conversations, by reviewing their written work, it's possible to identify those who need support to comprehend texts, take notes, complete an experiment, solve a math problem, or participate in a discussion (Graves and Graves, 1994; Goodman, 1985).

This watchful, responsive work we do is called *scaffolding*, a term with obvious links to the word scaffold, the framework that envelops a building while it's under repair. This metal or wood platform supports construction workers as they fix whatever is weak in the building's structure. In the classroom, teachers serve as this steady "platform," supporting instruction for those students who "don't get it" by giving them precisely the guidance they need to solidify their understandings of the concepts or strategies.

The need for scaffolding exists before, during, and after students learn, and responsive teachers work diligently to pinpoint those students who require additional help as they learn within the three-part framework (see pages 231, 245–249).

Scaffolding in Grade 4

I'm circulating around a room of fourth graders at work taking notes on the human body's systems. Each student has a book with information about the body part he or she has been assigned to research and several sticky notes. They write their name, date, and the title of their book, just as I'd modelled in my mini-lessons on how to pose during-reading questions, and I'm pleased to see so many students using the book index to locate specific information.

Then I pause at Colleen's desk, and the warm glow of feeling that my lessons have worked fades. Colleen is reading about the esophagus, but the questions she's jotted on her Post-its are: *What happens to food in the stomach? Why does your stomach make noises?* When I asked Colleen why she didn't have questions about the esophagus, she said, "I'm wondering about the stomach more."

My mind is like a maelstrom: What are other students writing? Why isn't Colleen posing more text-related questions? I move on to Nathan, who is reading about white blood cells. Here are the questions he's posed: *How do red cells help? What cells carry oxygen and food? How does blood clot?* When I chat with Nathan, he tells me that he was thinking more about the red cells and scabs than about white ones.

I continue to circulate. Most of these fourth graders had great questions, but their queries aren't directly related to their reading, and therefore *won't* help them take effective notes.

Clearly, my demonstration of reading for specific purposes (note taking) and raising text-related questions while reading hadn't been enough, and the note taking assignment I'd given them was too open-ended for this group.

Now, here's where the scaffolding comes in: I immediately shift gears and structure the note taking process further by creating lists of key terms that relate to the system each group is researching. The lists set a purpose for reading and taking notes. Groups divide the terms in each list among members, gather information, share their notes, then research the questions they posed in their inquiry notebooks (see page 75). When these fourth graders were given the lists of key terms, they were given the support they needed to complete the task.

Scaffolding: Some General Guidelines

Know Your Students. Custom-tailoring instruction can occur only if you have sufficient information and insight about a student. Collect data and interpret observations and assessments of students. Data to consider include written work, oral presentations, projects, quizzes, tests, and class participation. Invite insights from colleagues who've taught the student before. And last but not least, seek insights from students themselves. Schedule mini-conferences to gather students' feedback on their learning.

Scaffold one on one and in small groups. Some students benefit from 5 to 10 minutes of reteaching. Those with common problems, such as a lack of background knowledge and weak vocabulary, can work with you in pairs or groups of three. The scaffolding experience should be short and build on what students know and can do (Graves and Graves 1994).

Make the modelling of reading strategies clear and explicit (Pearson and Gallagher, 1983). Using a text the student is reading, think aloud and demonstrate how rereading or retelling supports comprehension and recall. Gradually move students from one level of competence to the next.

Prevent "The Matthew Effect." Keith Stanovich (1986) coined this phrase to describe the phenomenon where struggling readers are deprived of access to appealing texts. Traditionally, this group spends more time completing skill sheets, reading stilted, controlled texts, or not reading at all. We must nurture struggling readers' development and motivate them to practice reading by offering them the finest nonfiction texts they can read and comprehend (1986a).

Avoid teaching new strategies in an attempt to repair a student's difficulties. Doing so is time-consuming and can confuse students (Graves and Graves, 1994). Instead, reteach by repeated modelling of the strategies a student knows but has yet to "own," and then give him practice with using these strategies. If a student or small group still doesn't get the strategy, move on and come back to it later. Meanwhile, continue to teach the class new strategies for other topics and enlarge their repertoire of ways to improve comprehension.

Teach in the *Zone*. Whenever you scaffold instruction, you assist your students within a zone that Lev Vygotsky calls the *zone of proximal development* (ZPD). Students in the ZPD can do with teacher support what they cannot accomplish by themselves. In this zone, students learn new information and ways of completing tasks. However, asking students to do a task *beyond* their ZPD can be counterproductive. For example, asking a sixth grader reading three years below grade level to learn from a grade-level history textbook will result in student failure and frustration. Likewise, giving students tasks *within* their *zones of actual development* (ZAD)—the zone in which one can do something independently—means very little learning takes place, though such tasks may build confidence and fluency (Wilhelm, 2001).

Aim for independence. The goal of all scaffolding is to move students performing a new task from the ZDP into the ZAD. The end goal: ensuring that students have a full repertoire of strategies for reading and learning they can use independently.

Scaffolding: The Seven Basic Steps of the Process

To give you an overview of how to scaffold, I have adapted the seven steps that literacy researchers Taylor, Harris, Pearson, and Garcia have identified for the explicit instruction of reading strategies (1995):

1. Pinpoint what kind of scaffolding a student needs.
2. Help the student understand the need for and area of help.

Tips for Successful One-on-One Scaffolding

- **Motivate students.** Read a short, high interest selection. Invite students to look at photographs or share your experience. When you interest learners in the reading or a project, you can develop the desire to work hard even though the material may be difficult. Teachers can foster motivation among students by setting specific, short-term goals that lead to completing parts of a project successfully and by continually offering positive feedback when students' have earned it (Schallert and Reed, 1997; Schunk and Zimmerman, 1997; Wigfield, 1997).

- **Sit side by side as you explain.** Closing the gap between the student and your demonstration can help the student focus on what you are saying and doing and improve understanding.

- **Focus on one need and limit the encounter to 5 to 10 minutes.** I have found that students do best when working through one problem at a time. Jordan, a seventh grader, put it this way: "When she goes off on everything I've done wrong, I tune out. No way I can do it all."

- **Give students feedback.** Observe and inform students about what's working and how to improve and adjust their application of a strategy. Your comments can be oral and/or jotted on a Post-it. What you say celebrates students' progress, calls attention to their use of strategies, and tells them, "Aha, this is the way to do it!"

Here are some of the prompts I use:
- I liked the way you figured out a word and used…
- I'm pleased that you studied dialogue and inner thoughts to infer…
- I noticed how rereading helped you…
- Your retelling of that passage showed that you…
- You understand how to use chapter headings to…
- Your summary showed you could select key details because…
- I noticed that the questions you ask help you…
- I'm pleased that you made connections to…

3. Model the process, using strategies, skills, and techniques that the student owns. Students observe and listen.

4. Explain how the strategies support the learning and help students complete the task.

5. Work with students and observe them; guide them as they practice applying the strategy to similar learning tasks, i.e., taking notes, summarizing, solving word problems, long division, self-monitoring, answering questions, and so on.

6. Gradually release more and more of the responsibility for completing the task to the student. This might be completed in 3 or 4 meetings or over 3 to 4 weeks. Respond to the struggling readers' needs and give them the time they require to gain independence.

7. Invite students to complete the task independently, apply the strategy, solve the problem. The amount of time a student needs to move to independence varies with the task and the student's developmental level.

On pages 232–242, you'll discover how teachers adapt these seven steps as they help students learn in their ZPD. However, before we can help students, it's essential to learn how to identify which students need our expertise and guidance.

Identify Students Who Need Scaffolding—and Do It as Early as Possible

Most math, science, and social studies teachers in grades 6, 7, and 8 do not devote chunks of time at the start of the year to learning their students' strengths and needs. "After the first unit test, I pretty much know who can cut the work and who needs help," a seventh-grade science teacher once told me. But often four to six weeks have passed before that test—time that could have been used to support students. Discover students' strengths and needs early on, even prior to the opening of school, and continue the process throughout the year. Try some of the following suggestions and make gaining insights into students' performance an ongoing process.

Teaching Reading in Social Studies, Science, and Math

Study standardized-test scores before classes start. Before the school year starts, make a list of students whose scores have dropped each year and a list of students whose scores are consistently low. Many of these students will probably benefit from scaffolding.

When Dick Bell, sixth-grade history teacher, and I review the standardized-test score patterns in reading and vocabulary of incoming students, we discover that seven students have been in the bottom quartile since fourth grade, fifteen are in the middle, and four are in the top quartile. During the first month of school, Dick focuses on gathering data about the seven poor performers and any others he feels require close monitoring.

I recognize that this can be a daunting task for teachers with 130 to 150 students, but even a brief review of test scores and prior year achievements will give you a better idea of what your students will need from you.

Dialogue with the reading and/or learning disabilities teachers. Seek their guidance when planning scaffolding lessons. Invite them to read samples of students' written work and offer some suggestions. Their input will be particularly helpful with students they might already have worked with in the past and can also assist you with students new to your school.

Dick chats with Mary Hofstra, who has tutored four of the seven students whose low scores caught his attention. She gives Dick copies of accommodations she and other Powhatan teachers developed. She also discusses Richard, a bright learning-disabled student who reads independently on a third-grade level. Mary will continue tutoring Richard at his instructional level. A high-school student will read textbooks to Richard, and Mary asks Dick to funnel reading assignments to the student. Having this information enables Dick to care for the needs of the four students who already attended Powhatan. Dick will now monitor the three new students to discover ways to support their learning.

Discuss students who struggle at team meetings. When you check on students' performance in all subjects, you might find that a student is great in math and science but weak in history and reading. Input from others can provide you with fresh ideas.

At a sixth-grade team meeting in Johnson Williams Middle School, the math teacher discussed his concerns about Jason. "He can do computation and do it well. But give Jason a word problem and most times he writes nothing on his paper. I don't think he can read the textbook." The reading/writing teacher confirmed this hunch because she had just completed an Informal Reading Inventory on Jason and found his instructional level to be at beginning third grade. Here are some solutions the teachers brainstormed:

1. See if the reading teacher can work with Jason.
2. Pair all students and have them read the word problems to each other; the teacher will pair with Jason.
3. Try to get Jason into the before-school reading class that meets daily.

Administer a survey checklist. By the end of the second week of school, ask students to think about and indicate the strategies they use when reading a history, science, or math textbook. After students complete the checklist, ask them to explain, on the back, any adjustments they may have made in the list's wording, and why they do or do not read textbook assignments. A sample reproducible Content Area Reading Strategy Checklist is provided on page 229.

I have collected surveys from different middle schools. Students are generally honest and admit that they don't read their text but use it to study or look up answers. Every class has a group of students who read the words, so they can say they've read the pages, but don't understand or recall. A content area strategy survey can quickly spotlight students who require scaffolding that will enable them to learn. Here are some suggestions for probing deeper to discover more about students' use of strategies:

• Meet with students whose surveys indicate they lack strategies.
• Ask them to explain why they didn't check any of the statements.
• Ask students how they think you can help them.
• Observe students to collect more data.

The survey on page 230, completed by an eighth grader, illustrates students' honesty and underscores the need for teachers to scaffold instruction and teach strategies that support learning in history, science, and mathematics.

Content Area Reading Strategy Checklist

Name _____ Date _____

BEFORE READING

_____ I preview the section or chapter by looking and thinking about the bold face headings and vocabulary.

_____ I read the sentences around bold face words that are unfamiliar.

_____ I read the captions, charts, and graphs.

_____ I ask questions.

_____ I develop a general idea about the content I will read.

_____ I review the purposes that have been set before I start reading.

DURING READING

_____ I know when I'm confused and reread to understand.

_____ I continue asking questions and look for answers as I read.

_____ I look for information that relates to the purpose I've set, or that the teacher or class has set.

_____ I stop after each section and try to remember what I've read.

_____ I try to use clues in the sentences, charts, pictures to figure out new words.

_____ I take notes when the reading has lots of new information.

_____ I jot down questions to ask the teacher, especially when I'm confused.

AFTER READING

_____ I discuss ideas with a partner or group.

_____ I note new vocabulary in my journal.

_____ I use graphic organizers to note and organize information.

_____ I skim to find parts that might answer a question and reread these.

_____ I study my notes and skim the text after each assignment.

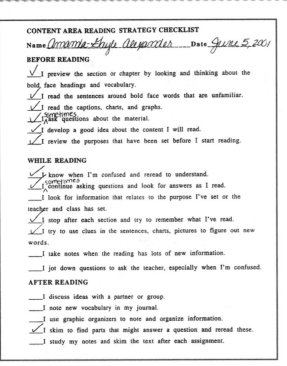

CONTENT AREA READING STRATEGY CHECKLIST

Name _Amanda-Gayle Alexander_____ Date _June 5, 2001_

BEFORE READING

✓ I preview the section or chapter by looking and thinking about the bold face headings and vocabulary.

✓ I read the sentences around bold face words that are unfamiliar.

✓ I read the captions, charts, and graphs.

✓ _sometimes_ I ask questions about the material.

✓ I develop a good idea about the content I will read.

✓ I review the purposes that have been set before I start reading.

WHILE READING

✓ I know when I'm confused and reread to understand.

✓ _sometimes_ I continue asking questions and look for answers as I read.

___ I look for information that relates to the purpose I've set or the teacher and class has set.

✓ I stop after each section and try to remember what I've read.

✓ I try to use clues in the sentences, charts, pictures to figure out new words.

___ I take notes when the reading has lots of new information.

___ I jot down questions to ask the teacher, especially when I'm confused.

AFTER READING

___ I discuss ideas with a partner or group.

___ I note new vocabulary in my journal.

___ I use graphic organizers to note and organize information.

✓ I skim to find parts that might answer a question and reread these.

___ I study my notes and skim the text after each assignment.

The only time I read the textbooks is when I am confused about my work, or when I need to understand something more clearly.

I like worksheets better than reading the textbook, because they are easier to transport, so I am more likely to do my homework. I also like worksheets because you can keep them to help you review for tests and future years.

An eighth grader comments on her strategy checklist.

TEACHERS SUPPORTING ONE ANOTHER

If content area teachers feel that there isn't enough time to give the survey to their classes, I sympathize with and honor those feelings. My solution is to have the reading/writing teacher administer the survey and share the results with the history, science, and math teachers. Then, all four can adjust instruction for students who need extra help in order to progress.

Scaffolding Is Powerful

Scaffolding instruction holds the potential of changing students' lives and diminishing the feeling that school and learning are frightening and frustrating. Sixth grader Mike summed it up this way in his evaluation of a before-school reading class: "When you put me in the extra class I hated coming early. I didn't think I could get better. Now [June] I am passing. I read better. I will come again next year."

Scaffolding Is Good Teaching

Sometimes scaffolding is simply the good teaching that you want to offer all students to ensure that they can learn new and unfamiliar material and topics. In the chart that follows, you'll find teaching tools to use with students who require extra help to experience success (Barr et al., 1990; Gillet and Temple, 2000; Graves and Graves, 1994).

Scaffolding Within the Three-Part Learning Framework

To Support Students BEFORE Learning:	To Support Students DURING Learning:	To Support Students AFTER Learning:
• Enlarge their background knowledge. • Preteach new concepts and connect to what students already know. • Preteach key vocabulary that students need in order to comprehend. Connect these words to students' prior knowledge and experience. • Preview text to help students understand its structure. • Connect the book or topic to students' lives. • Pose questions to engage students with the text while creating the purpose of reading to discover answers. • Be explicit about the strategies students will practice and employ. • Cue students in on transition words such as *however, because, in contrast, for example,* to build their knowledge of inter-sentence relationships. • Cue students in on words that signal information will be sequenced: *first, next, after that, finally.* • Set clear purposes for reading.	• Continue to set clear purposes for each section/chapter students read. • Encourage students to reread. • Model how to tune into what's understood and what's confusing, then access a fix-it strategy. • Teach students how to make mental images because "in-the-head" pictures promote comprehension and recall. • Pose questions and read on for answers. • Figure out word meanings using context clues. • Use text structure to determine main idea, essential and non-essential details. • Read and retell one to two sentences. Slowly increase the amount of retelling to one paragraph, two or more paragraphs, and finally an entire section of the textbook. • Read passages aloud to students. (This gives students information but does not improve their reading.) • Tape record chapters and have students follow along in the text while they listen. (Again, this builds listening comprehension, but does not develop reading skill.)	• Discuss to solidify recall of key details, concepts, and new words. • Discuss the process used to complete the task. • Skim and reread to locate key information and answer questions. • Reteach a strategy students have practiced. • Write about the reading by taking notes or summarizing. • Demonstrate the benefits of graphic organizers and show students how to use them. • Draw and label diagrams. These aid students in understanding and remembering complex information.

One-on-One Scaffolding in Action

To see how scaffolding works, step into Charlotte White's fourth-grade classroom and observe the process in action between teacher and student. Tim is experiencing difficulty answering questions in history. The class is studying the Westward Movement. While students work in pairs, looking up and answering "What Do I Want To Know?" questions (from the K-W-L; Ogle, 1986), Miss White takes ten to fifteen minutes to support Tim's learning. Although Miss White has the class answer questions from the textbook as a regular part of her instruction, Tim leaves answers blank instead of skimming to locate the information and rereading. Here's a summary of my notes documenting Miss White's efforts to guide and encourage Tim to try strategies that can help him answer all the questions.

First, Miss White thinks aloud to show Tim how she uses information in each question to skim the text and locate the page that answers the question.

MISS WHITE: *I'll read the first question to look for key words that might help me skim and locate.* [Why did people move to the West?] *I'll look for the words move and west as I skim. I'll look at bold face headings; these can help.* [She skims two pages.] *Here it is, under the heading "Reasons for Going West." Now I'll reread this part to get all the details.*

MISS WHITE (to Tim): *What did you notice?*

TIM: *You had to reread to get the answer.*

MISS WHITE: *How did I know what to reread?*

TIM: *You used words in the question. Headings, too.*

MISS WHITE: *Good listening and remembering, Tim. Now listen as I read the passage out loud. Here are the reasons: "to get rich, to have own land, for adventure, to escape punishment for a crime, etc."* [She keeps her hand in the book to hold her place and closes it.]

TIM: *Yeah, but you had to reread. You didn't remember.*

MISS WHITE: *I can't remember everything the first reading. Now I'll say, then write the answer in my own words without looking at the book. Saying things first helps me judge if I remembered enough. If not, I'll reread again.*

MISS WHITE: *People moved West for different reasons. Some to have their own land, some to escape being punished for a crime, some to get rich. Many people wanted an adventure. Then she writes as Tim watches.*

MISS WHITE: [Miss White models one more question.] *Tim, what do you notice about the way I look for answers to questions?*

TIM: *You reread, then say the stuff to see if you remember.*

MISS WHITE: *What have you been doing?*

TIM: *Leaving blanks if I don't remember after I read it.*

MISS WHITE: *What else did you notice?*

TIM: *Not much.*

MISS WHITE: *What did I do if I didn't remember the reasons?*

TIM: [reluctantly] *I guess you reread.*

MISS WHITE: *Good. Sometimes I have to reread two or three times.*

TIM: *It takes too long.*

MISS WHITE: *I understand that feeling. But the more you do it, the faster you'll get because you'll know how to skim, reread, then retell to yourself.*

TIM: *You write faster than I can. I spend time trying to remember.*

MISS WHITE: *It is easier to write when you know what you will say.*

The first time Miss White and Tim met, she modelled all three questions. The second time she modelled one, and then Tim completed one sitting beside her. Here's Tim's think-aloud for the question, "Why did many people travel west in groups?"

The words I'll look for are "travel" and "west." [Tim skims until he finds the page.] *Here, under the part about the dangers of travelling westward. Now I have to reread it. Now I say it and don't look. They stayed together because it was dangerous to go alone because it was land not known and there were Indian attacks. Staying together was good too 'cause if a family ran out of food or a wagon broke or got stuck others helped. It gave them company and made them less scared.*

MISS WHITE: *Tim, that was a top-notch job! You skimmed, reread, retold, and now writing will be a snap.*

On the next assignment, Miss White shifts the responsibility for answering all the questions to Tim, checking his work twice while she circulates around the room supporting others. "Good job, Tim, you've answered every question," she says. "Tomorrow, I want you to show Ricardo how you answer questions." Tim's grin is so wide it almost leaves his face. Not only does Miss White move Tim to another place, but she also honors Tim's careful listening. Her scaffolding has enabled Tim to overcome negative feelings about rereading and helped him apply strategies he understands but hasn't used. Then Miss White furthers her support by celebrating Tim's progress and designating him a peer helper.

Whole Class Scaffolding in Action: Grade 3

Sometimes it makes sense to scaffold learning for the entire class, especially when your observations tell you that all students will struggle because they need:

- more background knowledge
- instruction on how a strategy works and supports reading and recall
- concept building
- preteaching of tough vocabulary
- study skills and test-taking practice
- organizational and time-management skills.

Third grade is the first time that Nancy Roche's nineteen boys and girls read a history textbook. Nancy's class contains a wide range of reading levels, and eight students read from slightly below to two years below grade level. In addition to preparing students for concepts and topics, Nancy has them read then discuss small sections, using a "questioning the author" strategy (see pages 315–317) (Beck et al., 1997). All reading of the history textbook is done at school.

The section that Nancy plans to scaffold during reading is about indentured servants. She tells me, "I think it will be hard for third graders to grasp this part because the text switches from continual factual presentation of material to a story about an indentured servant that ends with the definition." Nancy wants third graders to understand the meaning of indentured servant and consider its drawbacks and advantages.

Before reading, Nancy scaffolds instruction by inviting students to brainstorm all they know about "servant" and "service." She wants them to come to this passage with solid background knowledge. Then Nancy follows the advice of Beck and segments the textbook section into two parts: the narrative and the definition. To support her students during reading, Nancy explains that they can question the author "to try to figure out what's important, to understand *indentured* servant, and to connect the definition to the story-example."

Nancy organizes students into pairs, so partners can read and use the questions raised to make meaning. Nancy starts the query process by inviting all pairs to consider this question as they read the first segment: *Why does the author bring in a real boy, Roger, who will become an indentured servant in America?*

Here are some of the questions partners raised for the first part:

- Why does Roger become an indentured servant?
- What does he think about when he sails to America?

- What was his life like before he sailed?
- How is an indentured servant like a servant or like a slave? How is he different?

For the second section, several students wondered, *Why did the definition come at the end?* The questioning and discussing of the first segment helped students understand what the term *indentured servant* meant. "Now," David and Jay agreed, "the definition is like a summary, and we understand it from thinking about Roger."

Segmenting texts, developing questions to use with segments, and creating follow-up queries to focus and broaden the discussion supports students as they deal with texts loaded with new vocabulary and concepts. The teacher decides where to break the text into sections and what understandings students should construct, then starts the questioning process and encourages discussion of the queries.

Learning Routines Help You Find the Time to Support Students

"I'd like to help every child, but I can't in 45 minutes." This comment echoes the feelings of many middle school teachers with short class periods and overcrowded classrooms. Finding the time to support students is an issue teachers wrestle with daily.

In a 40- to 45-minute class, it is possible to scaffold instruction for two individual students or two groups of two to three students, while others work in pairs or independently. The amount of time it takes to move a student to independence on a specific task differs for each child. Knowing in advance that this process takes several months (or several years, with students reading three to five years below grade level) can help ease your frustration.

Before setting students to work, reserve five to ten minutes over several days to teach students how to use independent learning materials (see the list below). Negotiate behavior guidelines with students and post these on the chalkboard. Reread guidelines two to three times a week before independent work begins and help students internalize them. The suggestions that follow are time-savers because students complete the tasks independently, freeing you to assist and guide those who need support.

Independent Learning Materials
- **Individual Student Folders:** Folders change weekly or twice a month. Math folders contain practice, reinforcement, and challenge materials. History and science teachers put magazine articles, map exercises, and puzzles in folders.

- **Free Choice Reading Book:** In science and social studies, students read books that relate to your studies (see Chapter 11).
- **Independent Writing:** Students take notes on their reading in their journals, complete a retelling or summary sheet, or a double-entry journal (see Chapter 6).
- **Vocabulary Builders:** Organize part of students' notebooks into a vocabulary section. In this section, students record new terms in math, science, or social studies and define each term in their own words.

Finding the time to scaffold requires adjustments in teaching practices. To what end? You can develop the students' motivation to work hard, improve their use of strategies, and foster self-confidence that is born of real success.

Scaffolding to Motivate Learning

Before I share other scaffolding techniques, I want to start with the one that threads through all the others: **motivation**. Use motivating techniques to engage your entire class, small groups, and individuals. Develop high interest activities that emerge from topics you're passionate about. Your enthusiasm for the topic can transfer to students and foster their desire to work hard even when the learning challenges them. For example, Josh Mosser loved teaching genetics and genetic mapping in high school. He wanted to motivate his fifth graders to study heredity and immerse them in problem-solving experiences that related science to the lattice multiplication they had learned. His pre-planning consisted of arousing students' curiosity with a coin-flipping game and introducing them to new vocabulary.

On the first day, Josh created a "predict and adjust" vocabulary chart to familiarize the fifth graders with new terms. Students predicted the meanings of words based on what they knew, using base words for clues, and by guessing. Josh started the refining process, and then the students continued to adjust words' meanings through-out the study. The chart that follows contains five of the eight words Josh introduced.

Predict and Adjust Vocabulary Chart

Word	Predictions	Adjustments
purebred	like a horse or dog	traits of a breed passed for many years--like a Labrador Retriever
heredity	what you inherit	passing traits from parent to child
dominant	dominate someone	traits that cover up recessive traits
recessive	I see recess in it	traits that are hidden
genetics	study of genes	how we inherit traits

The purpose of the coin-flipping game was to allow chance to help students create a human face with dominant and/or recessive traits. On the chalkboard, Josh listed these traits:

Dominant Traits
- dimples
- freckles
- full lips
- curly hair
- brown hair
- widow's peak

Recessive Traits
- no dimples
- clear skin
- thin lips
- straight hair
- blond hair
- straight hairline

Face students created by flipping coins.

Using two pennies, Josh explained that two heads or one head and one tail meant the trait selected had to be dominant. Twin tails indicated a recessive trait. Groups took turns tossing pennies, selecting a trait, and drawing a human face.

"Peer-Up" and Scaffold

I'm always looking for ways to reach more students, but at the same time remove some of the stress from my schedule. Pairing students during the scaffolding process frees me to attend to those who still require one-to-one support. Since I can not listen to these peer discussions while I am supporting others, I have to trust the way I've organized students.

Here are some guidelines to help you decide whether two students who are receiving extra support from you can help one another. I avoid pairing a proficient reader with a student who struggles because the partnership transforms into a tutorial. Peer-up when both students:

- have developed knowledge about the same issue.
- have observed you use the strategy in a specific context.
- have successfully completed one guided practice with you.
- can explain the strategy and how to apply it.

Working together, peer partners can accrue the extra practice necessary to internalize a strategy and make it their own. Moreover, students enjoy working with peers, and through their collaboration, they exchange processes and collect new ideas.

Ask partners to take turns reading short sections of a text and think aloud (see pages 142–145) to make visible the reading and self-monitoring strategies they are using (Baumann et al., 1993). This record of a paired-reading and think-aloud between fifth graders, Roger and Arnie, illustrates their exchanges about a paragraph from *Lewis and Clark* by George Sullivan (Scholastic, 1999).

ROGER: *Lewis realized almost from the beginning that he could not lead the* [pause, repeats sentence] *exitions* ["expeditions" is in the text] *by himself. I tried rereading but I can't say that word. I know I could put in trips and it makes sense, but trip doesn't start with "ex."*

ARNIE: [Says "expedition" for Roger.] *It does mean trips but it means trips to learn something. Like not a vacation. I looked at the "t-i-o-n" and know it always is "shun." I look at the whole* [word] *and find parts I can say.* [Next, Arnie reads from book.]

ARNIE: "He needed someone to share the burdens. He needed someone he could trust. He needed a friend." *I don't know what burdens means.* [Arnie rereads.] *Share means have others to tell things to. He wants friends to come* [pause] *he could trust friends.*

ROGER: *I got it. Friends that he could trust and share stuff—things—the things, maybe are burdens.*

ARNIE: *Maybe "burdens" means things that go wrong on the trip.*

Note how the boys listen carefully to each other, support one another and use the meanings of sentences they understand to unravel a good beginning definition of *burdens*. As students practice thinking aloud to make sense of short passages, they internalize the strategy and start monitoring what they do and do not understand, and they think about accessing strategies that can repair their confusions.

Scaffolding with Reteaching

Reteaching is appropriate when you observe that students have part of the concept. Turn to reteaching when one meeting, two at the most, can actually help the student better understand a strategy lesson, the purpose of a graphic organizer, or how to revise and rethink written work.

Dick Bell and I read his eighth graders' double-entry journals. We asked students to select a quote from the book about the Holocaust that they had chosen. After writing the quote on notebook paper, students explained its meaning, related it to the book's themes, and told why those words spoke to them. Four students explained why they chose their quotes, but they omitted the explanation of what they mean and their connections to the book's themes. While students read silently or rewrote their "Prejudice Interviews," Dick and I each met with two of those four students. Here's the conversation I had with Andy whose quote came from *The Upstairs Room* by Johanna Reiss (HarperTrophy).

Andy's Quote: "Darker. I stared at the stove. It gave off a red glow, the only point of light in the room. Once in a while a coal dropped. Thud." (p. 73)

ROBB: *Your reasons for choosing the quote are excellent. I like the way you talk about how the quote made you think of Sini and Annie in the underground hole with a flashlight. Let's read these words closely and see if you can connect them to a theme in the book. Pick out ones you feel are important.*

ANDY: *Darker, red glow, thud.*

ROBB: *Excellent choices. Now think*

> MArch 5
>
> This quote ~~better~~ made me see Sini + Annie in the hole under the ground. They were hiding and it was dark. The flashlight helped, but it's scary to be in a hole + not in a warm house. The hole is darkness, the house is light.

Andy's reaction to the quote he chose from *The Upstairs Room.*

about the connotative meanings—tell me what you associate with each word.

ANDY: Darker—*the hiding place in the closet. Their lives were darker because they had to hide. Red glow—maybe light they see from the window. Maybe hope that it will end soon. Thud— I'm not sure.*

ROBB: *Wow! You're on the right track! Dark hiding place and darkness in their lives—good connecting. Can you tell me some themes your group discussed?*

ANDY: *One was the courage of people like the Oostervelds who risked their lives to save Jews. The other was that the girls kept hoping and hope makes them believe the war will end.*

ROBB: *Both important themes in this book. Let me show you how I connect one of your words to these themes. "Darker" connects to how the light of life went out for the Jews when they had to wear yellow stars and lost all their rights. It also connects to the darkness or evil of those who murdered brave people. Now, can you do the others?*

ANDY: *"Red glow" connects to the light the Oostervelds brought to Sini and Annie, like when they could eat with the family. It also was the glow of hope that keeps them going. I think thud means like when the lights when out—that's what happens to the coal when it drops. That's the Germans searching the house and the concentration camps.*

ROBB: *You made superb connections, Andy. Thinking aloud and close reading can help you do that. Now you're ready to write.*

We all have students who don't absorb information presented on a chart, an overhead, or a chalkboard. Sitting side by side to review and reteach often moves students forward. Moreover, young adolescents in grades 6 to 8 are reluctant to say they don't understand or need extra help; they fear teasing and put-downs from peers in the locker room, the cafeteria, and while walking to classes. For these students, a side-by-side review is much less threatening.

Thumbnail Summaries of Other Ways to Scaffold Instruction

Before you begin scaffolding, isolate the student's problem (see pages 226–230); then decide what strategy or technique you will focus on as you move students through the seven steps to scaffolding on pages 224–226.

Scaffold with Discussion

Since discussion reclaims information and ideas and fosters making connections, "talk" is an effective way to support students (Alvermann, Dillon, and O'Brien, 1990; Gambrell,

1996; Tierney and Readence, 2000). Some students don't have one-on-one conversations in their minds about planning a solution to a math problem or chatting with the author as they read about the Industrial Revolution. In your classroom, you should strive to make in-the-head dialogue visible to your students by modelling how you:

- pose questions and read on to answer.
- make predictions and confirm or adjust them.
- connect your life and experiences to the text.
- pinpoint confusing words or passages.
- select key points.
- tell yourself it's time to apply a fix-it strategy.

Explain to your students that when the internal dialogue stops, they need to check their comprehension and recall. Students will probably need to practice for a long time to develop the "inner voice" that will enable them to interact with a text themselves.

Scaffold with Writing

Writing is the link that enables learners to explore, discover, and connect ideas and feelings; it should be integrated into all subjects.

When you provide a structure for note taking and writing, you are scaffolding the process. Heather Campbell does this when she helps a group of fifth

Lesson 3: The Country Pulls Apart

- **Free States And Slave States**
1- The Missouri compromise drew an imaginary line through the Louisiana Territory.

2- Slavery was allowed South of the line. North of the line slavery was forbidden except in Missouri.

- **Uncle Tom's Cabin**
1- Harriet Beecher Stowe fiercely attacked slavery in her book Uncle Tom's Cabin.

2- Southern slave traders Northerners feared that slaves and would not obey the Fugitive Slave law.

- **The Kansas-Nebraska Act**
1- This law left the choice of slavery up to the people in the territories.

2- Frontier farmers were worried that rich southern farmers would take the land away from them and use slaves to farm it.

- **Dred Scott and John Brown**
1- Dred Scott was a slave who was owned on free territory, he went to court, but lost.

2- John Brown raided Harpers Ferry arsnel but was caught and hanged

- **Lincoln is Elected**
1- Abraham Lincoln was a rebublician who was deeply against slavery.
2- Southerners feared that Lincoln would cause ruin to the South.
3- Many Southerners seceded from the North, and they chose Jefferson Davis as President for thier confederacy.

Heather Campbell scaffolds a note taking lesson by giving students a framework.

graders learn to take notes. First, she lists the bold face sub-headings in each chapter; then under each she writes the number of details students should record.

Offer a framework for writing a paragraph by separating each component and showing what details to include in each element:

- Topic sentence introduces the subject: jot down the subject.
- Body supports topic sentence with two or three supporting details: note two or three details that support topic sentence.
- Conclusion restates the topic sentence in a different way: reread topic sentence and body notes; then think of a different angle for the concluding sentence.

You should also explain (and re-explain, as necessary) how to set up and compose a double-entry journal (see pages 163–165). This format is extremely helpful in learning to analyze, connect and write about a topic. Teachers can also model how to create a plan to solve a math problem:

- **Read** the problem 3 to 4 times until it makes sense.
- **State** what the problem asks you to solve.
- **Select** data from the problem that will help you solve it.
- **Plan** by using the data to think of a strategy for solving it.
- **Check** your work to see if your answer makes sense.
- **Label** your answer.

Scaffold Through Drama

A relative of talking and writing, drama can deepen learners' understandings of characters in a biography or historical novel because it invites students to close read passages (see pages 145–150) and present what they have learned. It is a form of scaffolding that benefits all students as it:

- focuses students on understanding a character's personality, mood, emotional state, and inner life in order to project their interpretations to an audience.
- zooms students in on what the character says, does, decides,

SPEAKER TAGS

Sometimes, when writing dialogue, authors include speaker tags such as "yells," "whispered," "repeated angrily," that let you know a character's mood and emotional state.

Teaching Reading in Social Studies, Science, and Math

and thinks. They reflect on speaker tags (see page 242), motivations, and interactions with others. Struggling readers gloss over these narrative elements; participating in a drama nudges them to pore over these clues.

"I tried to become Atticus *(To Kill a Mockingbird),*" said Chris, an eighth grader. "I had to create his inner thoughts and figure out how he used his body so I could act it for everyone. I wanted them [students] to hear and look at me and know that Atticus was being kind but tough 'cause he wanted Mayella to tell the truth [at the trial]."

After presentations, the class (audience) questions student actors and actresses, who answer these queries in character, thereby extending the thinking and inferring experience.

Scaffold Organizational Skills for All Students

Most students in grades 3 to 8 lack or have underdeveloped organizational and time-management skills. The finest examples of scaffolding for reading and writing in all subjects will ultimately derail if students can't manage homework assignments, pack the books they need, and file papers so they can retrieve them quickly.

Organizing materials and managing time for long-term assignments are two areas where scaffolding can support students in grades 3 to 8. Here are some suggestions for using scaffolding to develop these important, lifetime skills.

- **Break Long-Term Assignments into Segments:** Teachers and students can negotiate due dates for each part of the project: a research report, post due dates for notes cards, report plan, illustrations, first draft, revised draft, and final draft.

- **Read and Comment on Each Part of a Project:** Establish criteria or specific guidelines students can follow as they complete work, then you or peer partners edit (see box on page 244). By reading the various stages of a project, you can support students who are off track and help them achieve success.

- **Set Aside Time and Review Assignments Daily:** Write homework on the chalkboard and review due dates with students. I suggest that students post these dates on a calendar at home in addition to writing them in their assignment books. For third and fourth graders, I recommend that teachers write down the homework and give a copy to each child.

- **Allow Time to File Papers:** Students need more time than adults to file papers in their notebooks or a special folder. And in large and small classes, there will be students who don't listen to and/or follow teacher directions. When I ask students to file materials, I circulate, supporting those who tend to stuff papers in their desks or drop them on the floor. Support also means giving a reminder and letting the child complete the task.

- **Help Students Pack Their Books and Materials:** At the end of a period or the day, take a few minutes to help students pack the materials they need. For students in grades 3 to 5, I like to write a list on the chalkboard and then ask two to three students to read the list. Involving them usually means students attend better.

The best plan for developing organizational and time-management skills is to integrate them into your daily lessons so students continually experience—by doing—how to accomplish these tasks and why they are beneficial.

Ideas for When to Scaffold and What to Do: A Strategic Resource

The behaviors described in this section signal a need for you to put on your detective's hat and hold a short meeting with a student. Start your conference by recapping what you noticed or heard, or review a piece of writing with the student. Responses such as: "I can't read a lot of words" or "This math problem is impossible," "I wrote this on the bus," "This topic is boring" or "I can't read at school" can help you decide whether scaffolding is appropriate.

The first column names the strategy, the second column describes scaffolding ideas, and the third column lists student behaviors that might signal a need for additional support.

SCAFFOLD TASK-EXPECTATIONS

Fifth-grade teacher Josh Mosser decides that scaffolding expectations makes good sense for all students. Together with his students, he establishes guidelines for partner research and presentations of Egyptian gods and goddesses. Josh writes the guidelines on chart paper so students can check their work against the criteria. The list helps Josh grade presentations.

- ◆ Draw a picture.
- ◆ Describe what your god/goddess looks like.
- ◆ Tell what your god/goddess controls.
- ◆ Tell how people feel about your god/goddess.
- ◆ Show how people honor your god/goddess.

Some Scaffolding Guidelines

Strategy	Some Instructional Scaffolding	Indicators of Scaffolding Needs
Activate Prior Knowledge	• Build background knowledge with pictures, read-alouds, film strips, talk, and field trips. • Use book title, chapter titles, bold face headings, pictures, charts, graphs, and captions to increase prior knowledge. • Work one-on-one to use prior knowledge from a text to predict and/or answer questions. • Think aloud and show how you use prior knowledge to preedict/support/ confirm/ adjust and/or answer questions. • List what you know and add to the list as you learn more. • Preteach key vocabulary. • Preteach key concepts. • Preteach text structure.	• Few ideas in brainstorming. • Teacher observation of prereading experience shows poor background knowledge. • Finds material boring. • Doesn't pose questions. • No ideas under the "Know" of a KWL. • Doesn't participate in prereading experiences. • Poor recall after reading. • Doesn't predict. • Doesn't make personal connections.
Decide What's Important	• Do a one-on-one think-aloud; then take turns with the student. • Set purposes and select details that relate to the purposes. • Preview titles, section headings, pictures, captions, graphs, and charts in a textbook. • Use boldface words for clues. • In an historical novel or nonfiction book, study the title, cover, illustrations, diagrams, photographs, and chapter titles. • Note important details on Post-its. • After reading, skim and create a "5 W's" organizer (see page 163). • Discuss and help student connect what's important to his or her life.	• Unable to select important details. • Doesn't set reading purposes. • Avoids previewing. • Doesn't skim and reread. • Doesn't know how to skim. • Sees no purpose in skimming. • Doesn't make personal connections. • Difficulty with webbing, mapping. • Difficulty with note taking or resists taking notes altogether. • Text too difficult too read. • Has little prior knowledge.

Strategy	Some Instructional Scaffolding	Indicators of Scaffolding Needs
Synthesize	• Read/Pause/Retell • Demonstrate how you select details that relate to the purpose for reading. • Think about purpose for reading and select key details. • Think aloud and show how you use details to create the main idea. • Paired questioning: take turns asking questions about short sections that help the reader focus on key points. • Paired summarizing: take turns summarizing the main points in short passages.	• Retells instead of summarizing. • Has difficulty selecting key events, ideas. • Has difficulty generalizing main ideas from details. • Doesn't set purposes or use purposes teacher has set. • Text too difficult to read. • Has little background knowledge.
Infer	• Help student understand that an inference is an implied or unstated idea. • Model how to draw inferences from data in a graphic, such as a chart or diagram. • Show how you use examples and anecdotes in nonfiction to draw conclusions. • Model cause/effect relationships. • Explain information sequencing and how understanding sequences can help you generalize. • Demonstrate how you connect two ideas to show the relationship between theories, topics, experiments, math problems. • Model how you infer what a character thinks and/or feels from dialogue, interactions with others, inner thoughts, conflicts, settings. • Study author tags in dialogue, such as "shouted," "wept," "muttered." • Show how you infer what a character thinks and feels, or why a decision was made by connecting the character's experiences to your own.	• Looks for literal meanings. • Has difficulty with analogous thinking or applying known data to a similar, but new situation. • Making connections between topics, ideas, and information is difficult. • Has difficulty connecting to characters. • Doesn't study character's thoughts, actions. • Doesn't create mental and sensory images. • Has difficulty using details to discover themes. • Has little prior knowledge.

Teaching Reading in Social Studies, Science, and Math

Strategy	Some Instructional Scaffolding	Indicators of Scaffolding Needs
Infer, con't.	• Model how you imagine a character's tone of voice and inner thoughts to help you make inferences. • Help student visualize a character's expression and gestures and decide what can be inferred from these. • Help students understand the meaning of themes: general ideas that a book explores through characters, plot, and settings. • Show students how you take details from a text to develop thematic statements.	
Self-Monitor	• Place tough words on Post-its, with page number and title of book. Help students use context clues in the text to figure out meanings. • Explain why it's important to identify confusing passages. Show how to access fix-it strategies, such as reread. • Read and summarize sections to see if you recall details. • Use INSERT to monitor understanding (see page 130). • Show how a preview of text structure can foster self-monitoring. • Use questions to self-monitor while reading.	• Skips confusing passages, new words. • Doesn't pause to figure out new words. • Doesn't self-check by pausing, rereading, and retelling. • Recall lacks details. • Does not connect material to background knowledge. • Has little background knowledge of the topic. • Doesn't understand how text structure can assist self-monitoring.
Ask Questions	• Show how questions foster self-monitoring while reading. • Model how questions prior to reading help set clear purposes for reading a text. • Show how texts don't answer all questions. • Model how questions posed while reading keep you engaged with the text and help make personal connections and access prior knowledge.	• Does not pose questions before, during, or after reading. • Texts are too difficult to read. • Uninterested in content of texts. • Does not make personal connections. • Does not connect material to prior knowledge.

Strategy	Some Instructional Scaffolding	Indicators of Scaffolding Needs
Ask Questions, con't.	• Use a Post-it to model pausing and posing questions with short passages. • Show how to raise after-reading questions for discussions. Let student know that talking about a text clarifies ideas, helps the recall of details, and enables readers to connect to self, to other books, to local and world issues.	
Skim	• Show how you use information in a question, a key word or phrase, to help you skim a text. • Show how you try to recall where you'll find the information: beginning, middle, end of a chapter, story, or book. • Use captions, pictures, charts, graphs, headings, and/or boldface words to think aloud, showing how each element helps you locate information. • Model how you reread small sections once you've skimmed and located the passage, explaining how the skimming and rereading support recall. • Demonstrate how skimming and rereading support answers rich in details. • Explain how skimming and rereading key points can help you review for a test.	• Can't determine what sections to skim. • Rereads everything instead of skimming. • Text is too difficult to read. • Lacks prior knowledge. • Has poor recall of where information is in the text. • Says that skimming is a waste of time. • Doesn't know how to use questions as an aid to skimming.
Make Connections	• Show how you make personal connections. • Model how you connect ideas, themes, and characters to other texts. • Explain how the information can be used in your life, and by family, friends, and community. • Model how you determine ways the information relates to world issues.	• Text too difficult. • Doesn't make personal connections. • Lacks background knowledge. • Can't select main ideas. • Doesn't understand theme. • Inability to see characters or historical figures as real people. • Doesn't set or use purposes to

Strategy	Some Instructional Scaffolding	Indicators of Scaffolding Needs
Make Connections, con't.		collect essential ideas. • Has information but it's difficult to link to self and others.
Build Vocabulary	• Preteach important words. • Preteach key concepts. • Create antonym and synonym webs. • Build words from Greek and Latin roots and demonstrate how a knowledge of the root meanings can help you understand an unfamiliar word. • Teach prefixes and suffixes and how these help you figure out a word's meaning. • Show how to use the dictionary to find the definition of a word that connects to the author's use of the word.	• Lacks knowledge of the book's concepts. • Has poor knowledge of roots, prefixes, suffixes. • Lacks strategies for figuring out words in context. • Doesn't know what to do when context clues aren't available. • Doesn't connect new words or concepts to prior knowledge. • Has poor dictionary skills.
Fluency	• Demonstrate repeated readings. • Use poems with strong rhythm and rhyme for repeated readings. • Read a phrase or sentence with expression and rhythm and ask the student to imitate. Continue practicing with short passages until students achieve fluency. • Have students gain fluency by reading easy books; then tape record stories for listening centers in primary grades. • Organize reading buddies so that non-fluent readers practice reading easy books with fluency and then read to younger students.	• Reads with many stops, hesitations. • Struggles to "sound out" many words. • Limited comprehension due to word-to-word reading. • Avoids oral reading to support a point. • Texts are too difficult to read.

In addition to the suggestions in this chart, refer to the prompts on pages 258–259, so you can honor students' progress and thinking.

Pause and Reflect on:
Giving Yourself the Gift of Time

When teachers risk change, support is a necessity that can come from a peer, a staff developer, or an administrator. It's like good writing—show me, don't tell me. And bear in mind that it takes time to change.

It's the same for the students we teach. Moving students who struggle with a task into their zones of actual development often requires that we take strategic action and support their learning one-on-one.

Furthermore, to reduce anxiety and that "Don't ask me to do one more thing!" feeling, set reasonable goals as you integrate scaffolding instruction into your day. Allow students and yourself three to four weeks to practice, accept, and feel comfortable with independent learning routines before you add the next layer: determining which students would benefit from scaffolding and working through the seven steps (pages 224–226).

❧ Chapter 9 ❧

Discussion as a
Way of Learning

The time has come, the Walrus said,
To talk of many things:
Of shoes—and ships—and sealing wax—
Of cabbages—and kings—

And why the sea is boiling hot—
And whether pigs have wings.
—From <u>The Walrus and the Carpenter</u>
by Lewis Carroll

The Walrus's invitation to the oysters to chat before he and the Carpenter devour every chubby one has always reminded me of the pleasures of conversation, and so I thought it a fitting way to open this chapter on discussion.

What are teachers doing—or not doing—in terms of classroom discussion? In some respects, "talk" as a way of learning isn't talked about much in our field. It isn't given the rigorous re-examination and spotlight it deserves. Talk is such a powerful tool for thinking and understanding, such a natural way to explore ideas and new information with others, and compose literate, oral texts (Tannen, 1988). Discussion is social, and every last one of us is a social animal. That's why Vygotsky's (1978) theory that social interactions are a key aspect of constructing meaning has always made sense to me. Social interaction enables learners to connect information to their lives and to others, to become aware of their ideas and beliefs, and in the process make new information their own (Wells, 1986; Short, Harste, and Burke, 1995). Research supports discussion as one of the best ways of improving recall and comprehension (see page 253).

And yet, in many classrooms, discussion is not encouraged, as this poem by a Navaho child reflects (Cazden, 1976, p.74):

> Our teachers come to class,
>
> And they talk and they talk,
>
> Til their faces are like peaches,
>
> We don't;
>
> We just sit like cornstalks

Lewis Carroll's Walrus would never survive in this classroom—a traditional environment where the teacher lectures and the students silently sit. From this child's perspective, the teachers have all the fun; the students' curiosity and urge to exchange ideas have been silenced.

When teacher talk dominates instruction, it stifles student learning in myriad ways. Among other drawbacks, the lecture mode makes it difficult for a teacher to know whether students are even listening, never mind understanding. Over the years, students have shared with me what they do during long lectures:

- I daydream and think of playing soccer.
- I plan the party that's this weekend.
- I think about eating lunch. If I'm hungry, sitting and doing nothing makes me more hungry.
- I fake taking notes, but I'm writing to my partner—she writes back on her paper.
- I talk and get in trouble. It's cool to be sent out. The hall's better than trying to look like I'm listening.

In this chapter, we'll explore the benefits of discussion in learning; the characteristics of and guidelines for good, purposeful discussion; and ways talk can be incorporated into your teaching plan.

What the Research Says About The Benefits of Talk

When teachers and students engage in dialogue to inquire, to explore information and feelings, to develop and test hypotheses, to make connections to self, others, and world issues, students can deepen their understanding of new information and ideas and remember this beyond the quiz or test (Alvermann, Dillon, and O'Brien, 1988; Mazzoni and Gambrell, 1996).

While a person reads, the dialogue between reader and author is silent (Rosenblatt, 1978), but present. Conversations with a peer partner or peer group extend these silent transactions because such conversations involve listening to alternate points of view, clarifying information, questioning and searching for answers, paraphrasing, understanding text structures, making connections, and reading between the lines in search of unstated or implied meanings. When students discuss a text, their talk moves them beyond their initial, silent dialogue with the author; they begin to construct a new set of meanings, new knowledge, and are better able to recall the information (Evans, 2001; Gambrell, 1996).

Recitation Versus Purposeful Discussion

"If I don't control the discussion, the noise levels will be unbearable. Besides, within two minutes, my seventh graders will be talking about a basketball game or the latest movie," said a teacher from Johnson Williams Middle School. For many teachers, giving up control of the discussion process is scary—but staying with a recitation model is scarier still, as it limits students' intellectual development. The recitation method—in which the teacher stays in control of a question and answer process—can reinforce a knowledge of factual information, but it will not develop using facts to infer and draw conclusions (Alvermann, Dillon, and O'Brien, 2000; Alvermann and Phelps, 1998; Vaughan and Estes, 1986). The example of recitation that follows shows a teacher in control, asking questions that put pressure on her sixth graders to recall facts from their reading rather than collaboratively build understandings.

Students have read a chapter on "Protists" and defined new vocabulary in their notebooks.

TEACHER: *What is a protist?*

STUDENT: *A single-celled organism.*

TEACHER: *Where do protists live?*

STUDENT: *In wet, moist places like ponds.*

TEACHER: *What is a plant protist?*

STUDENT: *Algae.*

TEACHER: *Why can algae make their own food?*

STUDENT: *They have chlorophyll.*

Recitation intimidates students and heightens their anxiety. Here's what students who I've interviewed in different schools say about recitation:

- I try to look like I'm with it so the teacher won't call on me.
- I get choked and can't remember. It happens so fast.
- We never get to the important stuff—how we feel about things.
- He [the teacher] says we need to know these dates and facts for state tests. It's all dumb [pause] and boring.
- I try to answer first thing if it's an easy one [question]. Then I look like I'm listening, but I'm not 'cause she [the teacher] probably won't call on me again.

Like a dead-end street, recitation goes nowhere. Elaborating and connecting ideas and other aspects of higher-level discourse are impossible because with recitation, there is only one response: the correct answer.

Real discussion, on the other hand, invites students to formulate their own questions and connections, think using what they have read as foundation, listen to others, then shape their emerging ideas into talk that transforms what they feel and think. Purposeful discussion thrives on diverse responses that can be supported with facts and implied ideas from a text as students explore, test, and evaluate interpretations on the way towards deepened comprehension.

Teaching Reading in Social Studies, Science, and Math

Purposeful Discussion in Action

Take a look at the following exchange among eighth-grade students who read *The Terrible Things: An Allegory of the Holocaust* by Eve Bunting. These students engaged in a purposeful discussion around two student composed questions: *Why don't you see the terrible things? Why didn't the animals learn from their experiences?*

LINDSAY: *I think that you never see the terrible things because if they're not described you can make them hideous.*

WARE: *Even the pictures don't give you a picture.*

CHRIS: *You see how powerful they are by what they do—take all the birds, all the fish. What do you think?*

WARE: *And their smell that stays even after they've left. There's something about disgusting smells that makes their horrible image worse.*

LIA: *It's what they do that makes them grotesque—they're not just Hitler and the SS, there are monsters everywhere that kill and murder.*

LINDSAY: *I think the book goes beyond the Holocaust. It makes me think of terrorists and how they attack people they don't know.*

WARE: *Well, they* [Hitler and terrorists] *have something in common. They both kill for control and for a belief.*

Notice how students built upon one another's comments. Chris asked, "What do you think?" prompting the group to maintain the discussion. After Lia commented that Hitler isn't the only terrible one, Lindsay and Ware extended her idea.

This was just one of many discussions that occurred throughout this study of the Holocaust. The class read and discussed historical novels, true accounts of the liberation of concentration camp victims written by teen-aged soldiers and prisoners, and poetry and paintings composed by children imprisoned in the Terezin Concentration Camp. The students also conversed with a concentration camp survivor and talked about their visit to the Holocaust Museum in Washington, D.C.

Throughout, the discussions helped these eighth graders make links between the past and the present that they wouldn't have made without the exchange of ideas. When students are given the opportunity to explore their own questions together, fluid ideas, sophisticated inferences, divergent thinking, and powerful connections occur between the content of school and the content of students' lives. For example, Lindsay told her group,

"The true accounts and historical novels we read were awful, but they didn't reach me deep inside. What really made me know how horrible it all was—what gave me nightmares—was Mr. Strauss's visit and our trip to the museum." Lia added, "It's in our country with the skin heads, white supremacists, the hate groups. It's scary. I think that it could spread today. Who would protect me, I wonder? Would I help others?"

Characteristics of a Good Discussion

Purposeful discussions have specific characteristics. What follows are some indicators that can help you evaluate the effectiveness of student discussions in your classroom. When discussion invites students to think, connect, and build comprehension, students:

- consider different points of view.
- raise questions.
- examine and probe information and ideas.
- demonstrate an interest in deepening their understanding of a concept.
- feel they can express their opinions freely without being criticized.
- talk longer because the focus is on thinking and exploration rather than on finding the one right answer quickly.
- explore opposing opinions.
- offer support for their ideas by referring to sections of their textbooks or other materials.
- reflect on learning outcomes after the discussion.

Once a teacher commits to holding rich discussions in math, science, or social studies, he or she has leapt over a huge hurdle. At this point it would be helpful to observe a colleague's class, then immerse yourself in the changeover. Be sure to observe students' reactions and tune into your gut feelings to make adjustments. If lecturing and recitation have been your teaching style, then I recommend that the change process start with improving whole-class discussions.

Teaching Reading in Social Studies, Science, and Math

Guidelines for Whole-Class Discussions

Helping students experience effective whole-class discussions is a way for both students and teachers to reflect on behaviors they want eventually to bring to small-group discussions (Robb, 1994). Unless students learn the elements of a purposeful discussion, create behavior guidelines, and learn how to maintain a meaningful discussion, noise levels will escalate, and students' talk will become social.

Here are suggestions that will enable you to help students value talk as a great way to learn:

Honor Wait–Time: Allow enough time for students to answer. Thirty seconds can feel like an eternity, making teachers rush into filling the silence with talk. I suggest that teachers slowly count to one hundred; by that time, students can gather their thoughts and respond. Explain the importance of wait-time to the class and discourage students from shouting out answers, which lets a few students control discussions.

Begin with a Strong Statement: Use a thought-provoking statement instead of a question to start the discussion (Alvermann, Dillon, O'Brien, 1988). In eighth-grade history class, John Lathrop opened a discussion of the plight of people in concentration camps with: "There are people today who say that the concentration camps did not exist and there was no Holocaust during World War II." In an eighth-grade humanities class, I generate thinking and talking with this statement about Atticus Finch *(To Kill a Mockingbird,* by Harper Lee, Warner, 1982): "Atticus is just too perfect to be real and believable." Fifth graders generate talk about budgets when their teacher, Josh Mosser, says: "A family of four can live well on $20,000 dollars a year." And in science, Ray Legge stimulates a discussion among sixth graders with these provocative words: "Recycling is a waste of time and too costly to be effective."

Restate What Students Say: Respond to students by restating what they have said, especially if you want them to clarify their ideas. If the student doesn't respond after the wait-time, ask: *Does anyone else see this from another point of view?* If no one responds, you can invite students to reread a section to discover additional information.

During a discussion of stereotyping that was part of a civil rights study, I responded to a student's comment about *To Kill a Mockingbird* this way: "So am I right in thinking that you believe it was okay for Jem, Scout, and Dill to play Boo Radley games?"

Nudge Students to Elaborate: Invite students to elaborate and develop an idea. Don't do it for them. Anna, a third grader, said, "In Virginia, the Native Americans lived in houses like we do."

Teacher Nancy Roche pursued with, "Tell us more about these houses."

At this point, Anna opened her textbook, skimmed, and stated, "Well, they're long houses and made of bark and animal skins. They had a fire inside and the smoke went out of a hole in the top." The discussion continued as others added more details and talked about comfort and keeping warm in the winter.

Use Discussion Prompts: If there is a brief lull in the discussion, use prompts that place the responsibility for thinking and speaking on the students. After modelling, encourage students to do the prompting. Writing prompts, like the ones that follow, on chart paper makes them available for students.

- Does anyone have another idea?
- Does anyone have a different opinion?
- Can anyone offer additional support?
- Can you give details that support the main idea?
- I don't quite understand the connection. Could you clarify your idea?
- What is the main idea?
- Can you give an example of how that concept affects your life?
- Why do you believe this word/concept is important?
- What other information did the book present?
- Can you explain what you mean by that statement?
- What exactly happened during that conflict? Event? Meeting?
- Can you tell us more about that person and his/her role?
- Why did you draw that conclusion from these facts? The experiment? The problem's solution?
- Where in the text did you find those examples?
- Was there misleading information? How did it affect your thinking?
- Can you tell us more about that idea? Conclusion?

Use Prompts that Affirm Students' Answers and Thinking: Avoid taking sides when students answer; as soon as you utter, "That's right," or "Great answer," you inhibit further thinking. Instead, use phrases such as:

- That's interesting. How did you form that idea? Can you connect the point to problems in today's world?
- You support that concept well using details from the text.
- It's clear you thought carefully about the main ideas.
- You showed the connection between the two topics well.
- I like the way you used the book's photographs to help us understand that process.
- You did a great job by quoting several passages that supported your explanation.
- I liked that you used details to find the main idea.
- You made good use of information in the sentence to find that word's meaning.
- You found examples that support the main idea.
- You were able to find unstated meanings by joining several ideas.

In addition, use words and phrases like *concluded, summarized, gained insight, convinced, persuaded, inferred,* and *read between the lines* as a way of honoring students' comments and naming the kinds of thinking and interpretations you want students to use and replicate.

Limit Teacher–Talk: A student discussion means that the teacher acts as facilitator, saying as little as possible, permitting students' talk and questioning to dominate. I recommend that teachers periodically invite a colleague to monitor the amount of teacher input during a student discussion. I do this periodically and find this feedback also lets me know whether I'm recognizing boys and girls equally.

Keep Records: It's easy to fall into the rut of letting those students who enjoy talking take over discussions. To avoid this pitfall, keep a list of students' names on a clipboard and check those who have responded.

Before discussions start, remind students to call on different peers whose hands are raised. When students remain silent over several days, I meet with them one-on-one to discover why they aren't participating. Reasons vary: *I don't want to sound stupid; I didn't read the stuff; I don't like to talk in front of everyone.* Once students observe that in your class it's safe to speak frankly, many will start to participate. Moving to paired discussions often helps students talk because they're less exposed and trust can build faster (see pages 261–262, 266–269).

Topic: Jamestown, Virginia

Book: *A Lion to Guard Us* by Clyde Bulla, HarperTrophy, 1981.

Introduction: Third graders have read the first two chapters of the book about Amanda Freebold, her sick mother, her brother Jemmy and sister Meg. Amanda's father left London three years ago and sailed to Jamestown. When Amanda's mother dies, Amanda decides to take her brother and sister to America to find their father.

During this discussion, which lasted 15 minutes, teacher Nancy Roche and I noted that 10 out of 19 students participated. What follows is a transcription of my notes of a small, but revealing part of this discussion.

RYAN: *I wouldn't want to be Amanda.*

JOSH: *Why?*

RYAN: *She works in the kitchen. The cook's mean.*

JENNA: *She can't even say a word to her brother and sister.* [very long pause]

TEACHER: *There are other reasons that made Ryan say she wouldn't want to be Amanda.* [many students skim through their book.]

JOHN: *She's a kid and she's the mom.* [long pause]

TEACHER: *John, tell us more about how you concluded Amanda's like a mom.*

JOHN: *Well, she takes care of her* [the mom].

ROBERT: *She wants her brother and sister to be in the kitchen.*

MEG: *Yeah. All they do is sit on the steps all day.*

JOHN: *She puts them* [brother, sister] *to bed and feeds them before and tells a bedtime story. That's what moms do.*

TEACHER: *Good job. All of you added many details that helped us see why Amanda is more like a mother than a child.*

Note that when Nancy steps into the discussion, it's only to help move it along. She also does something that a skilled discussion leader does: she describes John's thinking with the word "concluded" and at the end, shows the children what they did to support John's "reading between the lines."

Even though about half the class participated, that is not enough. The downside of whole-class discussion is that some students can and do remain silent observers. When used to model a discussion, to build prior knowledge, or to allow everyone to hear alternative ideas, whole-group discussion is effective. To encourage *all students* to participate in relevant discussions, have them work in pairs or small groups and then share their ideas with the whole class.

Partner Discussions

Paired discussions work well when teachers have a great deal of new material for students to learn within the limited timeframe of a 40- to 45-minute class and when class size is between twenty-five and thirty-five. (See pages 356–357 for guidelines on content area discussion groups.) Students can sit in rows or groups of four to six, pair up and discuss a passage from a textbook.

Pairing students can promote meaningful dialogue. When two students interact, participation is usually high (Alvermann and Phelps 1998). Moreover, it's easier for teachers to monitor behavior and observe whether both students are exchanging ideas.

Partner Discussion in Action: Grade 8

Subject: Science
Topic: Substances and Mixtures
Materials: Science textbook
Background Information: Eighth graders have just previewed the chapter called "Classification of Matter." The purpose for reading is to be able to distinguish between substances and mixtures.

Here's part of a dialogue between Josh and Sarah after they have read the two and a half pages. They talked, reread, and clarified their ideas for about 15 minutes. Then the teacher fielded questions from pairs, clarifying things they were still not clear on.
JOSH: *I get elements—it's matter that has one kind of atom.*

SET BEHAVIOR GUIDELINES

Negotiate some basic discussion guidelines with students; then on a bulletin board post a list that looks like the one below. Review these standards before students pair off to talk. Reread guidelines frequently; your students will benefit from the reminders.

◆ Take turns.

◆ Listen well.

◆ Value different ideas.

◆ Disagree politely.

SARAH: *It helps me to think of an example, like carbon in a pencil and oxygen.*

JOSH: *Copper in a penny is an element. Let's think about compounds. Compounds have two or more elements.*

SARAH: *Like a compound sentence in English—it has two sentences in it.*

JOSH: *That's confusing. Let's stick to science. Water and sugar are compounds.*

SARAH: *And it says here that the ratio of different atoms is always the same. Let's go to mixtures.*

[The pair uses their text to discuss this section.]

SARAH: *The purpose says we have to know how substances and mixtures are different.* [Both reread.]

JOSH: *Mixtures are made of substances like salt and water or sugar and water or perma-press material.*

SARAH: *Yeah, but here's the difference—compounds always have the same ratios of elements otherwise water would not always be water.*

JOSH: *So what's the difference?*

SARAH: *Mixtures—the ratio changes. Like you could put a cup of salt or a spoonful in water and it would still be a mixture.*

JOSH: *I get it. A mixture uses compounds but in different amounts. But could it have elements?*

SARAH: *I don't know, but let's ask in question time.*

Paired conversations don't have to occur daily. However, Mr. Green, the science teacher, explained why he started a reading of the chapter this way. "I knew the students had to understand certain terms to get the rest of the chapter. Taking time at the start really paid off. Every time I reserve part of a class to build understanding, kids are more successful with the experiments, and I can move through the chapter at a faster pace."

Keeping Track of Paired and/or Group Discussions

With large classes, it's impossible for teachers to monitor the progress of seventeen partners. Use the reproducible evaluation form (see page 263) to keep track of a student's participation. Invite students to complete a form twice a month (less frequently if groups work productively and smoothly).

Try to complete one form per student each semester or trimester. If that's too time-consuming, focus on students who require scaffolding through "coaching" or a brief conference; use your notes to discuss your observations with students. Evaluate the rest of your class the first and last part of the school year.

Evaluation for Discussions of Informational Texts

Name _____ Date _____

Selection:

Discussion Focus:

Key: A= Always S= Sometimes R= Rarely NA=Not Applicable

Content

_____ Focused on the question (s).

_____ Gave support from text (s).

_____ Connected ideas to self.

_____ Connected ideas to other materials.

_____ Connected ideas to world issues.

_____ Pointed out ideas that were new.

_____ Showed how new ideas affected thinking.

_____ Could paraphrase definitions.

Behaviors

_____ Came prepared with book and journal.

_____ Listened well.

_____ Valued other ideas.

_____ Made positive contributions.

_____ Asked follow-up questions.

_____ Encouraged others to talk.

_____ Encouraged others to find support.

Additional Comments:

Five Strategies for Encouraging Discussions

When I coach teachers and am helping them plan lessons, one question I always pose is, "Can you frame a lesson that takes the responsibility for students' learning off your shoulders and places it on the students?" To do so, teachers need a repertoire of strategies they can consider while planning a unit or themed study. The four strategies that follow are easy to implement and manage.

STRATEGY LESSON:
Jigsaw

How It Helps

Originally developed to promote positive race relations in public school classrooms (Aronson, et al. 1978), *Jigsaw* invites students to work cooperatively (Slavin, 1986). Pairs or teams are given a short text selection to read carefully. Once pairs or teams learn their material, they teach the parts of the puzzle (selected text) to others—often in the form of a presentation to the rest of the class. Each group member has to play an active role in the presentation. In so doing, each student fits the pieces of knowledge and concepts together until the puzzle has been pieced into a whole. If your class is large, jigsaw work is more manageable with teams of four to five students instead of partners.

With the jigsaw approach, science and social studies teachers can divide a textbook chapter, a nonfiction trade book, or a long magazine article into several parts. Or each group can work on a different article, some poems, or a chapter from a biography or historical novel related to a topic. Social and interactive, jigsaw encourages close readings, discussion, negotiating, and decision-making as groups plan presentations.

Purpose

To use a team learning and teaching approach that helps students comprehend material by becoming an expert on one part

Materials

The teacher selects part of or an entire chapter from a textbook, nonfiction trade book, articles from one or more magazines, several poems, chapters/sections from a biography, historical novel, or multiple texts—different titles that relate to a topic.

Subjects

The jigsaw works best with science, social studies, and literature where students have to learn concepts and a great deal of new information and vocabulary. In math, jigsawing is effective when groups reteach parts of a chapter to review a topic.

Time

Students can complete a jigsaw assignment in two to four days, depending on the length and complexity of the reading.

Guidelines

Teacher's Planning:

• Decide on the material to be jigsawed. Team presentations of small sections can make a complex chapter or article easier to understand because students listen to the information in short, manageable sections.

When using a magazine such as Scholastic's *Science World* or multiple texts, teams can make presentations first, motivating peers to read the entire magazine or additional book titles. Motivation develops from the excitement and enthusiasm presenters generate. A sixth grader put it this way, "After the groups did presentations on Jean Craighead George's books [related to nature], I couldn't wait to read *The Talking Earth* (Harper & Row, 1983)—surviving in the Everglades sounds great."

• Organize the class into heterogeneous, jigsaw teams.

• Negotiate a realistic amount of time for students to prepare presentations. I say "negotiate" because deadlines might require adjustments. When jigsawing short selections, it's possible to complete the process in one to two periods.

• Establish guidelines so students clearly understand expectations. For fifth-grade teams, using multiple texts on spiders, I set these guidelines:

—Name of spider, its habitat, appearance, web, food

—How helpful or harmful?

—You may draw on the chalkboard and use book photographs/illustrations.

—Each team member is to do part of the presentation.

—For planning, you'll have 30 minutes a day for three days.

- Have students read the entire textbook chapter, historical novel, biography or magazine before dividing the work among groups. Quickly reading all of the material gives students an overview and fosters deeper connections with each presentation.

Students' Planning:

- Read and discuss the material on the first day.
- Decide how to teach the material, prepare visuals, and have groups practice on the second day
- Teaching by teams on the third day or days three and four.

Advantages and Drawbacks:

The jigsaw fosters collaboration, reading and thinking deeply about small portions of text, managing time productively, decision-making, and problem solving, such as how the presentation will be divided among the team.

The main drawback is students' absences, since each team member has a job to be completed. And sometimes, no matter how carefully the teacher plans, groups don't interact well. Research completed by Battistich et al. (1993) noted that group members' friendliness and their desire to work cooperatively affected performance. However, I find that having content guidelines and time-management suggestions helps groups interact positively and manage independent work time well. Circulate among teams and pause to smooth disagreements, respond to questions, or tell groups how well they are cooperating. Circulate to insure that groups are following the guidelines and completing quality work. If one or two groups remain off task, sit with them and provide support (see pages 357–358).

STRATEGY LESSON:
Think-Pair-Share

How It Helps You

Fifth graders have completed reading a chapter about serfs' lives in the Middle Ages. First students think and jot down notes; then they discuss ideas with a partner. Here's part of

Teaching Reading in Social Studies, Science, and Math

Robin's and Jordan's brief exchange.

ROBIN: *Serfs were like slaves in the Civil War. They belonged to the lord they served.*

JORDAN: *Their lives were awful. They worked all day in the fields. Most of what they grew went to the lord. They couldn't hunt and would get punished if they did. They never had meat—mostly black bread, cabbage, and turnips.*

ROBIN: *Their houses were awful. One room with wattle walls that didn't let air in. In the cold, their animals stayed in the hut with the serf family. I read in a book that it was so smelly that even the devil wouldn't go in a serf's hut.*

JORDAN: *The only fun they had was on church holidays. Some lords had farm holidays. Then the serfs got food and danced and drank beer. It was like slavery. They would be killed if they ran away and got caught.*

ROBIN: *Also, if you were born a serf, you had to always be one. The only difference between serfs and slaves is their skin color.*

As students share ideas, they frequently make connections to similar situations, other historical periods and books, like this pair's belief that serfdom and slavery were the same.

A thoroughly versatile strategy because you can use it at any point in a lesson, Think-Pair-Share (Slavin, 1996) invites students to recall what they've read and formulate their own thoughts before discussing, which makes the exchange of ideas richer.

Purpose

To encourage students to think about their reading, then share and discuss ideas with a partner

Materials

Students can use selections from textbooks, poetry, or parts of a biography, historical novel, or nonfiction.

Subjects

All

Time

Set aside ten to fifteen minutes for partners to think-pair-share on a topic that can be discussed briefly. Add one to two 30-minute periods for all partners to share and discuss.

Think-Pair-Share

LEARNING PARTNERS

Pairing students can be tricky; it's helpful to know ahead of time how your students work with one another. Pairing a struggling or slow learner with a proficient reader and thinker often results in skewed sharing, for the stronger student dominates the discussion. As much as possible, try to pair students who can learn from one another. If your class has many struggling readers, you might want to scaffold the thinking part before pairing them to insure students have enough information to share.

Guidelines

Before Reading:

- Activate prior knowledge on a topic, such as weather, decimals, cell division, or earthquakes, by asking students to think about what they know.
- Have students jot down their thoughts in a journal.
- Share ideas with a partner and discuss.

During Reading:

- Help students self-monitor recall by asking them to read a section, think about it and take turns retelling to a partner. If recall is limited, then the pair should reread the passage and retell again.

After Reading:

- Have students write their own questions (see pages 79–80).
- Invite students to select one to two questions, think about the answer, then share and discuss with a partner.
- Ask students to prepare a joint response to share with the entire class or a small group.

Think-Pair-Share
Strategy Snapshot: Grade 6 Math

Topic: Decimals and powers of ten

Time: 15 to 20 minutes

Materials: Math textbook

Background Information: Mrs. Carnell frequently uses think-pair-share to help students read their math textbook

Sixth graders are starting textbook Chapter 2, "Large and Small Numbers." The first section of this chapter deals with multiplying decimals by powers of ten—10, 100, 1,000, and so forth.

Mrs. Carnell invited students to read pages 64 and 65, think about the information, then share new information with a partner. Then pairs will have a chance to ask questions. Here's a transcription of the sharing between Danielle and Robin:

DANIELLE: *I learned that it's easy to multiply a decimal number by 10. Just move the decimal one place to the right.*

ROBIN: *I think it's easy. One zero in ten, one move. Two zeros in 100, two moves.*

DANIELLE: *What do you mean by two moves?*

ROBIN : *I mean you move the decimal 2 places to the right.*

DANIELLE: *I found how to write out a trillion. It's got twelve zeros.*

ROBIN : *Did you see quadrillion and quintillion? I never heard of those.*

DANIELLE: *It shows how to shorten them with decimals, but I'm not sure about how to do it.*

ROBIN : *That's one question. I don't get it either.*

DANIELLE: *I don't really get the reason we move it. That's a question, too.*

This Think–Pair–Share enabled these students to share information, to pinpoint what still confused them, and ask their teacher to clarify it for them. This develops metacognition because students practice identifying what they understand and what confuses them.

STRATEGY LESSON:
The Discussion Web

How It Helps You

"It doesn't matter which group I place Kawan, Shaquetta, David, or Leah in, the four remain silent. They read the work; they listen; they never share. How can I get them to participate?" fourth-grade teacher, Mrs. Brown, had conferred with each one of the four to discover why, after three months of discussing literature, history, and science in groups, they were silent. Kawan and David said that their ideas were always put down. Shaquetta and Leah didn't think their ideas were good enough to share.

After Mrs. Brown read material on the discussion web, we planned a lesson. First, Mrs. Brown listed on chart paper the guidelines for using this strategy. Then she discussed these with the four students. Fourth graders had just completed reading about recycling and planning a campaign to convince other fourth-grade classes to recycle paper, cans, and plastic. Here's the question Mrs. Brown posed to her students: Should we recycle? What follows is the Discussion Web Mrs. Brown's students created.

Should We Recycle?

YES

- save trees by reusing paper
- save metals by reusing cans
- keep natural resources for future people
- keep the balance of nature by not taking
- all the forests and mining all the metals
- makes us aware of our environment
- makes us see how limited resources are

NO

- it takes too much time to do
- hard to drive to recycling places

Fourth Graders' Conclusion: No choice, recycling is something everyone should do. We'll use these ideas to get other classes to recycle.

The teacher points out how thoughtful these ideas are—so well done that Mrs. Brown presents the group's ideas to the entire class.

TIPS FOR SUCCESS

From my experience, the success of the Discussion Web depends on the time teachers give to modeling the process with students before releasing control to partners. Struggling learners will need more teacher scaffolding to show them how to skim, be selective, and jot down notes.

Designed by Donna Alvermann (Alvermann and Phelps, 1998), the Discussion Web is a strategy that encourages reading, thinking, speaking, note taking, and writing. The strategy builds on the premise that it's easier for students to discuss in pairs first, then in groups of four to six. Equally important, the Discussion Web invites students to think about an issue or problem, then gather proof for the "Yes" and "No" positions.

For students to be able to use the strategy effectively, it's important for teachers to model the entire process by collaborating with students—and writing ideas on chart paper for everyone to see—until students can complete this graphic organizer with less involvement from the teacher.

Purpose

To encourage meaningful discussion between pairs, among groups of four, and with the class; to teach thinking from opposite perspectives

Materials

Any reading or viewing material that contains two opposing perspectives

Subjects

The Discussion Web works well in history, science, and English.

Time

Reserve two to four class periods to complete the process.

Guidelines

- Prepare students for the reading or viewing material.
- Have students read the material and discuss the contents.

On the First and/or Second Day: (Younger students need a second day.)

- Organize class into pairs that will work well.
- Introduce the Discussion Web Graphic Organizer and the Question. Here's a question a fourth grade class worked on: *Should the Colonists Separate from England?* (See page 272, for students' responses.)
- Have students think, skim, and reread their texts to find support for both sides.
- Ask partners to share their ideas and jot notes on their Discussion Webs.
- Invite partners to join another pair, read their notes, discuss these, and add any new ideas to the web.
- Circulate as students work

On the Second and/or Third Day:

- Share points with entire class.
- Draw conclusions from points listed on the web. For example, if the "YES" and "NO" lists each contain several points, then students can own either position. However, if there are many notes under "YES" and only one or two points under "NO," (see earlier fourth-grade web on Recycling, page 270), then only the one position is logical.
- Debrief and discuss what worked well and what could be improved.

On the Fourth Day:
• Write a paragraph that focuses on one perspective (optional).

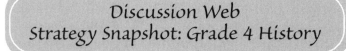

Topic: The American Revolution

Time: Two weeks to read and research; three 30-minute class periods to plan the debates; one 45-minute period to present the debate and have a follow-up discussion

Materials: Students notes collected from their textbook and library books

Background Information: Fourth graders in Debi Gustin's class have been studying the American Revolution. To prepare students for a debate, Debi used the Discussion Web with this question: *Should the colonists separate from England?* The arguments students developed from this question came from the Patriots who voted a resounding "Yes" and the Loyalists, who insisted, "No."

The web that follows illustrates the high-level thinking that the question stimulated.

Should the Colonists separate from England?

YES
• too many high taxes
• can only trade with Eng. now; should trade with other countries
• taxed without representation in parliament
• Eng. far away—why listen to rules Eng. makes
• have to feed and keep Eng. soldiers—costs $$ and food
• farmers will run out of food caring for Eng. soldiers
• we are different from Eng. and should be independent

NO
• Eng. helped colonies in French/Indian War
• we'll lose—Eng. most powerful empire
• we have no navy; Eng. has best navy—can't beat her
• we have no gov't—if we win what would we do?
• Eng. helped us come settle here
• we're English—we should stay faithful to mother country

Conclusion: It's possible to defend either position.

Students divided into two groups: Loyalists (devoted to England, their mother country) and Patriots (colonists who wanted independence from England). The debate was electric. Sally Goshen, with much drama, quoted some lines she memorized from Patrick Henry's speech (see margin box). "I quoted his words," Sally said, "because that's what happened in history. I thought his words said just what I wanted to say."

EXCERPT FROM PATRICK HENRY'S SPEECH

"Gentlemen will cry, 'Peace! Peace!' But there is no peace. Is life so dear or peace so sweet as to be purchased at the price of chains and slavery? I know not what others may think, but as for me, give me liberty or give me death!"

STRATEGY LESSON:
Collaborative Strategic Reading

How It Helps You

Developed by three university researchers working with fourth graders (Klingner, et al., 1991), this strategy aims to have students use several reading strategies *in concert* to help them approach, read, and reflect on a text as a group. Strategies include: Preview and Analyze, Read and Self-Monitor, Click and Clunk, Retell Key Issues, Make Connections, Wrap-Up, and Self-Evaluate.

Students should be familiar with using the individual strategies from past learning experiences before they combine them. And as is often true, it's important to model the process a few times, and gradually move students to use the combination strategy independently.

Purpose

To have pairs or small groups work independently on a combination of strategies that encourage discussion

Materials

A short chapter or a section from a textbook; a magazine article; a nonfiction trade book

ADJUST TO YOUR NEEDS

The main drawback of this strategy is that it's multi-faceted and can take up a great deal of class time. Consider using parts of the strategy, or use shorter sections of text so you can complete the strategy in a few class periods. Dick Bell's seventh graders, for example, completed the strategy in two 45-minute class periods using a three-and-a-half page history chapter.

Subject

Use this strategy with social studies and science texts that have bold face headings, vocabulary, photographs, charts, and diagrams with captions. Students in grades 3 to 5 will need more time than those in grades 6 to 8.

Time

Two to five consecutive class periods, depending on the length of the reading material

Guidelines

Before Students Read:

1. Invite students to brainstorm everything they know about the topic by talking to a partner, then writing their ideas in journals.

2. Collect students' brainstormed ideas on chart paper.

3. Have students preview the selection by reading the bold face title, headings, words, and studying pictures, charts, diagrams and their captions. Since many nonfiction trade books don't have headings, students can read first and last paragraphs of the selection.

4. Invite students to use their brainstorming and preview to predict what the selection will be about.

5. Have students note predictions in journals.

While Students Read:

1. Have students read silently, one section at a time, if the selection has several parts.

2. Have students put a light check next to parts that were tough to understand ("clunks").

3. Students should then fix the clunks by accessing a fix-it strategy. (Typically students reread, ask a peer/group member for help, or bring up the problem during whole-class discussions.)

4. Have students think about the most important (key) ideas as they read.

5. Students should repeat these steps until all the material has been read.

After Students Read:

1. Encourage students to seek support for understanding the clunking parts.

2. Ask them to adjust predictions and note their adjustments in their journals.

3. Invite them to discuss key points by retelling these to a partner in their own words. Have them jot some of these main ideas down in their journals, again recalling in their own words.

4. Ask them to make connections to self, friends, family, and/or world issues.

5. Have them self-evaluate the entire process, telling why it worked and explaining why parts did not work.

> ## Collaborative Strategic Reading
> ## Strategy Snapshot: Grade 7 History

Topic: Andrew Jackson

Time: Three 45-minute classes

Materials: A short textbook chapter about Andrew Jackson called "Old Hickory." The chapter opens with the inauguration ceremony that ushers in Jackson's Presidency. Throughout his campaign, Jackson promised his supporters to be a President of the people. Jackson's supporters followed their man to Washington, D.C. to watch him assume the presidency. That evening, while Jackson celebrated at the White House, an unruly crowd of his supporters crashed the party, destroyed furniture, spilled drinks, and almost crushed Jackson, who ended up spending his first night as President in a hotel. After describing these events, the chapter text then flashes back to Jackson's youth and summarizes the key events that lead to his election.

Background: After working through the process with seventh graders, Dick Bell moved the group to independence while he conferred with individuals on their research projects. Knowing that students would have questions, and knowing that he did not want to be disturbed while conferring, Dick pointed out how the strategy had a built-in student scaffolding system, and he encouraged students to help one another. He also told students that after he completed two to three conferences, he would check to see if anyone required his support.

The students' journal selections that follow show the predictions, adjustments, and key-point notes that they jotted down in their journals. I transcribed part of one group's discussion from my notes.

Adjustment

My prediction was correct. It was about Andrew Jackson's presidency and the events leading up to his presidency.

Evaluation

The process went very well. My prediction was correct. Andrew Jackson had a nickname "Old Hickory." Andy spent a lot of hard work, blood and sweat to get to the White House. He had many supporters along the way.

History Notes

February 14

Andrew Jackson
- nicknamed "Old Hickory"
- more a mountain man
- famous and an idol
- thousand of his supporters 'trashed' the White H night of inauguration
- 7th president
- 'King Andrew I' Powerful President
- 1812 war hero "New Orleans"
- Born 1767, died 1845
- S. Carolina militia 1780
- over a boot shining young Jackson is sabered by a British officer
- carries scar until death
- not good at school, but read well
- very popular in South and South West W Farmers & Factory Workers

History Class Work

Predictions- I think it is about Lewis and Clark searching and exploring the Lousiana Purchase. They met Indians (Sacagawea) It will be dangerous. (1804-1805)

I think this method was very effective. We all read and looked and had different opinions. After we put our opinions together we learned alot.

Lewis & Clark

Lewis & Clark exploring the West, Sacagawea helped Lewis & Clark cross the Lousiana Purchase, Took water rout to Pacific Ocean because of Rocky Mountains, Expedition lasted about 18 months, they had Indian encounters; Sacagawea helped them get horses and food from Indians during their long expedition, Thomas Jefferson sent Lewis and Clark on this expedition to discover the Lousiana Purchase.

Predictions: • I think Tecumseh is a great Indian cheif.
• I think he helps fight for Indian land.
• His brother Tenskwatawa is a intelligent man.
• I think Tecumseh fights a war for land against Americans but smart brother stops it.

Seventh graders' journal entries contain predictions, notes, and students' evaluations of this learning experience.

Procedure: Students use their questions for discussion, to select main ideas, and to make connections.

BOBBY: *I wondered why the people went wild in the White House?*

KATIE: *I think they admired him so much they all wanted to get up close to him.*

HEATHER: *Yeah, like when we go crazy over 'Nsync, the way people used to for The Beatles and Elvis.*

CONOR: *Why did Jackson get elected? I think that will help us get some main ideas.*

BOBBY: *He was in the senate, and the War of 1812 zoomed him to being a hero for everyone. That's where he got the nickname of "Old Hickory."*

KATIE: *He was a rich cotton planter and owned slaves.*

CONOR : *He fought with his men against the British in New Orleans and lost only 8 men. And the Brits lost more than 2,000. That would make him popular with the people.*

BOBBY: *Jackson won Florida for the U.S. and made Spain give it up.*

HEATHER: *Jackson developed the spoils system —we still have it today—where he gave his buddies good jobs in the government.*

As students discuss, they naturally connect to experiences in their lives and what they know about government today because Dick Bell continually offers time to practice this strategy. Notes in journals became starting points for rich discussions, and students elaborated ideas through the give and take discussion process.

STRATEGY LESSON:
Admit/Exit Slips Strategy

How It Helps You

According to Sharon E. Andrews (1997) the "Admit/Exit Slips" is a favorite strategy among her students because of its "brevity." The strategy provides an opening and closing structure to a lesson on material that students have read independently. In short, students are "admitted" to the discussion by writing down on a card one piece of important information that they recall from their reading (if they cannot recall anything, they can write that down). An opportunity for questions and discussion follows. Later, students "exit" the lesson after noting on the card the new facts and concepts they learned after discussing the topic.

Writing on index cards makes it easier for teachers and students to read and assess how much the students have learned from the process of composing their own questions and discussing them. The strategy is especially helpful for showing students the power of coming up with their own questions and exploring them together with others. It quickly highlights that a single reading, with no reflection, often results in limited recall of specific details.

Seventh-grade science teacher Kathleen Hobbs observed, "My students enjoyed the strategy because it showed them that to learn information, it really is helpful to discuss it with classmates." To stimulate discussion, Kathleen had her students create questions about the section they read, "Evolution of Stars." Kathleen then had students think-pair-share;

she reserved about fifteen minutes for pairs to bring ideas to the class.

"I couldn't believe how much more I could write on the 'exit' side after we wrote and discussed our own questions," said Bobby, a student in Katheen's class.

Purpose
To illustrate the power of discussion in helping students comprehend and recall information

Materials
A selection from a textbook, magazine, or literature that students have read but not discussed

Subjects
Science, history, literature, and math

Time
Five minutes at the start of the class and five to seven minutes before the end of class

Guidelines
Admit
- Give each student an index card.
- Have students write their names, date, and "Admit" at the top of the card.
- Ask students to write important information that they recall from their reading. If students recall nothing, have them write that.

During the Class:
- Have partners write several discussion questions for the section that they read.
- Ask partners to use each question to think–pair–share.
- Invite partners to select one question, read it to the class, then share the highlights of their discussion. Though some teachers use the end of chapter questions or ones they have created, asking students to *create* questions forces them back to the text to skim or reread sections, and the more students reread, the more they will recall details.

Exit

Ten Minutes Before Class Ends
- Invite students, about ten minutes before the class ends, to turn over their index cards and print "Exit" at the top.

- Ask students to write the new facts they learned in class from the discussion.
- Collect index cards and read.

On the Next Day:

- Debrief by inviting students to share how the strategy worked and helped them learn the material. Call for suggestions for improving the strategy.

Admit/Exit Slips Strategy
Strategy Snapshots: Grade 7/Grade 4 Science

Grade 7

Topic: The stars

Time: 30 to 40 minutes

Materials: Chapter from students' textbook

Background: Seventh-grade science teacher Kathleen Hobbs invited pairs to write questions for the section "Evolution of Stars" (see margin box). After pairs read and discussed their questions, Kathleen opened discussion to the entire class by inviting students to read their questions aloud. Kathleen noted that although many students' questions were similar, they nonetheless enabled students to engage in a comprehensive discussion.

Grade 4

Topic: The weather

Time: 30 minutes to read; 20 minutes to complete with the class

Materials: "The Weather Master," a folktale *(Ranger Rick's Nature Scope: Wild About Weather,* Judy Braus, ed., National Wildlife Federation, 1988).

Background: Debi Gustin decided to introduce the strategy by asking students to collaborate and create "Admit" state-

SOME QUESTIONS STUDENTS COMPOSED

- What is fusion?
- Why doesn't helium in the sun's core go through fusion?
- What kinds of stars are in the main sequence?
- How would we describe the fusion of a star—using drawings?
- What determines the life of a star?
- How does a neutron star develop?
- How does a black hole develop?
- How do nebulas get their matter?
- When does fusion stop happening?
- Why does a star become a supernova?

Admit/Exit Slips Strategy

Conor **[Admit]**

I found it interesting that the farthest out layer of the sun's atmosphere is hotter than the surface.

Why do some stars become neutron stars and other black holes?

[Exit]

I learned that large neutron stars become black holes. Smaller neutron stars stay neutron stars.

Seventh grader, Conor's, admit/exit slips.

ments as a whole class. "I think fourth graders need to see how the strategy works, then I can have them use it independently," said Debi.

Debi Gustin introduced the Admit/Exit strategy using a folktale about the Earth, Sun, Air, and Water called "The Weather Master." The students' "Admit" list consisted of retelling parts of the plot. At this point, most of Debi's nineteen students said that the folk tale confused them, so Debi engaged the students, who sit in groups of four, in a discussion with questions she wrote on the chalkboard.

Here's what students said after thinking about the questions and discussing the folktale:

JOHN: *I got different points that I missed.*

CARLIE: *I see what others think about the Earth and Sun and Air and Water and why they disliked one and like another.*

SARAH: *You can understand parts you didn't get.*

COLLEEN: *It made me think of parts I missed. It changed my mind about my first ideas about Earth.*

KEVIN: *I didn't understand the story until we discussed it—I didn't even see there was a party.*

By the time students were ready to complete the "Exit" part of the strategy, Debi felt that they could write these notes independently. However, since more than half the class asked if they could share what they learned from discussion *before* completing their cards, Debi wrote their ideas on chart paper. Their reason for this request was that they felt they needed to see all the ideas and then talk about some again.

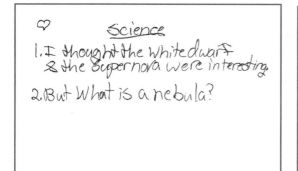

Science

1. I thought the white dwarf & the supernova were interesting.

2. But what is a nebula?

Exit

Write something you learned

I learned that a nebula is a kind of cloud or mist, & I learned the parts of the sun

Seventh grader, Sybil's, admit/exit slips.

Responding to the students' request for scaffolding, Debi collected their ideas, and encouraged additional discussion. At this point, students began making connections to other books and to people who act as vain as Earth did in the story. Here is one section of their student-controlled discussion:

JOSH: *Sometimes, in a book, there are lots of morals—different chapters have different points or morals.*

KEVIN: *The only books that I found that don't have more than one point are the* Goosebump *books (R.L. Stine).*

LIZZIE: *It reminds me of a saying from the Bible: The last will be first.*

JOHN: *It's like the morals in Aesop's fables.*

NATHAN: *And like the Greek myths about the gods and heroes.*

The focus of their Exit discussion centered around the fact that the story had morals or themes. The transcription of my notes reveals the kinds of connections students were able to make as a result of their teacher responding to their request and proving the scaffolding they needed.

Pause and Reflect on:
Discussion in the Classroom

Classrooms rich in talk *before, during,* and *after* reading, enable students to recall details and link new information to what they already know. The process helps students create new understandings and connect information to their present lives and other texts.

Periodically, you should take the inventory below; it helps assess the amount of and quality of student discussions in your class.

_____ Does student discussion or teacher lecturing dominate?

_____ Do you allow students time to think of their answers before responding yourself or moving to another student?

_____ Do students return to the text to find support?

_____ Do you use statements to encourage discussion?

_____ Do you prompt students, helping them move a discussion forward?

_____ Do students feel safe enough to share their ideas freely?

_____ Do students have opportunities to evaluate the effectiveness of their discussions?

Teaching Reading in Social Studies, Science, and Math

∽ Chapter 10 ∾

Exploring the Structure of Textbooks and Nonfiction

A key feature of effective planning is for the teacher to read the text that will be discussed in class while thinking about how the ideas in the text might be encountered by a young, less skilled reader.

—Beck, McKeown, Hamilton, Kucan

When teacher Nancy Roche introduces a study to her third graders, they can hardly contain their excitement. They know that whether they are about to study owls, trees, immigration, or life in Jamestown, their teacher will begin the study as she always does: by wheeling a squeaky, laden cart into the room. "When will the cart be ready?" Sudie asks Nancy excitedly. "Will it have as many as last time?" This drab grey metal cart is as enchanting to students as a jewel-encrusted carriage from a fairy tale because of its cargo—books piled high from the school library, the classroom library, and the local public library. "I bring in every nonfiction book and magazine article I can find on a topic," Nancy tells me. "I gather books the children can read, as well as some books for older students that are rich in pictures and photographs. The children can learn so much from pictures and captions."

For years the cart has been the centerpiece of Nancy's themed studies in science and history. But Nancy doesn't simply hand the books out for students to read. Instead, at the start of each study, she carefully weaves a strategy lesson on the structure of nonfiction texts. During two consecutive twenty- to thirty-minute class periods Nancy invites students to browse through books on the cart. On the first day, students browse freely, chat about pictures and interesting facts. On the second day, Nancy writes questions on chart paper and asks students to reflect on them as they browse (see below). The questions enable students to construct a mental model of the different ways authors organize nonfiction texts. She reserves 15 minutes for students to share what they have learned and what they recall from past experiences with nonfiction.

Here are questions Nancy uses to heighten her students' awareness of nonfiction and textbook structures:

- Is there a table of contents? How does it help you?
- Is there a glossary? What information does it offer?
- Is there an index? How does an index help you?
- Are there headings? What do you learn from these?
- Are there sidebars? Boxed photos and/or text? Why do you think the author included these?
- Does the size of print change? What can you learn from these changes?
- How is the print organized on the page? Does the print signal a genre?
- Do chapters have titles? What do you learn from these?

These questions not only familiarize students with various text structures, but also lead them to form personal preferences, a key book selection strategy. Third grader

Madeline says, "I like Gail Gibbons's books because there's headings and labeled pictures. They're fun to read, and I can find things I want to reread by looking for a heading." Jay, on the other hand, prefers books with "lots of boxes with pictures and extra stuff—I can learn tons. And I like the pages full of stuff to look at and read."

By mid-year, Nancy's strategy lessons and the browse and discuss work have paid off: all her students know about the table of contents, the index, captions, bold face headings and words, diagrams, graphs, photographs and captions, sidebars, and more. This knowledge helps them read and research.

The first part of this chapter explores the six basic structures found in informational texts as well as nonfiction genres. This will help you begin to plan lessons like the ones Nancy presents to her third graders. The second part of the chapter looks at textbook structures and provides strategy lessons that help students more effectively read their social studies, science, and math textbooks. But first, let's consider the advantages of informational trade books.

Textbooks and Trade Books: Weighing the Benefits

Though I believe we need to teach students to read textbooks, I'm compelled to voice this caveat: An exclusive diet of textbooks has many drawbacks. According to Freeman and Person (1998), science and math textbooks "do not portray the excitement of great discoveries and the impetus such discoveries give to other scientists" (p. 29). In addition, Freeman and Person state that social studies textbooks "do not transmit the flavor of an era or demonstrate the impact of literature, art, science, and architecture upon political ideologies of an era" (p. 29).

In light of these shortcomings, we need to expose students to a variety of informational trade books and explore their structures together. Unlike textbooks, which are written to grade level, trade books allow you to offer your students titles written at various grade levels on the same topic (see pages 336–345). Moreover, Beck and McKeown make the point that trade books offer students multiple perspectives on a topic, instead of the one perspective they find in their textbooks (1991).

Carefully researched and composed in a distinct narrative voice and literary style, historical texts can breath life into a topic for children because they can identify with the real people and events described (Meltzer, 1993). Informational books encourage inquiry and problem solving in science; they develop a sense of wonder with photographs, illustrations, and invite repeated readings (Nordstrom, 1992). In math, using children's literature can point out the connections between daily life and math and develop math concepts (Whitin & Wilde, 1992).

A Knowledge of Nonfiction Text Structures Improves Comprehension

We live in an age of information, and reading informational texts critically and analytically—gaining what Nell K. Duke (2000) calls "informational literacy"—is something every student must learn to do to succeed at school, in life, and eventually in the workplace. In an article in *Reading Research Quarterly,* Duke says: "A primary aim of U.S. education is to develop citizens who can read, write, and critique informational discourse, who can locate and communicate the information they seek" (p.202). Yet, when Duke studied 20 first-grade classrooms, she discovered that there were few informational texts "in classroom libraries, on classroom walls, or other surfaces, or in classroom written language activities." Of even more concern was the fact that children in low socio-economic areas had fewer informational texts; thus this kind of reading and thinking was not really available to them.

In middle school and high school, though research points to a strong correlation between students' comprehension and their understanding of expository text structures (Fielding and Pearson, 1991), too few students are taught to navigate a variety of structures.

According to Gillet and Temple (2000) "Problems in reading nonfiction text are most acute in the content areas of science, social studies, health, and math, in which students are expected to read a nonfiction text and acquire new information from it" (p. 33). Clearly, research points to the need for teachers to set aside time to familiarize students with textbook and nonfiction trade book structures. Richgels et al. explained that sixth graders who used a heightened awareness of text structures, especially compare/contrast, used this awareness to read more strategically (1987). Garner (1987) studied fifth and seventh graders' knowledge of text structures and concluded that when teachers explained text structures and modelled how each works, students benefit. However, when students read textbooks that are unclear and that assume a level of prior knowledge that students lack, they disconnect and fail to construct meaning (Beck et al., 1997).

The Six Basic Structures of Nonfiction Texts

All nonfiction, whether textbooks or literature, and all narrative texts contain specific patterns of organization authors use to inform, show, describe, and explain information (Alvermann and Phelps, 1998; Harvey, 1998; Vacca and Vacca, 2000).

The six basic structural patterns discussed in this chapter are:

- sequence,
- compare/contrast,
- cause/effect,
- question/answer,
- problem solution, and
- description.

Authors rarely use just one pattern exclusively throughout a text, but a section or paragraph might contain one pattern. In a chapter book and even a picture book, you'll find several patterns working together, much like the string, brass, woodwind, and percussion sections of an orchestra that play together to create the sounds of a symphony.

When you explicitly teach text structures, you offer students models for creating similar organizational patterns in their own writing. As you do this, also teach the words writers use to sequence, compare/contrast, show cause and effect, and so on. These help students identify a structure while reading, but they can also support expository writing by providing students with models (Freeman, 1991; Meyer and Freedle, 1984; Raphael, Engler, and Kirschner, 1989; Salesi, 1992).

The six structures that follow are found in narrative texts, too. (See appendix for books to model each text structure, page 374.)

(See appendix for books to model each text structure, page 374.)

TEXT WITH MORE THAN ONE STRUCTURE

Here is an example of a paragraph that includes description, cause/effect, and ends with a question. Remember, in a chapter or several pages of a book, authors can integrate all of the six basic structures.

…There were people, suffragists, who held other beliefs. For the past sixty years they had been demanding votes for women, but whenever they brought their petitions before Congress it was explained most patiently, and with the exquisite courtesy due to the gentler sex, that politics was a filthy business. Women were pure, motherhood a sacred calling, therefore they must be protected from politics, and in any case real women did not want the vote. Who would care for the children when they went to the polling places?

—From *We Shall Not Be Moved: The Women's Factory Strike of 1909* by Joan Dash, Scholastic, 1996, p. 55.

Text Structure Lessons:
General Guidelines for Getting Started

How do you raise students' awareness of how textbooks, nonfiction trade books, and magazine articles are constructed? Brief strategy lessons like the ones described in this chapter can be your mainstay. In grades three to five, there's a good deal of time to browse through books and explore structure by actively involving students in searching for and discovering the framework of a text. However, in middle school, where students change classes, you should familiarize students with the textbook in your subject in your first week's lessons (see pages 298–303). Reserve 10 to 15 minutes of your class to accomplish this through student scavenger hunts (see pages 302–303), by previewing and predicting (see pages 306–308), and with think-alouds (see pages 304–306).

In addition to familiarizing students with their textbook's structural features, familiarize them with short magazine articles (see page 299), newspaper articles and editorials, and the nonfiction texts you plan to use for research or to extend a textbook topic.

Some of the lessons that develop an understanding of text structure work well with a teacher think-aloud that calls students' attention to the structure. I've modelled the think-aloud process using sequencing. Cause/effect and compare/contrast require more in-depth probing to deepen students' knowledge; I included fully developed lessons for these as well.

The Structures

 SEQUENCE OR CHRONOLOGICAL ORDER: Details support a main topic and are presented in a specific or time order.

Example from *Experiencing Word History,* by King and Lewinski, American Guidance Service, 1991, in a section of the history textbook called "How the Church Was Organized" note that description is part of this sequence:

> The lowest level of the Church was the *parish*. Parish priests conducted services and taught religion to the people. The *bishops* supervised many parishes. The next highest church officials were the *cardinals*. They served as advisors to the head of the Church, the *Pope* (page 202).

Key Words That Signal Sequencing

until	before	after	next	finally	now
first/last	then	on (date)	at (time)	first, second, third, etc.	

Lesson: Using a Think-Aloud to Model Sequencing

Think-alouds are effective for modelling sequencing, problem and solution, question and answer, and description.

Purpose

To spotlight words in a text that signal sequencing and chronological order; to show the kinds of information that authors sequence

Materials

A section from a textbook, a magazine article, or passage from a trade book

Guidelines

1. Find examples of sequencing that use diagrams and illustrations with captions and sequencing written as a paragraph or two. Share with your students.

2. Read the text out loud and have students follow. If students don't have the text, write it on chart paper or use an overhead transparency. Here's what I put on a transparency from *Be Seated: A Book About Chairs* by James Cross Giblin, HarperCollins, 1995.

> First the designer [Danko] piled 180 pounds of lead bullets on the chair's seat. Then he attached a special machine he had made to the frame. Switched on, the machine rocked and twisted the chair more than 50,000 times. Only after it held up under this test... did the designer put the Waveform chair into production (pp. 118-119).

3. Think-aloud and discuss the structure. Here's what I say:

> It's easy to understand the sequence in these sentences. Words like "first, then, only after," let me visualize each thing Danko did and in what order. Creating a mental picture of the process helps me better understand it. I also noticed that each sentence dealt with only one part of the sequence.

4. Invite students to give you feedback and ask questions.

5. Have students skim their textbook or nonfiction trade books to discover sequencing in words, pictures, and diagrams. Ask students to share.

6. Discuss how illustrations and captions make the sequence of events clearer.

7. Reinforce reading with writing. Ask students to write a paragraph that sequences events in their lives, in history, cycles in science, how to complete a math problem or construct a cube. Encourage students to use "sequencing" words.

2 COMPARE AND CONTRAST: Presents and describes how two or more topics or ideas are similar or different.

Example from *Physical Science* by Smith, Ballinger, and Thompson, Merrill, 1993. A *solution* is another name for a homogeneous mixture. Particles in solutions are so small that they cannot be seen even with a microscope. The particles have diameters of about 0.000 000 0001 m (1 nm). The particles will also never settle to the bottom of their container. Solutions remain constantly and uniformly mixed. When you drink a glass of whole or low-fat milk, you are drinking a mixture of water, fats, proteins, and other substances. Milk is a colloid. A *colloid* is a heterogeneous mixture that, like a solution, never settles. Unlike the particles in a solution, the particles in a colloid are large enough to scatter light (pages 222-223).

Key Words That Signal Compare and Contrast

on the other hand	however	other	difference	differently
and yet	similar to	like	same as	different from
similarly	but	nevertheless	as opposed to	likewise
while	either...or	neither...nor	least	most
less than	more than	unlike	not only...but also	

Lesson: Teaching Compare/Contrast

Purpose
To show students how to determine whether two events, conflicts, characters, terms are alike or different; to show students that compare/contrast in a textbook is usually written within a sentence or a paragraph

Materials
A section from a textbook, a magazine article, or passage from a trade book

Guidelines
1. Repeat steps one and two from the think-aloud for sequencing (see above, page 289).

2. Discuss the elements that are alike and those that differ.

I use an article from Scholastic's SCOPE, March 20, 2000, about Elizabeth Murray's life on the streets of New York City.

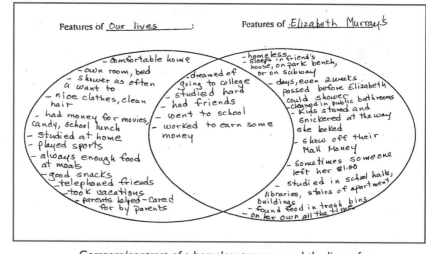

Features of <u>Our lives</u> : Features of <u>Elizabeth Murray's</u>

- comfortable home
- own room, bed
- shower as often a want to
- nice clothes, clean hair
- had money for movies, candy, school lunch
- studied at home
- played sports
- always enough food at meals
- good snacks
- telephoned friends
- took vacations
- parents helped - cared for by parents

- dreamed of going to college
- studied hard
- had friends
- went to school
- worked to earn some money

- homeless sleeps in friend's house, on park bench, or on subway
- days, even 2 weeks passed before Elizabeth could shower
- cleaned in public bathrooms
- Kids stared and snickered at the way she looked
- show off their Mall Money
- Sometimes someone left her $1.00
- studied in school halls, libraries, stairs of apartment buildings
- found food in trash bins
- on her own all the time

Compare/contrast of a homeless teenager and the lives of sixth graders at Powhatan in Virginia.

3. If you're using a paragraph, point out the words that signal compare/contrast.

4. Organize your compare/contrast into a graphic organizer called a Venn diagram. A visual way of comparing two concepts, characters, algorithms, or events, the Venn diagram consists of two concentric circles that overlap.

Sixth graders and I create a Venn diagram based on the SCOPE article.

5. Write common elements in the intersection of the circles; write elements that differ on each part of the circle that doesn't overlap.

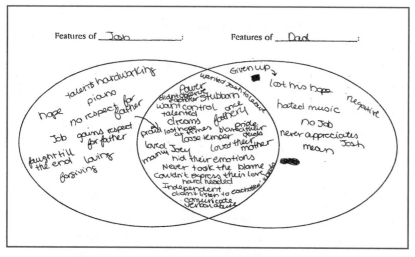

Features of <u>Josh</u> : Features of <u>Dad</u> :

talent, hardworking
piano
hope
no respect for father
Job gains respect for father
fought till the end
loving
forgiving

Given up
wanted Josh to leave
didn't deserve Power
Stubborn
want control once
talented
dreams
proud lost hope blame father
love their
loved Joey
mainly hid their emotions
Never took the blame
Couldn't express their love
hard headed
Independent
didn't listen to each other
communicate verbally

lost his hope
negative
hated music
no Job
never appreciates Josh
mean

Eighth graders compare and contrast father and son from *No Promises in the Wind* by Irene Hunt.

6. Note, if applicable, the words in the passage that signalled compare and contrast under the Venn diagram.

7. Continue to model and collaborate with students until you feel they can work independently.

8. Invite students to complete a compare/contrast using a Venn diagram.

CAUSE AND EFFECT: Presents and describes events and actions and gives reasons and/or consequences for these.

Example from *The Big Lie: A True Story* by Isabella Leitner with Irving A. Leitner, Scholastic, 1992

> For two days, we were given no food to eat, no water to drink. We ate only what we had brought for the journey—the bread, jam, and boiled potatoes. The food was not enough, but we made it last by nibbling.
>
> Many people fell ill. Mrs. Klein went crazy. She screamed hour after hour. Mrs. Fried's gone; Sarah died in her arms. Mrs. Hirsch's aged father died shortly after our journey began. But the train did not stop (pages 14–15).

Key Words That Signal Cause and Effect

since	because	therefore	this led to	due to
so that	for this reason	consequently	as a result	thus
nevertheless	if...then	then	so	

Lesson: Teaching Cause and Effect

Purpose

To deepen students knowledge of cause/effect relationships; to show that the cause/effect relationship occurs in history and science textbooks and in biographies and historical fiction

Materials

A section from a textbook, a magazine article, or passage from a trade book

Guidelines

1. Introduce cause and effect by explaining a cause statement and the term *effect*. Explain that cause statements result from actions and events, such as: *The hurricane's eye passed over our city;* or *South Carolina seceded from the Union.*

2. Help younger students and struggling readers understand cause/effect by starting with cause statements that relate to their lives. In fourth grade I write on the chalkboard: *It rained when we camped out in the park.*

3. Have students generate a list of effects. Here are the effects from fourth graders: *We got wet; We couldn't sleep; Our food got soggy; Our sleeping bags got soaked; We got cold.*

4. Continue using cause/effect statements from students' lives until they understand the relationship.

Teaching Reading in Social Studies, Science, and Math

On Another Day

1. Introduce cause/effect by placing text on a chart or transparency. I use *Hurricanes: Earth's Mightiest Storms* by Patricia Lauber, Scholastic, 1996, to model how some passages contain cause/effect signal words and others don't. My goal is for students to understand that the relationship is not always written explicitly. Here is an explicit sentence: "Because it was early fall, most of the summer people had gone home" (p. 8). Students point out that "because" introduces the cause and the result follows.

Here is the passage that doesn't include signal words, yet contains a cause/effect relationship:

> "The city of Boston was on the fringe of the
> storm, but it was shaken by winds of more than
> 100 miles an hour. At the airport, winds knocked
> down the radio tower and tossed an eight-ton air-
> plane into a slat marsh half a mile away" (p. 16).

One student commented that pinpointing the effects was easy: It's just all the things that happened after the cause statement: "Boston was on the fringe of the storm."

2. Use a double-entry journal organizer to log a cause and the resulting effects. On the lefthand side write the cause statement. On the right hand side list the effects.

3. Continue collaborating with students until they can independently select cause/effect relationships from texts.

Adapt the think-aloud lesson for sequencing on page 289 to develop lessons for these three structures:

◆ problem/solution

◆ question/answer

◆ description

Black Like Me - J.Griffen

Cause	Effects
Griff change from white to black and enters black society in the South.	- sits at back of bus - Followed and threatened by whites - has to use white only bathrooms & water fountains - can't get work - bus won't let G. off at his stop - gets hate stare from whites - has to stay in low standard hotels for blacks only - can't cash checks in stores or restarants

Cause/effect relationships from John Griffin's *Black Like Me.*

PROBLEM AND SOLUTION: Describes a problem and its causes and offers one or more solutions.

Example from "Mishaps" in *Daily Life in a Covered Wagon* by Paul Erickson, Puffin, 1994.

> Besides the weariness of months of travel, the overlanders had many other problems: Even if the driver was as good as Mr. Larkin, any wagon, however well made, could break down, and the oxen could become sick or exhausted. "Alkali water" killed many oxen. This water was full of chemical salts left behind as the lakes dried out in the hot weather. An ox that had drunk this water might be saved if chunks of bacon and swigs of vinegar could be forced down its throat to stop the salts burning its insides. Rough ground desert sands were also a hazard, as they often led to lameness and sore feet. The remedy for this was to put the ox in booties made of rawhide (page 30).

Key Words That Signal Problem and Solution

on reason is	a solution	a problem	solved by
outcome is	issues are		

QUESTION AND ANSWER: Poses a question about a topic, event, concept, or an idea, presents causes of the problem, and offers one or more solutions.

Example from *Cheap Raw Material: How Our Youngest Workers Are Exploited and Abused* by Milton Meltzer, Viking, 1994.

> Who was to blame for the children in bondage? Did poor families have any choice? At the wages a father worked for, he could not afford to send his children to school. Women and children had to work to keep the household going. The whole family was sacrificed to the drive of the business world for the greatest profit (page 60).

Key Words That Signal Question and Answer

how	when	what	where
why	who	how many	it could be that
it's possible to conclude			

6 **DESCRIPTION:** Offers information about a topic, concept, event, person, idea, or object by describing attributes, features, facts, details, traits, and characteristics. **Example** from *The Moon of the Owls* by Jean Craighead George, illustrated by Wendell Minor, HarperCollins, 1993.

> He stood tall in the pine tree. He pulsated the large patch of white feathers under his beak as he came awake in the roost tree. He had slept here almost every day for eight years. His reddish facial disc, rimmed with jet-black feathers, caught specks of starlight and directed them into his eyes. He lowered, then raised, the two ear-like tufts on his head that gave him the name "cat owl." He was not trying to hear better, for his ears were lower on his head, but to look more like the stub of a tree (page 12).

A knowledge of the key words that reveal a specific text structure heightens students' awareness of the structure and, according to research, does transfer to students writing of informational texts such as essays, news and magazine articles, and paragraphs (Maxim, 1998; Miller and George,1992).

Key Words That Signal Description

for example	such as	some characteristics are
look at	like, as	by observing

Provide Students With a Variety of Nonfiction Books

Curiosity is a characteristic of all children who delight in wondering about their world, themselves, the universe, and never tire of asking questions. Children turn enthusiastically to nonfiction in order to explore topics and search for answers to myriad questions.

"I know this book will have great photographs," Bernie, a fourth grader tells me, brandishing Seymour Simon's *Mercury* (Morrow, 1992). "Want to know how?" I nod, totally captivated by his words. "I read *Destination: Jupiter* (Morrow, 1998) and *Comets, Meteors, and Asteroids* (Morrow, 1994) both by Seymour Simon, and they had great photographs. This must, too."

Students who read many books by an author, as well as nonfiction picture and chapter books, can learn much about the text's organization and format. It's also helpful to read aloud and point out the structure of various informational texts as you use them for research or during a themed study in science, math, or social studies.

Common Structures of Informational Books

What follows are some common structures of informational books:

Nonfiction Chapter Books contain text organized into chapters. These usually include some photographs, illustrations, or diagrams, as well as texts rich with details on a wide range of topics. Examples include *Blizzard!* by Jim Murphy (Scholastic, 2000), and *Columbus and the World Around Him* by Milton Meltzer (Franklin Watts, 1990).

Science, Math, and Social Science Picture Books include many pages of photographs and/or illustrations and diagrams that help readers understand the information. Many, such as biographies and informational books on a wide range of topics, have rich texts and are ideal for grades 3-8. Examples are Seymour Simon's *Volcanoes* (Morrow, 1993), *Born in the Breezes: The Seafaring Life of Joshua Slocum* by Kathryn Lasky, illustrated by Walter Lyon Krudop (Orchard, 2001), *The Hershey's Milk Chocolate Multiplication Book* by Jerry Pallotta, illustrated by Rob Bolster (Scholastic, 2002), and books by Mitsumasa Anno, such as *Anno's Counting House* (Crowell, 1982).

Photo Essays contain a balance between the information presented in the condensed text and the photographs, which are detailed, informative, and offer the photographer's personal perspective of the topic. Some examples are Russell Freedman's *Lincoln: A Photobiography* (Clarion, 1987) and *When Wolves Return* by Ron Hirschi, photographs by Thomas D. Mangelsen (Cobblehill Books, 1995).

Biography is the life story of a person of the past or present (usually one who made a significant contribution to the world or had a destructive impact). Often the biographer commemorates the person by creating a portrait that includes information about family, education, experiences, influential people and events, and what this person did during his or her lifetime. Sometimes, as with biographies of Hitler and Stalin, the author's goal is to show the destructive nature of these individuals. Generally, a biography leaves the reader with a deeper understanding of the subject's character and motivation, but bear in mind that the biographer can skew his recreation of a person's life by omitting events, people who influenced the subject, positive or negative facts and opinions of the subject, and so forth. Examples of outstanding biographies for children are Russell Friedman's *Eleanor: A Life of Discovery* (Clarion, 1993) and Diane Stanley's and Peter Vennema's *Charles Dickens: The Man Who Had Great Expectations* (Morrow, 1993).

Ryan, a fifth grader dressed as Dr. Martin Luther King, discusses his life.

Autobiography is a person's account of his or her entire life, or part of his or her life. Written in the first person, autobiographies tend to be slanted because the writer tells his or her story, deciding what events to include or exclude, and interpreting these. Examples are Jean Fritz's *Homesick: My Own Story* (Putnam, 1982) and *Slavery Time: When I Was Chillun* based on oral histories of former U.S. slaves by Belinda Hurmence (Putnam, 1997). A memoir is also autobiographical, yet its scope has limits. Writers of memoirs focus their lens on specific places and times. They include events and relationships that enable readers to better understand a point in time.

Biographies and autobiographies focus on all or part of a person's life and are usually told in chronological order. Both can contain letters and diary entries, interviews and parts of conversations.

Fictionalized Biography contains narrative elements, where the author uses careful research to imagine conversations, dramatize events, and compose diary entries. The author recreates dialogue by using all the information related to each event or situation. Examples of fictionalized biography are *Stonewall* by Jean Fritz (Puffin, 1979) and *Behind Rebel Lines: The Incredible Story of Emma Edmonds, Civil War Spy* by Seymour Reit (Harcourt, 1988).

Newspaper articles open with a brief headline that announces the topic, a byline that gives the author's name, and a lead paragraph designed to grab the reader's attention and convey the message, "read on." Articles start with the most important details and tend to end with the least important ideas. All news articles answer the *Five W's* about a topic: *who, what, when, where,* and *why*. Newspapers often make an excellent resource for math, science, and social studies teachers because they can connect what students are studying to real world events and issues.

Magazine articles contain a title and often headings use a variety of type size and styles to highlight ideas. Told from the writer's point of view, articles are also based on research and may include facts, statistics, eyewitness accounts, interviews, the opinions of experts, and anecdotes.

Glossaries, Headings, and Other Basic Features of Textbooks

Textbooks in math, science, and social studies have common features that students should be able to recognize. Your instruction can help students appreciate how these text features discussed below can support their learning of the information in their textbooks.

Table of Contents: Found in the front of the textbook, the table of contents contains the unit headings, chapter titles, section headings, and the pages on which their text can be found. *Benefits to Students:* Develops an overview of the information to be studied; helps students locate the pages of specific chapters and sections.

Glossary: Found at the back of the textbook, before the index, the glossary lists and defines, in alphabetical order, each boldface key word that appears in the book. Many glossaries show the page number where each word can be found.

Index: Located at the back of the book, the index, in alphabetical order, lists the major topics and names of persons in the book and the page numbers you'll find information on entries.
Benefits to Students: Glossary and index enable students to locate information on a specific topic quickly and easily; ideal for finding key topics to review for a quiz or test; the number of pages devoted to a topic indicates the depth the book goes into each topic.

Some Excellent Magazines and Newspapers

Students enjoy magazines because articles are usually short and contain many interesting photographs, illustrations, maps, puzzles, diagrams, and charts. Here are some excellent resources:

Calliope is a 48-page, themed magazine about people and events of the past.
Cobblestone Publishing, Inc., 7 School St., Peterborough, NH 03458

Cobblestone is a 48-page, theme-related magazine. It offers an imaginative approach to teaching history and those people, events, and ideas that have shaped the American experience.
Cobblestone Publishing, Inc., 7 School St., Peterborough, NH 03458

Field & Stream, Jr. has articles on hunting, fishing, conservation, sporting ethics, and nature.
Times Mirror Magazines, Inc., 2 Park Ave., New York, NY

Ranger Rick helps deepen children's understanding of nature. National Wildlife Federation
8925 Leesburg Pike, Vienna, VA 22184-001

Scholastic Dynamath contains 16 pages of word problems, test prep ideas, and computation for grades 5 and 6.
Scholastic Inc., 557 Broadway, New York, NY 10012

Scholastic Math has articles that offer strategies for problem solving, computation, statistics, test prep, consumer math, and real-life math applications.
Scholastic Inc., 557 Broadway, New York, NY 10012

Scholastic News is a weekly classroom newspaper for students in grades 3–6.
Scholastic Inc., 557 Broadway, New York, NY 10012

Science Weekly motivates students to learn about their world and develops science and technology awareness. The magazine is available for grades 3–8.
Science Weekly, Inc., 2141 Industrial Parkway, Suite 202, Silver Spring, MD 20904

Science World is published biweekly and has several feature articles and brief newsworthy items based on current research in all the sciences. It is ideal for grades 7–10.
Scholastic Inc., 557 Broadway, New York, NY 10012

The Wall Street Journal, Classroom Edition is for students in grades seven through twelve and tries to improve their business and economic literacy.
The Wall Street Journal, Classroom Edition, P.O. Box JJ, Sonoma, CA 95476

Zoobooks offer entertaining and informative full-color articles about wildlife and are ideal for students in grades 3–8.
Wildlife Education Limited, 3590 Kettner Blvd., San Diego, CA 92101

Large, Colorful Unit or Chapter Title: These show the "big picture" or the main concept that several chapters will explore such as "Life" in a science textbook and "Patterns Leading to Subtraction" in a mathematics textbook.

Benefits to Students: Helps students quickly locate a theme or topic and the related sections; enables students to locate specific sections to read, reread, and review.

Bold Face Words: These occur at the start of a section or chapter and appear again in bold face or italics within the text. The list contains words that relate to the concepts and main ideas students must learn.

Benefits to Students: The list enables teachers to engage students in vocabulary learning before they read; then, as students read, they can refine their understandings. Allows students to read and think about the new words they will meet. Offers students clues to the main ideas and concepts they will learn.

Photographs and Illustrations: From these, students can collect information about a topic that the textbook does not describe in detail. Enhances students' visualization of concepts, details, ideas, and descriptions, thus enabling students to recall better the specific facts and ideas.

Captions: These are the words written beneath a photograph or illustration or diagram.

Benefits to Students: Captions often provide additional information and also clarify the point or meaning of the photograph, diagram, or illustration. Students can figure out the gist of a chapter's content by studying pictures and reading captions, and thereby build prior knowledge and improve comprehension.

Graphs and Charts: Included in this genre are line, picture, pie, circle, bar graphs, and tables that organize as well as compare and contrast data.

Benefits to Students: Data written in the text becomes clearer and easier to understand when organized in a graph or chart. Provides opportunities for students to evaluate and think with information as well as compare data—skills they need for standardized tests.

Review Questions: At the end of each section and/or chapter there are several review questions that test students' recall of key information.

Benefits to Students: A helpful way for students to check on how much they recall from

Teaching Reading in Social Studies, Science, and Math

their first reading. Partners can review together in a think-pair-share, then skim and find sections that need rereading. Students can also work independently.

Structural Features Associated with Math Textbooks

The question/answer accompanied by written explanations and the problem/solution structures are prevalent in math textbooks. In addition to one or more sample solutions of problems, sections and chapters contain highlighted summaries of a process, such as multiplying numbers by powers of 10. There are also applications for students to solve, a review section and, at the back of the book, answers to selected (even or odd) problems in each chapter. Some texts also contain hands-on classroom activities and links to real-life situations.

Students who understand the structure of their math textbook can be taught how to study by rereading and reflecting upon written information, sample problems, process summaries, and by completing several problems that have answers in the back so work can be checked. Harry Holloway, a math teacher at my school, has students complete even numbered problems for homework and asks them to use the odd numbers, with answers in the back, to review and study for tests.

Structural Features Associated with a History Textbook

When history textbooks include anecdotes about historical figures, places, and events, students can use their experiences with narrative to connect to new information. Readable and interesting history texts contain primary sources that help learners gain insights into the tone and flavor of a period. Therefore, selections from diaries, letters, speeches, pamphlets and documents, such as treaties, court decisions, the *Declaration of Independence,* and the *Constitution,* make it easier for students to step back into another time.

Maps are also an important part of history textbooks, for they enable students to visually understand what the world looked like in the past and how land boundaries and countries have changed over time.

Structural Features Associated with Science Textbooks

A good first resource for reading and gathering background information is the students' textbook. Many science textbooks contain sidebars that connect a science topic to math, computers, history, people, literature, art, and related sciences. Some sidebars invite students to use a photograph to write a poem or journal entry or to pose questions that encourage critical thinking. Texts also contain suggestions for hands-on experiments under headings such as "Explore Activity," "Mini-Lab," or "Problem Solving." Often, these are listed in a separate Table of Contents, making it easy to locate a specific item. It's impossible to do every activity in a science textbook; it's more of a full menu to pick and choose from. But by jigsawing activities, pairs and/or groups can investigate different areas and present their findings to the class, enlarging everyone's knowledge and understanding (see pages 264–266).

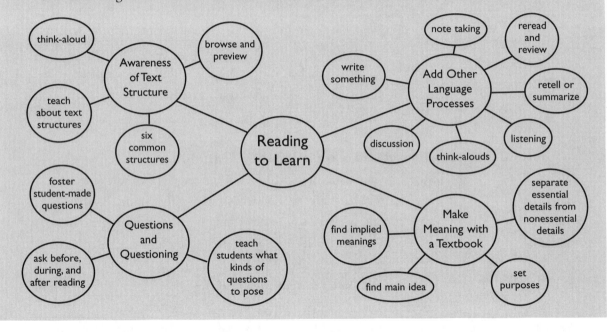

Strategies for Reading Textbooks to Learn Information

By modelling and thinking aloud, then inviting students to practice during class, you can deepen their knowledge of how to read in order to learn information from content area textbooks.

Some Strategy Lessons to Try

I recommend having students go on a textbook scavenger hunt to familiarize themselves with the basic features of their textbook. Take part of two to three class periods to complete. Here's how it works:

- Divide the class into teams of four students.
- Give each team a reproducible to complete (see page 303).
- Have teams share one or two items with the class.

Teaching Reading in Social Studies, Science, and Math

Textbook Scavenger Hunt

Name _____ Date _____

Directions: Use your textbook to answer the questions below. Use separate paper to answer each one.

1. Find and check out the index. How many pages of index are there? Where do you find the index? Locate and write a key topic that has several pages of information. Find a topic that has single pages listed.

2. Stroll through the Table of Contents. Where is it located? How many units does it include? List three units you would like to study.

3. Glance through the glossary. Where is it located? What information does a glossary contain? Select and jot down two words you know something about and two that are unfamiliar. How can a glossary help you?

4. Check out the first page of a chapter. List all the information here.

5. List three boldface words in that first chapter. Find out what each one means and write the explanation in your own words. What else can you use in this textbook to find the meaning of a word?

6. Scan the textbook and find a photograph. Note the page number. Study the photo and read the caption. Write what you learned.

7. Introduce yourself to a graph, chart, diagram, or map. Note the page it's on. Now, study it and read all the print. In your own words, write what this feature can teach you.

8. Flip through two chapters. What other features do you find in your textbook? How do these features help you learn new information?

9. Take a look at the last page of a chapter. What do you find there? How can this help you?

10. Skim through a chapter. Is there anything that confuses you? Note the page and ask your teacher about it.

STRATEGY LESSON:
Seven Steps to Reading a Graphic

Purpose

To show students that graphics contain key information presented in a visual; to show the importance of reading all the print in a graphic

Materials

A map, diagram, chart, or graph

Guidelines

1. Look at the graphic and read the title. Think about the title's meaning and what it tells you about the graphic.

2. Read all of the text in the graphic.

3. Think about the information. Ask yourself how it relates to the chapter or article.

4. Ask yourself, "what's important?"

5. Make sure you understand all the words. Work with a partner to figure out the meanings of tough ones.

6. Connect this information to your life and experiences and to issues and problems in your community and the world.

7. Paraphrase what you learned from the graphic.

STRATEGY LESSON:
Interactive Think-Aloud

Purpose

To show how a think-aloud can deepen knowledge of text structure and support learning; to help the teacher determine students' level of understanding.

Materials

Chapter from a textbook

Guidelines

1. Think-aloud to show students how you use text structure to understand elements better and to improve learning.

2. Encourage students to offer feedback and pose questions.

3. Invite students to think-aloud about a section of text. For students reluctant to talk out loud, have them jot ideas on Post-its or in a journal, then share with a group or class.

> ## Interactive Think-Aloud In Action
> ## Sixth Grade Math Text

Textbook: *Transition Mathematics,* University of Chicago Mathematics Project, Scott Foresman, 1995

Teacher's Goal: To introduce and review structural elements with each of the ten sections in Chapter 1, "Decimal Notation"

Time: 5 to 8 minutes at the start of each class

TEACHER: *On page 6, the section title, "Decimals for Whole Numbers" gives me the topic of this section—I'll learn to use decimals to write whole numbers. The first page of each section in this textbook starts with a question and offers an answer in one or more paragraphs. In the answer are boldface terms that tell me these are important. What are the boldface terms in this paragraph?*

DAVID: decimal system, decimal notation, *and* whole numbers

TEACHER: *Note the box at the bottom of the page, highlighted in green. It shows how to write a large number using words. Highlighted boxes in this book show or summarize a process. Look at page 7. There's a heading called "Covering the Reading" that poses questions about the reading and provides examples to make sure you understand these ideas. Turn to pages 8 and 9. What other headings to you see and how can the work under each help you?*

ANGEL: *On page 8, it says "Applying the Mathematics." Looks like word problems.*

LEROY: *It says to go back and study the examples if you can't do these. These make you think.*

LIA: *Yeah, and show whole decimal numbers in real life.*

TEACHER: *Good analyzing. What about page 9?*

KATE: *It says "review." This is for practice. If you can't do these, you probably need help before the test.*

CHRIS: *The last one is "Exploration." It makes you explore things. It says you might need a dictionary or other stuff.*

LIA: *Or an almanac or atlas, or maybe the* Guinness Book of World Records.

TEACHER: *Who can summarize what you learned about the structure of this section? [several students recap and teacher makes notes on chalkboard.] When we look at section 2, we'll search for repeated features, note any new features, and focus on sample problems.*

STRATEGY LESSON:
Preview and Predict

Purpose

To extend the preview from reading headings to reflecting on their meaning, connecting preview information to the chapter's title, and predicting what the chapter's about

Materials

A textbook chapter

Guidelines

1. Have students read each bold face heading and the sentence that follows it as well as the last sentence in the section. Invite students to discuss what they think each section will be about.

2. Next, ask students to read the captions, study the pictures, and explain how they relate to the chapter's topic.

3. Then, have students take the information gathered and write a "gist statement"—the main ideas or points they will learn in this section.

4. Have students adjust their gist statement after the first reading.

Teaching Reading in Social Studies, Science, and Math

Preview and Predict In Action
Fourth Grade History Textbook

Fourth-grade teacher Diane Sanders and I agree that simply previewing a text is never enough. "Unless there's more to a preview," Diane tells our study group, "my students just go through the motions. They soon learn that they read all bold face and italicized headings, words, and captions. But this doesn't encourage thinking." Right on! I say to myself.

Diane has added the element of "analyzing" to previewing a strategy. At first, teachers in the study group were skeptical of the analyze element. "It will take too much time," or "My students can't do that," were typical comments from teachers after they worked through the strategy with me.

Diane's fourth graders study Virginia's history. To build background knowledge for a study of Native Americans that uses poems, legends, and informational texts, Diane started with the section in the students' textbook.

First Diane reviewed the guidelines for Preview and Analyze (see page 306). Then she asks students to read information in the short overview called "Focus Your Reading."

From detailed notes, Diane reconstructed this thirty-minute lesson which opened with an explanation of the strategy and clarification of the guidelines by responding to students' questions. Students volunteer to comment on each section. Everyone does the previewing, and students help one another. Diane makes it clear that they are not looking for right or wrong answers, but they are trying to figure out what they will learn.

Once students understand how the strategy works, they can complete a three-page text section in 10 to 15 minutes.

Part of a Fourth Grade's Preview and Analyze of the Section Titled "Native Americans"

DOMINIQUE: *It says "tribe, longhouse, wigwam" under vocabulary. I know a* wigwam *is a kind of house they lived in, a* longhouse *must also be one 'cause it ends in house.*

DAVID: *Don't know it for sure.*

ERNESTO: *It's also about different kinds of Native Americans—like the Mohawks or the Shoshones—I read about them in the summer.*

RITA: *Under "Focus Your Reading" it says: "What was life like for Native Americans living in Virginia at the time of the first English settlement?" That's what we'll learn about—maybe about houses and families and hunting and cooking.*

JOSE: (Reads the headings "Virginia's Many Tribes" and "The First People"; then he reads the first and last sentences): *"Long before any European set foot on Virginia soil, people were making their homes there.... There were now two groups of Indians—those underground and those above the ground." Well, we weren't the first here is one idea. I never knew people lived under the ground. I want to read it now.*

By adding the analytical component, exciting things happen. Jose expresses his desire to find out more about information that intrigues him. Rita knows that the "Focus on Reading" gives clues to the purposes or what they should learn. Students gain a beginning understanding of terms that are new or need refining. Students' sentences range from a restatement of the "Focus Your Reading" to thoughtfully predicting what will be learned.

• I think were gonna read about how tribes lived here before they [English] came to VA.
• We'll learn about why some tribes lived underground and some on top and also how they got their food.
• This part is about tribes and how they grew food, what they ate, and where they lived.

Diane convinced our teacher study group that investing time to analyze had much merit, as it is a great way to build background knowledge and create a strong desire to read the entire section. Gist statements revealed that students had begun to process some key points in the section—points that prepared them to read and connect to the new information.

STRATEGY LESSON:
Taking Notes by Posing Questions

Purpose
To teach students how to use text structure to raise questions; to show how a preview links to an effective note taking strategy

Materials
A textbook chapter or chapter section

Teaching Reading in Social Studies, Science, and Math

Guidelines

Part I—Preparation:

1. Fold a notebook page in half, lengthwise. At the top, write name, date, and pages from text the students are using.

2. Organize students in pairs or have them work independently.

3. Have students create questions from bold face headings, words, information in diagrams, charts, and graphs, and captions that are unfamiliar or that they know little about.

4. Write questions on lefthand side of page, leaving several lines blank between questions.

Part II—Read the Selected Pages:

1. Jot down, in short phrases, some answers to the questions.

Part III—Discuss with a Partner, Group or Class:

1. Note additional ideas, information, or clarifications on the answer side of the journal page.

Eighth graders preview and pose questions, then read and take notes.

Question/Note Taking In Action
Sixth Grade Science Textbook

Ray Legge teaches science to sixth and eighth graders. One of his favorite preview strategies is Question/Answer, which he calls "Qs and As." This strategy appeals to Ray because "students preview the section, raise questions about things that arouse their curiosity or that are unfamiliar, and start jotting down notes that answer their queries." Often, Ray has partners complete the "Question" part together, as their interactions stimulate better questions and more talk about the text (see below).

After reading, students skim to find answers to their questions and jot these down. After discussing the sections, students return to their "Q & A Journal" entry to add more details.

What follows is a transcription of the interactions between Ali and Kate as they created questions for this section.

Partners Raise Questions on the Section "Seed Plant Reproduction"

ALI: *All these words—I only know the ones about pollen and pollination 'cause we live next to an orchard.*

KATE: *You think the ovary in a plant is like ours?*

ALI: *I'm not sure. Let's make that a question and ask if it's like ours.*

KATE: *I think we need to know what "Gymnosperm Reproduction" is.*

ALI: *Yeah. Never heard of that word.*

KATE: *Same for "Angiosperm Reproduction."*

ALI: *Agree. Look at the picture. Did you know that flowers got pollinated at night? I wonder why?*

KATE: *Don't know. But now I want to know why there are different kinds of reproduction for plants.*

ALI: *It seems more complicated than with people and animals.*

Questions Kate and Ali Posed

- Is a plant ovary like ours? Does it have the same purpose?
- What are ovules, stamens, and pistils?
- What is Gymnosperm Reproduction?
- What is Angiosperm Reproduction?
- Why are there so many kinds of reproduction with plants?
- Why does some pollination happen at night?

Sixth graders help third graders read books about natural disasters.

- How does a seed develop?
- How do seeds germinate and what does germinate mean?
- How do seeds travel to different places?

Exchanges like those between Kate and Ali show the benefits of talking through this process. Students slow down to think and discuss ideas, decide what they truly know, and ask questions that the preview suggests to them. Talking with a partner encourages students to be thoughtful and selective, thereby refraining from turning everything into a question. It doesn't matter that partners' questions are similar. The point is to think about headings, words, captions, diagrams, then make decisions and formulate questions.

Thinking by Questioning Moves Students Beyond Text Structure

In addition to vocabulary deficits, a lack of understanding of text organization and relationships among text parts and sentences impedes comprehension (Barr et al., 1990). Once students understand the framework of a text and how to use that framework to read and comprehend, they are better equipped to put the facts they've collected to work. The two questioning strategies that follow foster comprehension, analytical thinking, and even enable students to identify authors' biases.

Critical Analysis of Text

It's important to teach students specific strategies for reading and evaluating informational texts,

A seventh grader studies an article on the Internet.

articles from magazines, newspapers, the Internet, and advertisements (Freeman and Person, 1998; Keene and Zimmermann, 1997; Tierney and Readence, 2000; Zarnowski, 1998a).

Critical analysis of texts is a problem-solving experience that invites readers to compare and contrast information in books on the same topic, note various authors' points of view, evaluate whether the information included is fact, opinion, biased or accurate, and whether the author has expertise on the topic.

SOURCES FOR CRITICAL ANALYSIS

Textbooks, trade books, newspaper and magazine editorials and articles, advertisements, propaganda posters, as well as articles on the Internet are excellent for developing students' ability to evaluate passages critically. I maintain a file folder of short pieces to use for this purpose.

STRATEGY LESSON:
Questions That Foster a Critical Analysis of Texts

Purpose

To teach students how to analyze and evaluate a text for accuracy; to differentiate between fact and opinion and identify stereotyping and bias

Materials

A biased or skewed reading selection that relates to the curriculum

Guidelines

1. Have students read a short passage that has bias, opinion, or stereotyping. A short text helps students to understand the process.

2. Select questions (from those that follow) that are appropriate to the texts students are reading.

3. Think aloud to show students how you go about answering the questions. Modelling is important, since many of these questions require close reading and the ability to judge and evaluate texts.

4. Here are some questions, followed by examples in italics, that foster critical analysis:

- What is the purpose of the text?

  Does it entertain, inform, persuade, promote a political or social perspective?

- Who is the author? Is he or she qualified to write about this topic?

  Does the author have expertise in and/or experience with the topic?

- Does the author have a vested interest in the topic?

  Does the writer work for the company whose opinion he's promoting? Will the writer make lots of money by persuading others?

- Are sources of information given? Are they reliable?

  Is there a bibliography? Are sources provided within the text?

- Can you separate opinions from facts?

  Does the author use words and phrases, such as might, probably, could have, from my perspective, *to signal an opinion is coming?*

- Is there an abundance of stereotyping or generalizations?

  Does the author take one event and make sweeping statements about a group of people, historical figures, and minority religions that lead to prejudice?

- Are there "loaded words" that have negative and/or emotional connotations?

  Words such as nonsense, ashamed, harebrained, ridiculous, baloney, *all have negative and insulting connotations.*

- Given the facts, are the conclusions drawn valid?

  For example, if data show that a drug that's been tested is harmful, does the writer maintain that it's okay to use because only a small percentage died?

- Does the author make valid connections between past and present?

  Is key information ignored in order to make a biased connection?

- Does the piece/article stack the deck in favor of one point of view?

  If the writer favors nuclear power plants, does he only give information that supports his belief?

HELP STUDENTS IDENTIFY DIFFERENT INTERPRETATIONS

Invite groups to read several nonfiction titles on a science topic, history event, or about a famous person. Have students identify inconsistencies. Students can check to find additional resources on the Internet or at a local or university library.

Questions

- Do texts have different interpretations of the same event? *Will a text about the American Revolution written by a British author interpret events leading up to the revolution in the same way an American author will interpret those events?*

- Do other texts offer conflicting accounts? *When two books offer differing accounts of the same event, it's time to investigate additional sources to root out the accurate data.*

Integrate Critical Analysis of Texts into Your Curriculum

"I love Jean Fritz's history books. They're like reading a story, and I feel I'm there." This fifth-grade student has connected to the narrative or story elements in nonfiction. Many authors use research to recreate conversations among characters and include narrative elements to relay factual information; these books are classified as narrative nonfiction or "faction" (Lynch-Brown and Tomlinson, 1999). Examples are *Tituba*, by William Miller, illustrated by Leonard Jenkins (Harcourt, 2000), *Traitor: The Story of Benedict Arnold* by Jean Fritz (Puffin, 1981), *Cathedral: The Story of Its Construction* by David Macaulay (Houghton Mifflin, 1973). It's important to read narrative nonfiction to insure that the author has done the research necessary to accurately recreate events.

Engage students in critical reading of texts throughout the year; it only takes 10 to 15 minutes to focus students on some of the questions on pages 312 to 314. Sixth graders studying nuclear power searched an Internet article from *The Detroit News* called "Build More Power Plants" for loaded words and phrases. Students targeted: "local scuttlebutt, instigating delay, crimps consumers pocketbooks, a slew of regulatory obstacles, and lower our standard of living." The class rated this editorial as inflammatory writing aimed at citizens against nuclear power.

Practicing critical analysis of texts can result in students like eighth grader, Heath, and his group concluding that Whitley Strieber knows more about wolves than nuclear winter *(Wolf of*

An eighth grader's critical analysis comparing Strieber's knowledge of wolves and nuclear winter.

Wolf-Nuclear Winter Discussion

This was one of my most favorite discussions of all year. I really liked the way it was set up. We would list the facts that *Wolf of Shadows* gave us on wolves and nuclear winter and then we researched to find out if that information was correct. Surprisingly, we agreed that most information the book gave on nuclear winter was inaccurate. When we researched we found this to be true. When we researched about wolves we found out that the book's information was factual.

I can safely assume that the author knows more about wolves than he does about nuclear winter. However, he made an effort to show the effects of nuclear war and I think this counts for something. Who knows, there is a chance he could be right. Afterall, we've never had a nuclear war before.

Shadows, Ballantine, 1985).

Beck et al. (1997) point out that constructing meaning from a text is more than recalling some facts or one to two details. Strategic reading, making connections, and self-monitoring comprehension can all derail if students are in a tough, fact-laden textbook. Beck et al. also developed an interactive strategy called "Questioning the Author." QTA engages students in an active search for meaning, inviting readers to explain information in a text to themselves. For expository texts, QTA includes questions that start the probing-for-meaning process as well as follow-up questions (p.45).

STRATEGY LESSON:
Questioning the Author

Purpose

To offer students a strategy that enables them to connect to and understand a text; to foster self-monitoring and independence

Materials

A reading selection that relates to your curriculum

QUESTIONING THE AUTHOR

Initiating Queries

◆ What is the author trying to say here?

◆ What is the author's message?

◆ What is the author talking about?

Follow-Up Queries

◆ What did the author mean here?

◆ Did the author explain this clearly?

◆ Does this make sense with what the author told us before?

◆ How does this connect with what the author has told us here?

◆ Does the author tell us why?

◆ Why do you think the author tells us this now?

Guidelines

1. Write the initiating and follow-up questions on chart paper (see margin).

2. Model how you use these questions to interpret and comprehend a text.

3. Encourage student feedback and questions.

4. Organize students into pairs and invite pairs to use QTA with a short passage.

5. Keep practicing until students can apply the strategy to their own reading.

Questioning the Author In Action Sixth Grade

Learners who construct meaning reach beyond recapping some of the text's facts to connecting facts to community and world issues and to developing hypotheses and supporting them with text. They also discover the difference between what the author says and what the author means.

A conversation between a pair of sixth graders in Dick Bell's history class illustrates how QTA drives students to explore the authors' meaning. Note how Mr. Bell's use of QTA follow-up questions connects students to what was previously read and what students will learn as they read on.

Here is the text students use.

> Luther intended that these ninety-five statements should be discussed by Church officials. His ninety-five statements were printed and quickly spread throughout Germany. The sale of indulgences decreased. The Church officials in Rome became concerned about the loss of money. More importantly, they were concerned about Luther's ideas. Steps were taken to stop Luther's influence.

(p. 313, Experiencing World History, AGS, 1991).

JOHANNA: *I think the author is trying to tell me that Luther objected to Tetzel's indulgences. But the author says there were ninety- five statements, so I bet Luther objected to lots of things in the church.*

CLINT: *It also means that the church lost money because it didn't sell that many indulgences.*

MR. BELL: *How do you think the people felt?*

CLINT: *Well, it said before that you could get a relative's soul out of purgatory if you bought an indulgence. I bet people didn't like not having that chance.*

JOHANNA: *But it says that Tetzel was a great salesman. Maybe it was more due to his selling than to people wanting to save relatives.*

MR. BELL: *Good thinking. But why do you think the author tells us "they were concerned about Luther's ideas."*

JOHANNA: *Maybe to let us know that Luther would be punished.*

Questioning the author is an effective strategy for focusing students on the essential points and big ideas; it drives them to use this information to make connections and draw conclusions about historical events and the people who shaped them.

Pause and Reflect on: Teaching Text Structures

The more students understand the formats of textbooks and informational books, the better equipped they are to construct meaning and new understandings. Start the school year by focusing on structure, then sprinkle the year with reviews of text structures. What students learn about text structure can support their ability to choose and write in the structure that will best convey their ideas to others.

Capitalize on read-alouds to point out how writers organize informational texts. Gina, a sixth grader, put it this way: "When I know what to expect in a book, I can spend time thinking about what I'm reading instead of struggling to figure out how the stuff is put together."

Teaching Reading in Social Studies, Science, and Math

✤ Chapter 11 ✤

Using Literature in Social Studies, Science, and Math

He ate and drank the precious words,
His spirit grew robust;
He knew no more that he was poor,
Nor that his frame was dust.

He danced along the dingy days,
And this bequest of wings
Was but a book. What liberty
A loosened spirit brings!

—Emily Dickinson

I've always liked quoting this poem when I speak about reading, but I don't believe I really felt the power of Dickinson's message until I read the following words of one of my students.

Here's what Frances Woods wrote in her journal in response to my question: *What do you value in your life and why do you value it?*

What makes this eighth grader's letter remarkable is her literacy history. Until seventh grade, Frances struggled with

> **My Love for Reading**
>
> Frances   Feb. 9
>
> For me reading is my world. Ever sence my parents took our TV away about a year ago I have found reading as an ecape from my boring life. When I read though I imagen myself as the charecters and everything is eysiting.
>
> If I had one wish, it wouldn't be for $ or anything. It would be for every book I read I would go into the 🅱 storys and be the main charecter.
>
> I also think reading helps my imagination and personality some what, because they inspire me to do new things in life.

In her evaluation of what she values, Frances celebrates her love of reading.

reading. From third grade on, during the year and for several weeks each summer, a reading specialist tutored Frances. Progress was slow, and by fifth grade, Frances resented reading what she called "easy books"—books two to three years below her grade level.

In fourth and fifth grade, when Frances worked with me on spelling and writing, she'd wistfully say, "I want to read the books my friends read. When will that happen?" Frances was making progress; all her teachers conveyed this to me and to Frances. But I worried that if she did not make the leap to grade-level books soon, Frances might give up. However, I learned that these were *my* worries; Frances' enthusiasm and effort flagged occasionally, but she always recharged her energy and worked hard. With her teachers' and parents' help, Frances gradually progressed and by the end of sixth grade, she read at a fifth grade level. That summer, Frances read book after book.

Now, as an eighth grader, Frances keeps two to three books with her all the time. "If I finish one, I've got another," she tells me. "I can read what I want to. And if it's hard, I read it again." As we teachers provided the scaffolding to help Frances learn skills and tools to improve her reading in general, we used the opportunity to transfer/incorporate these lessons into her reading of textbooks as well. While learning to interpret and infer meaning, support assumptions with text, pinpoint main ideas, distinguish fact from fiction, summarize and synthesize, Frances also practiced applying these strategies to her reading of nonfiction texts. Moreover, specific genre assignments led Frances to enjoy nonfiction texts as much as narrative texts. "My favorite [nonfiction] book this year was *No Pretty Pictures* by Anita Lobel," she told me.

The Role of Voice, Verse, and Story in the Content Areas

In *The Call of Stories* (1989), Robert Coles talks about a deep and consuming connection readers make with written narratives. He shares the words of one of his wife's students, Linda, who eloquently captures the reading process:

> ...the story becomes yours. I don't mean "your story"; I mean you have imagined what those people look like, and how they speak the words in the book, and how they move around, and so you and the writer are in cahoots. (p. 64)

To generate this wonderful reader-author collusion in your own classroom, try integrating poetry into your content area teaching; it's an easy, first step toward bringing literature into the classroom and encouraging your students to think about their textbook readings in new ways. For example, *A Book of Americans* by Rosemary and Stephen Vincent Benet (Holt, 1961), *Singing America: Poems that Define a Nation* by Neil Philip (Viking, 1995), and *We The People* by Bobbi Katz, illustrations by Nina Crews, (Greenwillow, 2000) all entice students to explore the essence of an historical figure in a way no textbook can.

COLLECT POEMS!

Skim anthologies of poetry to become a collector of poems that relate to your subject. Build a file folder of poetry that motivates students to learn and that you can read aloud while studying a topic.

Introduce a topic or theme with poetry; invite students to dramatize a poem, reading it as if they were the narrator or author, or perhaps that event brought back to life (Robb, 1990). You can motivate students to learn United States geography by sharing "Traveling" by Eve Merriam (*Jamboree,* Dell, 1984) or introduce variables and equations with Lillian Morrison's "Number Theory" *(Overheard in a Bubble Chamber and Other Science Poems,* Lothrop, Lee & Shepard, 1981). These poems are reprinted in the margin.

Invite students to move beyond the facts in their textbook and relive the past through historical fiction, biography, and autobiography. Books such as Katherine Paterson's *Lyddie* (Lodestar, 1991) can enlarge students' knowledge of family, education, and social boundaries during the industrial revolution in Lowell, Massachusetts. Kathryn Lasky's *True North: A Novel of the Underground Railroad* (Scholastic, 1996) is a portrait of Afrika's

"Traveling" by Eve Merriam

Click, clack
train on the track.

Conductor has to
know
where you want to go.

Tap your toes,
tap, tap,
clap your hands
clap, clap,
add a little ginger
with a fingersnap.

Meet sister Mattie
in Cincinnati.
Brother Ben
in Cheyenne.
Flip a coin
in Des Moines.
Thanksgiving turkey
in Albuquerque,
eat red-hot beans
in New Orleans.
Fetch some hay
in Santa Fe.
Lose a loose tooth
in Duluth,
open a store
in Baltimore.
Be noisy in Boise.
Nitty gritty
in New York City,
dance in a disco

in San Francisco.
Go, go, go, go.

Tap your toes,
tap, tap,
clap your hands
clap, clap,
add a little ginger
with a fingersnap.

Click, clack,
train on the track.

Full steam ahead
and don't look back.

> **"Number Theory"**
> **by Lillian Morrison**
>
> "To be is to be the value
> of a variable,"
> say the new philosophers.
> Oh, so variable
> and so valuable,
> and I must solve
> how not to be a
> function of this varying
> as you soar, sink, simulate
> in brilliant semi solutions
> to difficult equations.
> I plan to be
> a necessary integer among
> them,
> independent, varying
> within my own harmonic series
> of events
> but reappearing
> as a welcome constant
> in yours.

courage and determination to be free and the people who made her dream a reality. Sharing primary sources, such as letters, diary entries and speeches with students, will also help them understand history, science, and math by listening to the voices of men and women who made history and whose discoveries changed our lives.

Harness the Power of Peer Recommendations

Be sure to build time into your lesson plans for students to share what they are reading with peers; this is a great way to inspire students to read authors and study topics they haven't before. Listen in on fifth graders James and Sara discussing their favorite science writers:

JAMES: *When I read Seymour Simon's books about the planets and looked at the great photos, I feel like I've stood on and explored Mars and Jupiter.* [James shows Sara some favorite photos.]

SARA: *Those photos are cool. I could just look at them and learn stuff about Jupiter. My favorites are Jean Craighead George's "Moon"*

> **RESOURCES FOR PRIMARY SOURCES**
>
> Consider using Scholastic's Primary Sources Teaching Kit series. Each book has many primary source documents and covers a different topic, including The Westward Movement, Explorers, Colonial America, Civil War, Civil Rights, and Immigration.

books and Bianca Lavies' books. They're about animals and birds and snakes. I love animals and being outside. Look at this photo of garter snakes (from Bianca Lavies' *Garter Snakes*, Dutton, 1993). *It's so gross, but I love to look at it. I can feel the mass of them squirming.*

JAMES: *Can I read that book about the snakes now?*

The more students read nonfiction science trade books, the better they can understand new concepts in physics, chemistry, astronomy, biology, botany, earth science, and mathematics.

Encourage and help your students to create a genre palette splashed with poetry, nonfiction picture and chapter books, biography, autobiography, and historical fiction.

Dynamic Ways to Use Nonfiction in Social Studies

During a study of World War II in a humanities class I team teach with history teacher John Lathrop, eighth grader Jaime read an article about the Japanese relocation camps and *The Children of Topaz: The Story of a Japanese-American Internment Camp* by Michael Tunnel and George Chilcoat (Holiday House, 1996). His journal entry opens:

> The article & book that I read both astonished and confused me. I was astonished at the fact that Americans condemned the Nazis, but treated Japanese-Americans in much the same way. With little notice, they rounded up families. Jobs, homes, important possessions were left behind and people were taken to remote areas. Crowded together with dozens of families in one barrack, fear and anxiety filled people's hearts. Here's what confused me. How could we shed tears for the Jews suffering in death camps, but watch dry-eyed as the same injustices occurred right under our noses?

It's clear from Jaime's journal entry that these two texts provided him with an opportunity to reflect on history, digging deeper beneath the facts to ponder the messiness of—and ignobility of—a nation's attitudes and actions. He's understandably confused by the apparent hypocrisy of many Americans who attempted to rationalize the internment of Japanese Americans. After Jaime read his journal entry aloud to the class, students posed these questions, "Why did we pick on the Japanese? Why not German Americans? Italian Americans?"

Jaime's question and the discussion that ensued reflect insights that students probably wouldn't have arrived at had they not been reading informational texts. When you plan your teaching, look for books and articles that work well together; these sources might have similar or divergent points of view on a topic. What's important is that together they create a synergism of information that leads to insightful student discussions.

Insights Students Gained

- It was easy to target Japanese-Americans because they look different—eyes, skin color, hair.
- American propaganda machines built distrust of Japanese-Americans saying that they were a threat to our nation's safety.
- We stereotyped a whole culture. We said all Japanese-Americans were spies involved in anti-American activities. They stopped being individuals.
- The bombing of Pearl Harbor was directed at the United States. Italy and Germany had not made direct attacks on us on that scale. That's why we went after Japanese-Americans.
- Our textbook has one paragraph about the internment camps—doesn't that make a statement.
- We imprisoned Japanese-Americans—and this wasn't right. But we did not exterminate them as the Germans did Jews.

Using Nonfiction with Sixth Graders

Dick Bell and I have been working together to bring more literature into his sixth-grade history class. I offered him three books about the Age of Exploration, and he chose *Around the World in a Hundred Years: From Henry the Navigator to Magellan* (Putnam & Grosset, 1994) by Jean Fritz because "All twenty-two of my students can read the text well." Dick used the "five finger method" to determine that all sixth graders could successfully read this book (see margin box, next page).

Dick's goal in social studies class is to illustrate how studying the past can offer insights into our world. That's why he takes the time to demonstrate how he uses parts of a text to support the connections he makes to self, community, and world issues before inviting students to make similar connections from texts.

When Dick pre-planned this lesson on the Age of Exploration, he had several goals for

THE FIVE FINGER ASSESSMENT METHOD

Dick asked each student to read any page he opened in the book. The rule is that if the student can not pronounce and/or doesn't understand five words on that page, then the book is too difficult. Six students had problems with three words, and Dick felt that since the book was an instructional text, he would make sure this group would receive solid support from him.

his students. In order to achieve these goals, he:

- Selected the chapter.
- Organized students into groups of three and four.
- Asked each student to find a passage that spoke to him or her.
- Had students take turns reading aloud their passages to the group, then connect them to their lives or community and world issues.
- Invited group members to discuss each example.

Students' discussions not only revealed their knowledge of the information Fritz offers in her book, but their talk touched upon the *way* Fritz said things and showed how her style made students think and make connections. Here are the prompts, posted on chart paper, and part of a conversation that I noted among three students, Tim, Winston, and Clint, about the chapter called "Prince Henry the Navigator."

Prompts Posted for Students

- Do you see any personality traits in Prince Henry that are similar to your own personality?
- Did people in Prince Henry's time deal with issues and problems your family and community wrestle with?
- Is slavery an issue in the world today? In your community?
- Can you connect what you have read to other historical periods?

Sixth Graders' Conversation

The boys decide who will read his passage first, second, etc.

TIM: *I related to this part on page 20: "He [Prince Henry] became obsessed with that mysterious African coastline which the mapmakers had never been able to finish."*

The word "obsessed" is what got to me. She [Fritz] shows how Prince Henry never gave up—sent men out again and again.

WINSTON: *Yeah. They figured out how to sail around the storms* and they mapped the end of Africa. *Obsessed is a good thing to be if you want to do something. It's like wanting to be an astronaut or an artist or a great skate boarder.*

CLINT: *Do you think leaders of countries are obsessed? I mean like Bush and Gore wanting to win and all that campaign stuff.*

WINSTON: *Like terrorists or the Kamikaze pilots in WWII. Their missions obsessed them. It also says on page 27 that the Portuguese were not interested in Africa's coastline and weren't happy about the amount of money Prince Henry was spending. But it didn't stop Prince Henry from his mission. That's a real obsession.*

CLINT: *Here's the part I picked on page 29: "The African slave trade now became big business in Europe." I didn't know that the slave trade went on so far before the Civil War. Prince Henry wants to convert the Africans, but he lets them become slaves. Fritz puts her opinion in when she uses the word "probably" to show that maybe Prince Henry felt okay about slaves because he saved their souls. I don't buy that.*

TIM: *My dad says we still have slaves. Like very poor people who have no health insurance and not enough food.*

WINSTON: *Yeah, but no one owns them. They're free.*

TIM: *I'm not sure if you can be free if you're so poor.*

When students close-read texts and discuss what they've learned with classmates, they become better at articulating ideas, thinking critically, and making connections. Moreover, listening to peers offers opportunities to observe classmates' thinking and analyzing processes (see pages 264–269). Indeed, finely crafted literature, Myra Zarnowski points out (1998, p. 107) has the power to introduce students "to social studies as a vibrant, living, relevant subject—one that requires active thinking."

Kids often pick up on an author's language.

Makes text-to-world connection.

Clarifies and deepens understanding of "obsessed."

Student examines, evaluates, and judges.

Thinking critically to draw a conclusion.

SOCIAL ACTION MOVES LEARNING BEYOND THE CLASSROOM

Involve students in social action projects, such as collecting food for a local food bank. Have them write letters to their congressmen or the president about educational issues, such as overcrowded classrooms, no school library, or lobbying for after school programs in sports, music, or art.

Social action is also appropriate in science where students can write letters to congressmen on issues they feel strongly about, such as keeping drinking water pure, protecting the rain forest, or not drilling in Alaska's national parks.

For a book that can help students take social action, I recommend: *The Kid's Guide to Social Action: How to Solve the Social Problems You Choose—and Turn Creative Thinking into Positive Action* by Barbara A. Lewis (Free Spirit, 1991, Grades 5 and up).

And remember, while it's impossible to sit in on every group in your class to evaluate the level of discussion, it is feasible to assess what pairs and groups have learned by inviting them to list, in their journals, five or six key points the discussion made.

A seventh grader's notes show key points learned about types of rocks.

A third grader's notes taken after reading.

Biography-Based Projects Put Students in the Shoes of History's Greats

My eighth graders groan and mock yawn when I announce, "We're going to study biography." Obviously, they've written one too many traditional biography book reports in their long and illustrious school careers.

I want my students to see *biography* in a new light, to think about what the subject's life was like "day to day" and how this shaped his or her contribution to history. I don't want them to get hung up on dates, or memorize them mindlessly, but to use their energy to learn about the personal and public world that enveloped that person. Only by knowing the wider social/cultural/political context of a person in history can we even begin to assess his or her character, thoughts, and influence.

In this section, I'll share some projects that enable students to step into the skin of a great person, or a character in a novel. In this way, students can collect information that fosters thinking and feeling about that person's life in order to understand his or her decisions and actions, and the impact these had on his or her world and ours.

Reading Biography in a Fourth-Grade Class

"I want students to get to know the men and women who made history," Debi Gustin tells me. Her students read the encyclopedia for an overview of a person's life, but then deepen their knowledge by reading a biography and articles from the Internet. Debi's goal is to introduce fourth graders to an array of research tools, then have them organize their notes into an interview, a news article, or a monologue, where students become the person they are studying.

Colleen, a fifth grader, discusses photographs that chronicle Helen Keller's life.

Students receive a time line of due dates for note cards, their plan, and their first draft to support their planning and research. Debi reviews students' work after each due date, helping them make revisions and adjustments after each deadline. Their work illustrates the excellent research young students can complete over a two-month period. These fourth graders enjoyed this experience so much that Debi repeated the process when the class studied the Civil War.

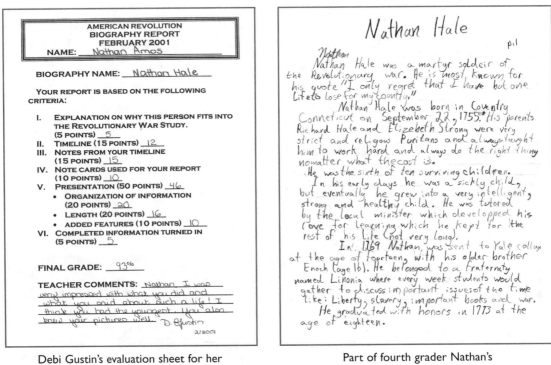

Debi Gustin's evaluation sheet for her fourth graders' biography reports.

Part of fourth grader Nathan's biography report on Nathan Hale.

Eighth Graders' Interviews and Dramatic Monologues

In addition to basing interviews on research, students can conduct interviews and write monologues using characters and events in a book. To support a study of natural science, I invited eighth graders to read *California Blue* by David Klass (Scholastic, 1996). The book is about John Rogers, who finds a new species of butterfly in the woods surrounding the mill town where he lives. The conflict between mill town workers and scientists mirrors current environmental issues that continually make newspaper headlines.

Groups of three students took turns being interviewer and subject. Here are the notes and the interview questions one group wrote.

Several students decided to write and present monologues that chronicled key events in a character's life. Together, the students and I established guidelines that enabled them to meet specific goals.

Dramatic Monologue

By Lindsay Gibson

My name is John Rogers. When I found out that my father had leukemia, I knew I should feel bad about it- I really tried. But you see, my father and I had never been very close, and I always felt he was disappointed in me. My brothers and sisters were all basketball or softball players or cheerleaders, and my father still holds the record for most yards gained in a football game. And there I was, a middle distance runner, which I suppose my family considered to be a pretty lowly sport. My dad never even came to one of my track meets. About the only other thing I was interested in was studying bugs, and my family found this certainly no better than track running, if not less worthy of my time. So, when I found this chrysalis after falling into some bushes, I saw no real point in telling my parents about it. They would probably have the same reaction as my brother, who was both perplexed and grossed out at the idea of anyone keeping a bug in their room. So, as I like to do with bugs, I tried to identify it with my field guide, but couldn't. So I took it to Miss Merrill, to see what she though about the butterfly. She got in touch with Dr. Eggleson, and he could not identify it either. So, when he called a town meeting about *his* butterfly and all the kids were hoping he wouldn't get out of town in one piece, I felt that it was my responsibility to acknowledge that it had been me who found the butterfly. I felt that it was time to stand up for something that I believed in. I was willing to forsake all my connections to my town, even my family, for the sake of that butterfly. Then, this happened again when I decided to go to the protest with Dr. Eggleson and the other people concerned about the butterfly. I didn't really care what my parents or

A dramatic monologue by an eighth grader based on *California Blue*.

Lia
Mrs. Rogers' Interview

Lia: Why didn't you want John to go to San Francisco?
Thea: answer We thought he wouldn't get anything out of it. He would more work done at school & his father didn't want a big commotion.
Lia: What would you have done if John didn't come home?
Thea: answer I don't know if I could ever really forget about him but things in the family just haven't been going well.
Lia: Do you agree with your son or the mill?
Thea: answer I've been trying to avoid the whole situation although I understand both sides.
Lia: In your oppinion, what makes John different from his brothers and sisters?
Thea: answer John is a lot less like his father than his other siblings. He's so much more independent & devoted to schoolwork
Lia: What do you think Miss.Merril has done in your sons life?
Thea: answer She's taught him many things I wouldn't have been able to explain as a mother.
*get 2-gether w/Eric and answer Miss.Merril? 4 interview! She's a very bright & kind young woman.

Eighth graders' notes for their interview based on David Klass's *California Blue*.

Using Biographies as Models for Writing

Third-grade teacher Nancy Roche has students read biographies of men and women for an additional purpose: writing. Besides wanting her students to learn about the lives of men and women who changed history, science, math, and the fine arts, Nancy helps her students understand the structure of a biography, then invites students to write biographies of their own lives. For six to eight weeks, students take notes, formulate writing plans, create first drafts, confer with Nancy, then complete illustrated final drafts.

"I do this every year," Nancy tells me. "The children love predicting their adult lives."

Monologues, interviews, oral presentations, and students' biographies share a common benefit: they move students beyond collecting facts in a notebook and writing a report. Once students absorb information and make it their own, like alchemists mixing ordinary metals to create gold, students can select and transform information about a person (or themselves) into dramatic presentations for others to learn from and enjoy.

Several excerpts from Jessica's autobiography.

Jessica Krasich designed clothing for animals. Jessica Danielle Krasich was born on March 18, 1992. She went to Bradock Street for preschool, Wakefield country day school for Kindergarten and Powhatan for 1st thru 8th grade. On the weeck end one day wen Jessica was 12 she started her career. Jessica was playing with clay and brier horses designing saddles and bridles.

This would be the beginning of Jessica's career. After graduating Powhatan Jessica went onto a designing school. When Jessica went on to another designing school for graduates

Jessica got first place in the art show When Jessica graduated she went on to be a famous animal clothing designer. When Jessica was 36 she married John Cole a famous horse back rider. Two years later thay adopted a six year old girl named Mary Aann. Fourteen years later when Mary was 20 Jessica was 51 and John was 60 he died of a heart attack. At his funeral Jessica and Mary hit his pet rock in the head with a saddle. Even with the death of her husband.

Teaching Reading in Social Studies, Science, and Math

Dynamic Ways to Use Nonfiction in Science and Math

Integrating trade books and poetry into science and math can be done in such a way that it doesn't make teachers feel ever more pressed for time. Simple, brief assignments can go a long way to enhance a core textbook. For example, when seventh graders study astronomy, space, and the solar system, Ann Kiernan invites her students to use the knowledge they have gained in science to craft poems. In English class, Ann reads aloud all the poems in Myra Cohn Livingston's *Space Songs* (Holiday House, 1988).

In science, both sixth and second graders study the natural world. As part of a larger, mentor-like project, sixth graders use one class period to ferret out poems about nature that they can read to and discuss with second graders. During a second class, older students read poems to their younger buddies, then discuss the poems with them. Pairs illustrate their favorite poem and share this with the entire group.

Eighth graders expand their investigation of inventions related to biology, chemistry, physics, oceanography, astronomy, space, and botany, by researching their topics with trade books. Their purpose is to create a set of invention cards for fifth graders to use in a science center. Here are the guidelines teacher Ray Legge set for this project:

- Consider your audience when you write.
- Choose an invention that will interest a fifth grader.
- Use Who, What, When, Where, Why as part of your description.
- Complete a write-up that has fascinating facts.
- Include references to research

by Ogden Nash
The camel has 1 hump,
The Promedary has 2,
Or else it is the other way around,
I am never sure,
Are you?

A poem selected by a sixth grader.

An illustration drawn by a sixth and a second grader.

materials when appropriate.

- Draw and label a picture of your invention or trace a labelled diagram of it.

This has become an annual project because students give it high ratings. Moreover, it makes up for the limitations of a textbook, which can only address a few inventions, and invites students to research for a specific purpose.

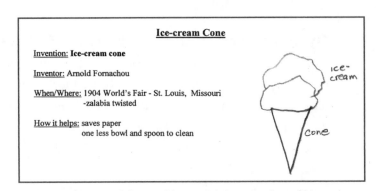

An invention card designed by an eighth grader for a fifth grader.

In math, you can use children's literature to deepen mathematical understanding. (Wilde, 1998). While most informational books about mathematics are picture books for younger students, there are more sophisticated picture books available. Books by Japanese author and illustrator Mitsumasa Anno, for example, explore factorials, logic, permutations and combinations—all subjects studied by older students.

Science books can also help deepen mathematical understandings (Wilde, 1998). In Seymour Simon's *Oceans* (Morrow, 1990), for instance, students can explore how the author uses numbers to discuss oceans. One teacher I know used dozens of books about different kinds of whales to study scale. My colleague Harry Holloway invites sixth graders to read about famous mathematicians and present oral reports about their lives and contributions to the field.

While teaching fifth grade, I used *How Much Is A Million?* (by David M. Schwartz, illustrations by Steven Kellogg, Lothrop, Lee & Shepard, 1985) to help students understand big numbers. One year, students created a set of math problem cards related to very large numbers and decorated them with some of the book's illustrations. Recopied many times, teachers still use these cards.

Creating the cards helped students better understand exponents and scientific notation, and they read a book that inspired them to think about large numbers in our world.

Students broaden their knowledge of a topic and view of their world when they read informational books to learn how scientists and mathematicians classify, observe, experiment, hypothesize, and infer from data (Fredericks, 1998). One fifth grader clearly explained the need for nonfiction in the classroom when he said, "This book [class textbook] doesn't answer half my questions."

Teaching Reading in Social Studies, Science, and Math

Several math cards fifth graders created using *How Much Is a Million?*

Teaching Partnerships

Teaching partnerships can help middle school teachers enrich the content in textbooks with literature and writing. For example, a math, science, or social studies teacher can ask the English teacher to support one or two themes a year. For example, when eighth graders study the Depression in history, they read *No Promises in the Wind* (by Irene Hunt, Berkley, 1987) or *Bud, Not Buddy* (by Christopher Paul Curtis, Delacorte, 1999) in English class. For another good example of a partnership in action, see page 337–338, "Multiple Texts and Individualized Strategic Teaching." Partnerships among teachers enhance student learning through the dialogue and a shared experience among students and between teachers (Alvermann and Phelps, 1998; Tierney and Readence, 2000).

HOW TO CHOOSE THE BEST BOOKS

If you're just embarking on a journey to integrate nonfiction into your math, science, or social studies curriculum, it's helpful to have some guidelines for selecting the best available literature. See pages 346–349 for information on how to select excellent nonfiction trade books.

Using Multiple Texts

A typical mix of students in middle school classes often includes students who read on grade level, some who read two to four years below grade level, and others who read above grade level. Given this wide range, use materials that match students' independent or instructional reading levels to engage *all* students in a themed study or unit (Robb 1994, 2000a). This way, even when districts mandate that teachers help students unpack meaning from textbooks too difficult for them to read independently, teachers can fill their classrooms with multiple texts that vary in readability levels, allowing every learner to read and participate.

Whether your focus is space, the Holocaust, or a literary genre, you'll want to include a wide range of materials: informational picture and chapter books, fiction, historical fiction, biographies, photographic essays, and primary sources as well as Internet, newspaper, and magazine articles.

Example: Grade 7 Civil War Unit

During a study of the Civil War that is built upon multiple texts, I bring in many and varied materials: articles from *Cobblestone* Magazine; biographies of generals and Abraham Lincoln; nonfiction chapter and picture books about the Underground Railroad, Jim Crow laws, the battles and military strategies; historical fiction; folk tales about slavery; and primary sources, such as letters, diaries, and speeches. These texts range from three years below to three years above grade level so that every student can participate. "I can read and say things in the discussions," Jared wrote in his journal. "I feel part of this class, not like when everyone could read the textbook except me."

Jared raised an issue that multiple texts remedy: students who can't and don't read the text feel like outsiders in a class community. Some retire into silence, distancing themselves from the learning; some become disruptive, saying things like, "This stuff's dumb," and "I hate science," or "What a waste of time," and "Who cares about this stupid stuff?" Others escape by visiting the bathroom, removing themselves to break the anxiety and tension that builds from not knowing information, being disengaged, and hoping that no one will call on them. One student admitted, "I go to the bathroom to get out of the room when I feel that everyone's on the page but me." Using multiple texts will make learning new information accessible to all students.

Guidelines for Getting Started

Before initiating your multiple-text unit, set aside time to build students' background knowledge of the topic. Next, think aloud and show how you compose open-ended questions that can be used with any topic-related text (pages 344–345). Invite the class to generate the essential questions you'd like students to ponder as they read and discuss. List the questions on chart paper, so pairs or small groups can use them to plan and prepare for discussions.

Help students choose materials they can read by organizing the books and articles on four desks. On two desks, display materials for students reading below grade level. Place materials for students reading at or near grade level on a third desk. Fill the fourth desk with materials that proficient readers might enjoy. Send four to five students to the desk that has materials appropriate for them. Let them browse through books and articles and select one to read. (Those waiting at their desks complete class assignments or work on writing projects.) In plastic crates or on a shelf, stack extra books from each desk, so that when students have finished one, they can check out another. This system offers students some choice within a group of books they can read, think with, and enjoy.

Negotiate with each student to determine a reasonable number of books and articles to complete. Set aside 20- to 30-minute blocks at least three times a week for students to read and note responses on Post-its (Harvey and Goudvis, 2000). Students stick Post-its on the page that generates responses, such as questions, making connections to other books or experiences, or noting new and fascinating information.

Notes become springboards for paired and small group discussions. For student-led discussions, I organize heterogeneous groups and change these every 4 to 6 weeks.

Multiple Texts and Individualized Strategic Teaching

Multiple texts do place greater instructional demands on teachers than using the same expository text for everyone. The broader the range of materials, the more you will have to familiarize students with their structures in order to help them navigate through new territory. In this section I'll show you ways to adjust reading lessons and tasks to meet each student's needs and offer everyone opportunities to improve through individualized strategic teaching (Keene and Zimmermann, 1997; Robb, 2000a; Wilhelm, 2001).

Let's take a look at how individualized strategic teaching plays out. History teacher Dick Bell invites me to support his study of World War II by bringing related multiple texts in for a reading-writing workshop. This enables me to improve students' application of strategies to their reading of nonfiction texts.

While these eighth graders read their Holocaust books, I hold short, one-on-one conferences. In one class period, I can meet with four to six students. To determine the strategic support each student needs, I observe and note students' reactions to whole-class or small-group strategy lessons. Reading journal entries and listening to student-led discussions also provide me with valuable information on how students are applying strategies, such as making connections, summarizing and synthesizing, or finding the main points.

A strategy log enables me to keep track of the strategies each student practices during our mini-conferences. On a clipboard are the log sheets of students I plan to meet with while others read independently. I file logs in each student's reading folder so I can refer to them when deciding what to focus on next.

One-on-One Assistance

First I stop at Frances's desk. She's reading *The Big Lie: A True Story* by Isabella Leitner. Together, Frances and I have been practicing finding and explaining cause-and-effect relationships. Using a passage from her book, I think aloud to explain cause and effect. During the next two mini-conferences, I skim to find the cause, and Frances skims the text and explains the effects. The fourth time we meet, I ask Frances to find a cause event and discuss the effects. Here's what she says (based on pages 34–35): "They're on the train to the camps, packed in like cattle and they get no

Name _Jake_ _____

Date & Focus of Meeting:
12/5 Using context clues

Comments:
- if not in sentence with word, gives up
- tends to skip new words
- practiced reading around word
- meet tomorrow – more practice

Date & Focus of Meeting:
12/6 Using C. Clues

Comments:
- improved – reads before/after word
- next time – work on situation
- pair with H. – help each other
- put tough words on post-its for partner work.

Date & Focus of Meeting:
1/9 Connect to issues on chart

Comments:
- Found sep. abuse + poverty issues for Maya Angelou – said got it from class discuss., when others shared issues
- Check journal entries for writing abt. issues

Date & Focus of Meeting:
1/10 Using C. Clues

Comments:
- great job – fig. meaning from text.
- talked abt. things to do when text has no clues.

A focus meeting record sheet

Teaching Reading in Social Studies, Science, and Math

food—that's the cause. The effect is the people got sick [pause] from no food or drink and being so close."

"Can you read the last paragraph that starts on page 34 and find other effects?" I ask.

Frances skims. "It makes me want to puke, so many died. They give people's names and that makes it more real. I guess the Nazis never heard of human rights."

"You made such a good connection to human rights, an issue we've been discussing. Excellent work, Frances. You're understanding cause/effect so much better." Next, I walk to Bobby's desk.

One-on-One Assistance

Bobby is a proficient reader. Multiple-texts work permits me to stretch his ability to connect his book, *Darkness Over Denmark* by Ellen Levine, to other texts he's completed. First, I model how I connect this book to a recent read-aloud from Milton Meltzer's *Rescue: The Story of How Gentiles Saved Jews in the Holocaust*. Bobby immediately brings up *No Pretty Pictures,* an autobiography by Anita Lobel. "There wasn't a lot about resistance in Poland [in Lobel's book], but there was a lot about rescuing Anita and her brother. Their nanny hid them in the country and then got them into a convent. I guess that is a kind of resistance—going against the Nazis and saving Jews. The Danes, like Leif Vido, stole weapons for the resistance from German soldiers. A big connection is that if you hid a Jew or hid weapons to resist the Nazis and they found out, you were finished. I guess there are different kinds of resistance."

I tell Bobby, "I like the way you connect different kinds of resistance and the examples were excellent." Then I move on to work with David, who needs help with selecting essential details, and Maria, who needs to practice using context clues to figure out the meaning of new words.

Using multiple texts drives me to consider and meet the needs of each student by helping them practice and apply reading strategies to texts they can read. In addition, reading materials become the grist for discussing varied interpretations of the same topic.

Multiple Texts, Multiple Perspectives

Multiple texts introduce multiple perspectives on a topic rather than limiting students to the viewpoints in their textbook or the one biography or nonfiction book an entire class reads. According to Tunnell and Ammon (1996), multiple perspectives are "fundamental to good history teaching" (p. 212). I would extend this to mean that in studies of science, the environment, influential men and women, discrimination and human rights, any issues that include multiple interpretations of events provide the diversity for the discussion of social, political, and economic issues. Such studies compel students to consider these questions: What really occurred? Are there other solutions? What do primary sources say? Is the author changing events and why? Why did the author omit some events? What's the author's agenda? Why were specific decisions made? Did others suggest different ways of dealing with issues? Why were alternate solutions abandoned? How did past decisions/discoveries/inventions affect our lives?

Multiple Texts Help Us Rethink the Past

Dick Bell and I use biographies, informational picture and chapter books, diaries, letters, speeches, and historical fiction to study the Civil War with seventh graders. A transcription from my notes of a discussion among three students illustrates that exposing students to varied perspectives through multiple texts resulted in learning ideas and concepts that textbooks didn't provide. The students discussed how the war affected children based on these works: *Drummer Boy,* a picture book by Ann Turner; a description of a slave auction from Chapter 12 of *Uncle Tom's Cabin* by Harriet Beecher Stowe from *Words That Build a Nation;* and chapter one of *The Boys' War* by Jim Murphy.

JAIME: *Stowe shows how fearful mothers were in a slave auction. Haley [a master] refuses to buy the mother with her son. It ends with the mother asking, "Couldn't dey leave me one?" And they tell her to trust in the Lord. What good will that do? She's alone with no one to love and love her.*

RACHEL: *Slaves had no rights.*

KATIE: *Yeah, like kids in the war. The boy was property, too. Murphy says in the first chapter that grown-ups writing about the war soon after it was over never mentioned the young boys fighting. Maybe no one wanted us to know about them. Lots of boys signed up and died before they had a chance to live.*

JAIME: *Do you think that could happen today?*

KATIE: *I'm not sure. I guess someone could forge papers. But they'd have to look older. These looked like ten or twelve.*

RACHEL: *In my book, a thirteen year old lies and signs up. He becomes a drummer boy and hears cannons roar, and the screams of shot horses and men crying for their mothers. Here [shows picture] the drummer boy is crying. He never expected war to be death—thought it would be glory.*

KATIE: *War takes your childhood away.*

JAIME: *So does slavery. I think they're alike. The drummer is a slave to the side he signed up for.*

RACHEL: *The men that took the boys—I blame them too. They knew what war was really like. The slave auctioneers knew that families would be separated, people whipped and starved. But they still did it.*

Multiple texts enabled these students to make connections between boys sold into slavery and boys enlisting in the army, and to understand the drummer boy's disillusionment.★

Multiple Texts Raise Awareness of Public Issues

Teaching with multiple texts doesn't mean you always have to gather materials from many genres. In history or science, you can also focus on a particular genre, such as biography, informational chapter books, or magazine articles.

Reserve two class periods for students to list and discuss important public issues that they hear on the news, read about in books, and study in history and science (Parker, 2002). You might start the list by writing a topic, for example "poverty" or "prejudice," on a chart. As students construct the list, it becomes clear that biographies might show how such issues had an impact on people's beliefs, values, and their chosen career.

Important Public Issues

poverty	prejudice	diversity	unity
environment	health care	education	homeless
American dream	civil rights	women's rights	service
equal opportunity	crime	discrimination	power
taxation	prisons	peace	safety

★ Pages 336–341 contain excerpts from "Multiple Texts: Multiple Opportunities for Teaching and Learning" by Laura Robb, which appeared in *Voices From the Middle,* Vol. 9, No. 4 (May, 2002). Copyright 2002 by NCTE. Reprinted with permission.

Specific Purposes
Create Active Readers

During the weeks that students read the biographies, reserve 15 to 20 minutes of class time for independent reading. Have students jot notes on Post-its whenever they find a section that addresses the public issues on our chart. They read to explore how their subjects dealt with an issue or how specific issues affected those people's lives. Post-its remain in the texts so students can cite specific examples

April 10, 1943

Dearest Franklin,

I have just completed my inspection of the New York State Penitentiary and was compelled to write you while the horrific images were still fresh in my mind. Even though the prisoners confined there have committed very serious crimes, the institution itself is committing the most serious crime imaginable, the violation of basic human rights. The prisoners are treated unthinkably, like they are no better than the homeless mutts that roam the Manhattan streets. The guards seemed quite proud that the convicts cowered in fear at their every word. The guards curse and otherwise mentally abuse the poor prisoners. They shout vulgar words and phrases in the prisoners ears at such a high volume that the prisoners' ears sometimes bleed! The guards are physically abusive as well. I saw one guard beat a convict over the head with his food tray while he was patiently waiting for his meal. I quickly confronted the guard about his shocking actions and he replied, "He wasn't moving".

The meals at the New York State Penitentiary are disgraceful as well. The menu stated that the afternoon meal was to be chicken with various vegetables and applesauce, but to my utter dismay, the food that was prepared was almost unrecognizable. The chicken was old and moldy, the vegetables had worms crawling among them, and the applesauce was simply sludge with chunks of apples floating along the top. I was forced to cover my nose with my handkerchief to keep from retching. The prisoners' cells were simply unlivable. The hanging beds were unstable and rusted, and the mattresses were infested with fleas. The lavatories were foul with waste and the floors of the cells were filthy as well. They were covered with dirt and rat droppings and I was so horrified I nearly grabbed a broom and cleaned them myself!

The New York Sate Penitentiary is in violation of basic human rights and should be shut down immediately. It is dangerous, possibly deadly for the prisoners to be kept there. Until improvements are made, they should be moved to various other penitentiaries in the New York area.

On a lighter note, I hope you are well and I miss you with all of my heart.

Your loving wife,
Eleanor

Sage, an eighth grader, steps into Eleanor Roosevelt's shoes and expresses her feelings about the state penitentiary.

Michael Jordan   December 17
BY Mitchell Krugel

The issue of dishonesty and cheating comes up in my biography. In one season Jordan broke a bone in his foot. He missed 64 games because of this. When he finally came back, his coaches wanted him to sit out the rest of the season. Jordan worked out a deal with them allowing him seven minutes a game.

Jordan contended that his not playing was messing up the chemistry of the team. He lashed out at his coach, saying that he was being held to a minimum of minutes because the manager of the team thought if they didn't make the playoffs, they would be elligible for one of the first picks of men straight out of college. It got ridiculous when he was taken out of a win over Indianapolis with :31 seconds left in the game. Finally the coaches let him play. My biography is pretty good as biographies go, and I'm glad I picked this book.

Bobby's journal entry spotlights issues that affected Michael Jordan.

while discussing the issues with a partner and completing journal entries. After reading Russell Freedman's biography, Sage composes a letter to Franklin Roosevelt that Eleanor Roosevelt might have written. The letter shows Sage's understanding of how an issue shaped Mrs. Roosevelt's thinking and her demand for action.

Relating biography to public issues helped students view their texts as more than data about an interesting person. "At first, I thought looking for issues would

Teaching Reading in Social Studies, Science, and Math

be boring," Bobby admitted. His first journal entry celebrated Michael Jordan's talent, but a later entry explained that Jordan stood for more than basketball (see page 342).

Multiple texts enable teachers to offer students books they can read (and want to read), to improve students' application of reading-thinking strategies, build confidence, develop the motivation to learn, and provide their students with opportunities to make meaningful contributions to discussions. Moreover, varied texts provide multiple perspectives to help students rethink events and issues that impact everyone and to deepen their knowledge of literary genres.

Seventh Graders' Questions for Their Civil War Study

- What were the differences between the North and South states?
- Why did the war start?
- How did the Underground Railroad work?
- Were slaves' lives different and why?
- Why was the South for slavery?
- Why was the North against slavery?
- How did the war affect families?
- What were the important battles?
- Why did the North win?
- What did the Emancipation Proclamation say?
- How did Lincoln's assassination affect the country?
- When did the slave trade start?
- Why did young men want to sign up for the army on both sides?
- How did the secret codes work for the Underground Railroad?
- What did this war have in common with other wars?
- Could the differences have been solved a different way?
- What can we use from this war to help us deal with conflicts today?

In this case, the teacher added the last question because she wanted students to apply their knowledge to current events. For a study to be constructivist and centered around students' inquiries, they should generate most of the questions.

Refining the Questions

An eighth-grade history student from Warren County Junior High wrote on the back of her "Content Area Reading Strategy Checklist":

> The stuff I didn't check is because asking questions doesn't work b/c I
> don't really know what kind of info I'm going to get. I have to read it
> before I really know what it's about.

This and similar comments helped the history teacher recognize that he needed to spend more time preparing students for a study so they could pose meaningful questions prior to reading (see pages 74–83).

The open-ended questions that follow have been composed by students with guidance from their teachers. Use them to generate discussions when students read multiple texts to study a theme or topic.

Open-Ended Genre Questions and Prompts
Biography
- Are there primary sources, photographs, or narrative elements? How do these help you better understand the person's life and times?
- Does the author differentiate between fact and opinion? How?
- Did your opinion of this person change as you read the book? Point out the change and explain what caused it.
- Why is this person important?
- Identify and discuss three problems this person overcame.
- Explain how two to three key events and people influenced this person's life.
- Evaluate some of the key decisions this person made, and explain how each decision influenced his or her life.
- Why do you think this person was able to realize his or her personal dreams and hopes?
- Has the book affected or changed your way of thinking? Explain how.

Historical Fiction
- Show how events and people in the past are similar to those in the present.
- Compare and contrast family relationships and people's values in the novel to your own family life and values.
- Do you believe that the same situation(s) could occur today? Explain your position.
- How do people cope with economic problems, such as scarcity of food, finding a job, obtaining housing?

- What did you learn about a different culture and way of life?
- How are you like a specific character? Do you face similar problems? Do you solve them in similar ways?
- Do the events in the book create social, political, and economic change? Discuss the changes.
- How are women and minorities portrayed? Are they stereotyped? Give examples to support your opinion.

Science Fiction

- Point out the scientific advances in society. How do these advances in technology affect the characters' decisions and actions?
- Compare the problems characters face in the story with problems people face today. Show how they are they alike and/or different.
- Evaluate life in the future as described in your book. Would you like to live there? What are the advantages and disadvantages?
- Does the story offer hope for humanity or is it a warning? Explain.
- Why might you consider this future world alien?
- How do people fit into this futuristic society? Are they subordinate to machines? Has democracy vanished? See if you can identify changes and offer reasons for these changes.

Discussion questions and prompts for Information Books can be found on pages 80, 171, 312–317.

TRY LITERATURE CLUSTERS TO EXTEND LEARNING

By blending a group of eight to twelve books of varied literary genres that relate to a topic, you create a *literature cluster* (Hancock, 2000). Clusters enrich and support a topic because students read narrative, poetry, and nonfiction that relate to and widen the lens focused on that topic. Clusters extend content area learning and can be organized to meet a wide range of reading abilities. Read more about literature clusters in *A Celebration of Literature and Response: Children, Books, and Teachers in K–8 Classrooms* by M.R. Hancock (Merrill, pages 291–302).

Evaluating Nonfiction Books

Your librarian is an excellent resource for helping you choose high-quality nonfiction literature for your students. You'll also find resources in your school and/or public library (see box, page 349) that offer reviews of children's literature for math, science, and social studies.

As you read and integrate literature into your curriculum, you'll also need some guidelines that will help you pick books that are worthy of reading and discussing. Strive to offer your students a variety of books ranging from satisfactory to outstanding. Such a mix can compensate for a book you rate "good" but want students to experience (Bamford and Kristo, 1998; Brown and Tomlinson, 1998).

Two fifth graders partner read.

Teaching Reading in Social Studies, Science, and Math

Guidelines for Selecting Nonfiction

When selecting nonfiction trade books for students, consider these elements as you review titles:

Accuracy

So you can offer books based on what is true and timely. Here are quick tips to rating a text for accuracy:

- When the book was written will tell you if the material is current or outdated.
- The author's experience in the field helps you determine his or her qualifications.
- The acknowledgments offer others in a specific field who have supported the author's research.
- Information at the back or in the introduction that explains the writer's research process.
- A list of additional readings.

Example: *There Goes the Neighborhood: Ten Buildings People Loved to Hate* by Susan Goldman Rubin, Holiday House, 2001.

Clear, direct, and easy-to-understand writing style

Reviewers favor a less-is-more approach, where the style is conversational but compressed, where word choice is interesting and sentences varied.

Example: *Red, White, Blue, and Uncle Who? The Stories behind Some of Americas Patriotic Symbols* by Teresa Bateman, illustrated by John O'Brien, Holiday House, 2001.

Informative captions and labels

These brief snippets of text should be written in clear prose because they are often the key to helping readers understand the significance of a chart, graph, photograph, or picture. The question to ask is: Do captions extend the text or merely repeat it?

Example: *Wild, Wet, and Windy* by Claire Llewellyn, Candlewick, 1997.

Fact, opinion, and theory are clearly differentiated

For example, the author hedges using qualifiers such as "maybe" or "perhaps" or "might be" or "can be inferred" to distinguish between facts and hunches the author offers.

Example: *The Great Little Madison* by Jean Fritz, Putnam, 1989.

Anthropomorphism

Making animals and non-living things appear human by having them talk and feel like people is fine for fantasy, fairy and folk tale, but not for nonfiction texts. Examples of anthropomorphism are writing that a worm enjoys eating soil or a dog feels happiness when he finds his master. It is also unscientific to explain the forces of nature in human terms, saying that autumn wears its colorful robes or that spring has painted bright colors on plants and trees.

Visual appeal is important to readers of nonfiction.

Attractive covers, intriguing photographs or illustrations, and a careful balance of text and visuals grab and hold readers' attention.

Example: *Ms. Frizzle's Adventures: Ancient Egypt* by Joanna Cole, illustrated by Bruce Degan, Scholastic, 2001.

Visuals should be appropriate to the content.

Sometimes, as in Seymour Simon's books, photographs are more appropriate, especially when excellent ones are available. However, drawings can call attention to specific details, too, and sometimes nonfiction uses art and engravings created in the past to recreate an historical period or reactions to an invention.

Example: *The Universe* by Seymour Simon, HarperCollins, 1998.

Text and visuals avoid stereotyping.

Look to see whether the book contains positive images of different cultures and historical periods; images in text and pictures that avoid stereotyping are essential.

Example: *Christmas in the Big House, Christmas in the Quarters* by Patricia McKissack and Frederick L. McKissack, illustrated by John Thompson, Scholastic, 1994.

The topic should be appropriate to the age of the audience.

Giving students books on subjects that are too difficult for them to comprehend creates frustration, anxiety, and turns students away from books. Offer books on topics that children can relish.

Example: *The Magic of Mozart: The Magic Flute and the Salzburg Marionettes.* Photographs by Costas, Atheneum, 1995.

Resources to Help You Select Nonfiction

If your school library does not subscribe to these resources, encourage your librarian to reserve funds for some of these. Many schools have Parent–Teacher organizations that raise money for books, and local public libraries often have many of these resources.

- *The Best in Children's Nonfiction: Reading, Writing, and Teaching Orbis Pictus Award Books,* J. M. Jensen, R.H. Kerper, & M. Zarnowski, (Eds.), National Council of Teachers of English, 2001.
- *Book Links: Connecting Books, Libraries, and Classrooms.* A bimonthly magazine that explores themes, many in science and social studies. Includes annotated books lists and teaching ideas. (American Library Association, 50 East Huron St., Chicago, IL 60611.)
- *Eyeopeners II* by Beverly Kobrin: Includes an introduction to nonfiction for children and an annotated list of 800 recommended books. New York: Scholastic, 1995.
- *The Horn Book Guide,* published by The Horn Book, Inc., is a biannual publication that organizes books by genre, subject, and age appropriateness. Reviewers rate books from 1 to 6. I urge teachers to order books with ratings of 1, 2, or 3, but the best books are those rated 1 and 2. (The Horn Book, Inc., 56 Roald St., Suite 200, Boston, MA 02129.)
- *It's the Story That Counts: More Children's Books for Mathematical Learning K–6,* by Whitin and Wilde, Portsmouth, NH: Heinemann.
- *The Kobrin Letter: Concerning Children's Books About Real People, Places, and Things.* Uses a newsletter format to review new and top-notch old information books on selected topics (732 Greer Rd., Palo Alto, CA 94303).
- "Notable Children's Trade Books for a Global Society" is an annual annotated list published in *The Dragon Lode,* the magazine for the international Reading Association's Special Interest Group on Reading and Literature. This biannual magazine contains annotated lists of outstanding fiction and nonfiction on various topics. (Obtain the name and address of the current Membership Chair from IRA, 800 Barksdale Rd., P.O. Box 8139, Newark, DE 19714.)
- "Notable Children's Trade Books in Social Studies" is annotated and published annually in the April/May issue of *Social Education,* 3501 Newark St. N.W., Washington, D.C. 20016.
- "Outstanding Science Trade Books for Children" is an annual annotated list of science books published in the March issue of *Science and Children,* NSTA, 1840 Wilson Blvd., Arlington, VA 22201.
- "Orbis Pictus Award-Winners, Honor Books, and Notables" is published annually in *Language Arts.*
- *Read Any Good Math Lately? Children's Books for Mathematical Learning* by Whitin and Wilde, Portsmouth, NH: Heinemann, 1992.
- *Searchit.heinemann.com.* A website that contains the newest and best science trade books.
- *The Wonderful World of Mathematics,* edited by Thiessen and Matthias, Reston, VA: National Council of Teachers of Mathematics, 1992.

Nonfiction Read-Alouds

Many teachers shy away from reading nonfiction aloud because they feel reading an entire text will bore students. However, unlike narrative stories, you don't have to read an entire nonfiction book. (Taberski, 2001; Vardell; 1998). Vardell points out that, in fact, "most nonfiction books do not lend themselves to cover-to-cover read-aloud" (page 153) because the amount of new information and vocabulary in a text can overwhelm students, and they stop listening once they're on overload.

You can introduce students to the variety of nonfiction by reading part or all of a letter, a diary entry, newspaper story, famous speech or political document, biography or autobiography, interview, even part of an almanac. The more students experience nonfiction, the more they internalize how the structure of different texts works. When students develop a deep knowledge of how a biography or diary entries work, they have a wider choice of what form their own writing should take.

One year, a sixth-grade teacher asked students to write autobiographies; the class had three weeks to complete this assignment at home. When the teacher showed me the papers, her face sagged with the disappointment she felt. "No one wrote more than half a page," she moaned. "Half a page in three weeks!" We chatted for a while, and she vented her anger and frustration. Then I gently asked, "Do your students really know much about the structure and purpose of an autobiography?" A long pause ensued; it felt like infinity, but I said nothing. "I better find out," she said between tightened lips and marched down the hall to her room.

A week later, the teacher stopped me in the hallway and continued our conversation as if no time had lapsed. "Not one student had ever read an autobiography," she said. "Less than half had read a biography. No wonder I got nothing." How right she was.

Through read-alouds, you can expand students' knowledge

Teaching Reading in Social Studies, Science, and Math

of how nonfiction texts work, providing them with background knowledge about different genres so they can make informed choices. This translates into students choosing,
even daring, to try a newly understood genre in their writing.

Recommended Read-Alouds

Nonfiction: Grades 3 to 5

- *And Then What Happened, Paul Revere?* by Jean Fritz, Harper, 1987.
- *Flight: The Journey of Charles Lindbergh* by Robert Burleigh, illustrated by Mike Wimmer, Philomel, 1991.
- *Faithful Elephants* by Yukin Tsuchiya, illustrated by Ted Lewin; translated by Tomoko Tsuchiya Dykes, Houghton, 1988.
- *Bill Peet: An Autobiography,* by Bill Peet, Houghton, 1989.
- *So You Want to Be President?* by Judith St. George, illustrated by David Small, Philomel, 2000
- *Wild and Swampy: Exploring With Jim Arnosky,* HarperCollins, 2001.

Nonfiction: Grades 6 to 8

- *The Chimpanzees I Love: Saving Their World and Ours* by Jane Goodall, Scholastic, 2000.
- *Letters from a Slave Girl: The Story of Harriet Jacobs* by Mary Lyons, Scribners, 1992.
- *Leonardo da Vinci* by Diane Stanley, Morrow, 1996.
- *Through My Eyes* by Ruby Bridges, Scholastic, 1999.
- *The Mystery of the Mammoth Bones: And How It Was Solved* by James Cross Giblin, HarperCollins, 1999.

- *Traitor: The Case of Benedict Arnold* by Jean Fritz, Putnam, 1981.

Historical Fiction: Grades 3 to 5

- *Bound for Oregon* by Jean Van Leeuwen, pictures by James Watling, Dial, 1994.
- *Coolies* by Yin, illustrated by Chris Soentpiet, Philomel, 2001.
- *The Fighting Ground* by Avi, Lippincott, 1984.
- *Our House: The Stories of Levittown,* illustrated by Brian Sleznick, Scholastic, 1995.
- *Pink and Say* by Patricia Polacco, Philomel, 1994.
- *Sees Behind Trees* by Michael Dorros, Hyperion, 1996.

Historical Fiction: Grades 6 to 8

- *Adjeemah and His Son* by James Berry, HarperCollins 1992.
- *Lyddie* by Katherine Paterson, Lodestar, 1991.
- *The Librarian Who Measured the Earth* by Kathryn Lasky, illustrated by Kevin Hawkes, Little Brown, 1994.
- *Pharoah's Daughter: A Novel of Ancient Egypt,* by Julius Lester, Harcourt, 2000.
- *Sacajawea* by Joseph Bruchac, Harcourt, 2000.
- *The Watsons Go to Birmingham—1963* by Christopher Paul Curtis, Delacorte, 1995.

Read-Aloud Selections and Primary Sources

**Read-Aloud Selections
From Top-Notch Primary Sources**

- *Hold Fast to Your Dreams: Twenty Commencement Speeches,* collected by Carrie Boyko and Kimberly Colen, Scholastic, 1996. Grades 5 and up.
- *Anne Frank: Diary of a Young Girl,* by Anne Frank, Simon & Schuster, 1958. Grades 6 and up.
- *Zlata's Diary: A Child's Life in Sarajevo,* by Zlata Filipovic, Viking, 1994. Grades 4 and up.
- *Slavery Time: When I Was Chillun,* by Belinda Hummence [based on oral histories of former slaves], Putnam, 1997. Grades 6 and up.
- *Words That Build a Nation* by Marilyn Miller, Scholastic, 1999. Grades 5 and up.

**Read-Aloud Selections
That Include Primary Sources**

- *At Her Majesty's Request: An African Princess in Victorian England,* by Walter Dean Myers, Scholastic, 1999. Grades 3 and up.
- *Christopher Columbus: Voyager to the Unknown* by Nancy S. Levinson, Dutton Children's Books, 1990, Grades 3 and up.
- *Keeping Secrets: The Girlhood Diaries of Seven Women Writers,* by Mary Lyons, Henry Holt, 1995. Grades 3 and up.
- *Now Is Your Time! The African-American Struggle for Freedom,* by Walter Dean Myers, HarperCollins, 1991. Grades 6 and up.
- *Starry Messenger: A Book Depicting the Life of a Famous Scientist, Mathematician, Astronomer, Philosopher, Physicist,* by Peter Sis, Farrar, Straus, Giroux, 1996. Grades 3 and up.
- *Voices from the Civil War: A Documentary History of the Great American Conflict,* by Milton Meltzer, Crowell, 1989. Grades 5 and up.

Student-Led Book Discussions: A Key Piece to Using Literature Successfully in the Content Areas

That the desire, the urge, to talk and share great parts of a book, ask questions, and exchange opinions with someone who has read it is a common experience among readers, is evident from the great number of adult book clubs. Our students share the same desires. Janice Amalsi ("A New View of Discussion," in *Lively Discussions: Fostering Engaged*

Reading, 1996) points out that when students exchange ideas about their reading, they "collaboratively construct meanings or consider alternate interpretations of the text in order to arrive at new understandings" (page 2). Conversations also start with the reading of a text, when the reader interacts with the author's words.

Louise Rosenblatt showed that reading is not a static experience, nor is there one interpretation of a text (1983; 1978). Instead, the reader transacts with the text, talks to the author using what the reader knows, has experienced and is learning, while reading to shape these transactions and constructed meanings. Rosenblatt's research forms the foundation of the importance of discussing texts because each reader brings a different perspective, making collaborative dialogue diverse (Beck et al., 1997; Evans, 2001; Gambrell, 1996, Weaver and Alvermann, 2000). The example of three eighth graders discussing different books on the Holocaust, each one at student's independent reading level, highlights the benefits of using multiple texts that relate to a theme.

Books read by Sally, Sloan, and Ryan:

- *Nightfather* by Carl Friedman, Sundance, 1992.
- *The Upstairs Room* by Johanna Reiss, HarperCollins, 1972
- *The Endless Steppe* by Esther Hautzig, Harper Collins, 1968.

Student-Generated Discussion Question:

Can you show how the Holocaust affected the main character's life?

What follows is an excerpt from a long discussion:

SLOAN: *Ephraim,* [Nightfather] *survived the concentration camps. He's married and has children. In our world that never had to endure beatings, starvation, sleeping in feces, Ephraim seems crazy. His family says his disease is "camp."*

SALLY: *What's "camp?"*

SLOAN: *It's acting crazy. Yelling. Hiding. Saying things that don't make sense. Thinking the Nazis are everywhere trying to get you. I guess you could say the experience made him paranoid. But I can see why.*

SALLY: *It's weird, in my book* [The Endless Steppe], *Esther leaves a comfortable home and is sent to Siberia to the frozen wasteland—steppe country. She works in potato fields, lives in a crowded cottage with another family, but when she's free to return to Poland, Esther wants to stay. She's in school and has made a life. It's like Esther adapted more than Ephraim did.*

RYAN: *I think that's one of the important ideas. The ones who survived it [the Holocaust] were changed, but for each one it was different. Even though the two girls [in* The Upstairs Room*] had to hide in a tiny room, the Oostervelds treated them like their own children. They didn't want the girls to leave when freedom came. The end [of the war] was sad for the Oostervelds like for the Jews.*

Different texts enabled students to collect a variety of ways that imprisonment and survival affected Jewish prisoners. Students came to understand that each type of prison caused different reactions, but all three agreed that the concentration camps caused the greatest emotional scars.

Suggestions for Scheduling Student-Led Book Discussions

There's no right or wrong way to integrate the discussion of nonfiction and historical fiction into your curriculum. Here are some suggestions to consider:

- Schedule, on a regular basis, discussions of parts of your textbook in history or science. In math, students can talk about diverse ways to solve a problem, the meaning of an explanation or sample problem, or share journal entries (see pages 60–61).

- Integrate literature into your program all year long, setting aside two to three discussion sessions each week. Time constraints and limitations may stem from schedules, the goals set by teacher and students, the riches (information) within the text, and the age of students (younger students might not be able to sustain a conversation as well as older students). It

RESOURCE TO CONSIDER

Great Grouping Strategies: Practical Ways to Group Students Flexibly for Social, Emotional, and Academic Growth by Ronit M. Wrubel (Scholastic, 2002).

may be impossible to feel that a book has been totally and thoroughly explored. But that's the joy of literature!

- Reserve one period every six to eight weeks for students to discuss books they have read that relate to a topic or theme. Choose from the open-ended prompts on pages 344–345 to stimulate discussion or invite students to create their own questions.
- Focus your integration of literature in a four- to eight-week period and during that time, hold short discussions.
- Make nonfiction literature the centerpiece of your studies and your reading program, and invite students to discuss materials daily.

Organizing Student-Led Groups for Book Discussions

When John Lathrop or Dick Bell and I team-teach combined history and English, students sit in six groups of four. We change groups every four to six weeks so students gain experience learning with many personalities and abilities. As Michael Opitz recommends (1998), when choosing groups, we create a flexible, heterogeneous mix of students who will share the work load equitably and support one another. Reasons for grouping depend on the nature of the work and/or study, including:

- a common book
- similar interests
- an author study
- same project or experiment
- a common problem to solve
- jigsawing a text (see pages 264–266)
- a research project
- same topic.

"Some students in my history class always complain that they do all the work. I hear groans from them when I organize groups. That's why I've decreased the amount of group work and discussions," Bill Schriber, said. "It's always the same kids who present the groups' findings to everyone and the same ones who do the talking and thinking." Many teachers feel like Bill. I have travelled that road, too. However, I have found that groups work successfully and distribute the work evenly when there are specific guidelines and roles for students. Rotations for specific jobs can occur weekly, after two to four sessions, or by negotiating changes with your students.

Some Guidelines for Group Book Discussions

The tips that follow will enable you to negotiate guidelines with students before engaging them in discussions.

- **Choose a group leader** and rotate this position, so every student experiences this role. The leader checks that everyone has read the material, has a journal, pencil, etc., and is prepared to work. If a student hasn't read the work, they should do so before returning to the group. Participating when unprepared is unfair to those who have completed their work and also offers an opportunity for a student to gather enough information to continue to avoid reading.

  Group leaders review the negotiated guidelines for discussion, the behavior guidelines (see page 261), and distribute the work among members. This can mean creating x number of questions, selecting main ideas and supporting details, designing and completing a graphic organizer, taking journal notes of key points, or coming up with a plan to share with everyone.

- **Invite a student to be the group's spokesperson,** and rotate this position, too. The spokesperson summarizes the group's discussion during a whole-class share. Group members can add points after the spokesperson shares.

- **Require that all group members take notes** on the main points covered in the discussion and those points they will present to the class.

- **Pace the work** by asking students to prepare and discuss one day and present to everyone the next day. This way you can also cover other material with students, such as previewing a new chapter, developing or extending a concept, or pre-teaching vocabulary, etc.

- **Note which students aren't involved** in the conversation as you circulate around the room. Join one or two groups as a member. Your job as "facilitator" is to ask an occasional question when conversation lulls and model how to move the discussion forward.

- **Post prompts** on chart paper (see page 258). These help students maintain the momentum of a discussion.

- **Develop behavior guidelines** with students (see page 261).

- **Offer positive feedback** that honors students' thinking and encourages diverse interpretations (see pages 258–259).

When Students Aren't Engaged in a Book Discussion

If your classes are like mine, every year there are students who don't join in discussions, even when you establish guidelines to engage everyone. Don't get frustrated; give students time—four to five discussion meetings. Then meet privately with each student and ask, "Can you tell me why you aren't participating?" Responses will range from "I don't want to look stupid," to "I don't like to talk in class," to "You can't make me talk."

True, it's impossible to make a student participate. What's helpful is to build their trust in you and create a "safe" classroom, where risking an answer doesn't result in students shouting put-downs, such as "That's dumb," or "Can't you read?" Seventh grader Dave was honest in his evaluation of group discussions when he wrote in his journal:

> I hate group discussions. I don't want to talk. They always say: come on, don't you have something to tell us or what is your opinion. They make fun of me when no teacher is around. Discussions make me miserable.

Dave wrote this entry at the end of February. He opened the door for a series of conversations with me. During our meetings, Dave and I would discuss a book, and I worked to build his confidence. Finally, Dave agreed to participate, and I gave him the open-ended question to prepare at home. The next day, I joined Dave and his group, and pointed out how well Dave used text details to support his idea. When Jimmie said, "You found three pieces of support—that's great," I looked at Dave and watched him grin. One positive experience is not enough to transform students' perceptions, however. Dave received my support several times before I felt he was ready to tackle a response without a question and my presence.

Helping students like Dave participate comfortably takes time and patience. Here are some helpful and encouraging measures to take:

- Have several brief meetings.
- Get to know students and let them know you.
- Discover their hobbies, favorite sports, extracurricular interests, and movies they have enjoyed. Open conversations with this information to build trust.

- Invite students to prepare for the discussion at home. Knowing a question in advance makes taking the plunge easier. (But allowing students to prepare at home should never take the place of creating a "safe" environment in your classroom.)
- Stop students' critical comments immediately; hurtful words will play over and over in students' minds.

Samantha, a sixth grader, was only interested in talking about her boyfriend or her weekend plans. "When I meet with my group," she told me, "I don't want to talk about my ideas. I want to talk about Jason and the movie we saw." Every class has its share of Daves and Samanthas who challenge us daily. Expecting the entire class to participate fully and freely is an unrealistic goal. Based on my experience and observations of other teachers' struggles, a wide range of students' reactions toward discussions are the norm.

Pause and Reflect on: Integrating Nonfiction Books

Ray Legge invites his sixth and eighth graders to read biographies and nonfiction chapter books, poetry, and historical fiction that relate to their studies of the natural world and physical science. After negotiating a due date, Ray sets aside one class period for pairs or groups to discuss their reading and share one to two memorable points with the class. "One period, three to four times a year doesn't cut into my curriculum—it adds to it," Ray points out. "Besides gaining knowledge, my students are learning how nonfiction texts work, and this improves their writing and reading."

You can develop a curriculum based on informational texts, or like Ray Legge, periodically bring your students and informational books together. In either case, you will broaden their understanding of the world while introducing them to the great variety of the nonfiction genre.

Here's a checklist I recommend teachers visit at the start of the year, and at least twice during the year, to evaluate how they are using nonfiction.

_____ Do I bring informational texts into the classroom to offer students multiple reading levels and perspectives?

_____ Do I set aside time for students to collaborate to construct meanings?

_____ Do I model and invite students to practice close readings?

_____ Do I invite students to dramatize events so they experience the past?

Final Reflections

Taking the Journey

The teaching journey has been *the great adventure* of my life. Every day I step over the threshold of my classroom, I walk off the map into unknown territory. I can't predict what my middle school students will say, feel, or whether all of them have completed their reading or journal work. Like chameleons, students' emotions change color, depending on what happened at breakfast, on the bus, and between classes. To a certain extent, unpredictability is part of life in the classroom—no matter how expert a teacher you are. I like it that way. It forces me to listen, watch, think, and use what I know about how children learn to draw conclusions and make impromptu decisions and revise others.

But teaching is also more than me and my students. It's curriculum, bus rides, recess, and lunch duty, filling out forms, keeping attendance records, writing report cards, conferring with happy and disgruntled parents, and planning lessons that actively involve students. It's learning new content, grading tests and written work, and meeting state standards. My day starts early, ends late, and students and curricular issues even invade my dreams. The journey envelops me day and night, and I've had to find ways to reduce frustration and feelings of being overwhelmed by too many tasks. Like you, though, teaching is only one part of my life. I'm a mother, daughter, sister, wife, grandmother. I love to walk, hike, listen to music, see shows, and eat out with friends. Juggling all these roles is tough, but doable, especially once I recognized that I need a personal life.

Resist buying into that joyful and wild thought we all have after completing a book or attending a conference: *I can't wait to get back to school and do it all.* Think it and enjoy the moment of willow-wild energy. But resist temptation. Instead, I offer these suggestions:

If You're a First-Year Teacher: Take an inventory of what you know about strategy lessons and your practice-teaching experiences. Consider your subject and how many different preps you have each day. Pick one strategy you would like to try. Model, collect student feedback, jot down in a notebook what worked and what still needs refining. Question an experienced peer and gather feedback on your teaching.

Once you're comfortable, add a second learning strategy. It's fine if you can only manage one new strategy your first year. In fact, you're doing great! Don't try more than two.

If You've Taught for a Few Years: Now that you know your colleagues, find a peer partner, someone you trust, someone you can talk to candidly and from whom you can expect supportive feedback. Choose two strategies you'd like to try, but make sure you work through each one separately. If all you can manage is one new strategy, feel good about yourself. Jot down notes relating to what worked with that strategy and what should be fine-tuned.

Develop the habit of reading two to three professional journal articles and one professional book each year. Invite your peer partner to read the articles and the same book so you can discuss ideas and reactions. Ask your librarian or a colleague to recommend two to three children's books that relate to your subject. Read them and share with your students.

If You're an Experienced Teacher: Beware of hooking into the temptation to do too much. Each year, I like to bring two to three new strategies to students and improve one I've already tried. Introduce one at a time. If the demands of your personal life dictate doing less, then do less and put aside those guilty feelings.

Try to read one professional journal article a week. Share top-notch articles with colleagues, especially inexperienced teachers. Set the goal of reading at least one to three professional books and several children's trade books that relate to your subject. Integrate trade books into your curriculum.

Throughout your teaching journey, remember to take time to nurture your soul and do things beyond teaching—things you love. These experiences will give you riches to share with students and others. They will ground you in what's important and meaningful. They will enable you to reflect and create, dream and hope. They will be the beacon that guides your teaching journey.

Bibliography of
Professional Books & Articles

"Adolescent literacy comes of age." (1999). In *Reading Today.* Newark, DE: The International Reading Assoc., (17) (1).

Allen, J. (1999). *Words, Words, Words: Teaching vocabulary in grades 4–12.* York, ME: Stenhouse.

Allington, R.L. (1998). Introduction, In *Teaching Struggling Readers: Articles from the reading teacher,* R.L. Allington, ed. Newark, DE: The International Reading Assoc.

Almasi, J. (1996). "A new view of discussion." In L. Gambrell & J.F. Almasi (Eds.) *Lively Discussions: Fostering Engaged Reading.* Newark, DE: The International Reading Assoc.

Alvermann, D.E. (2000). "Classroom talk about texts: Is it dear, cheap, or a bargain at any price?" In B.M. Taylor, M.F. Graves, & P. Van Den Broek (Eds.), *Reading for Meaning: Fostering comprehension in the middle grades.* Newark, DE: International Reading Association and New York, NY: Teachers College Press.

Alvermann, D.E., O'Brien, D.G. & Dillon, D.R. (1990). "What teachers do when they say they're having discussions of content area reading assignments" In *Reading Research Quarterly,* 30, 314–351.

Alvermann, D.E. & Phelps, S.E. (1998). *Content Reading and Literacy: Succeeding in today's diverse classrooms,* (2nd ed.). Boston, MA: Allyn and Bacon.

Alvermann, D.E., Dillon, D.R. & O'Brien, G.E. (1988). *Using Discussions to Promote Reading Comprehension.* Newark, DE: The International Reading Assoc.

Anderson, R. (1984). "Role of reader's schema in comprehension, learning and memory." In R. Anderson, J. Osbourne, & .R. Tierney, (Eds.), *Learning to Read in American Schools.* Hillsdale, NJ: Lawrence Erlbaum Assoc.

Andrews, S.E. (1997). "Writing to learn in content area reading class." In *Journal of Adolescent & Adult Literacy,* (41), 141-142.

Armbruster, B.B. (1991). "Silent reading and learning from text." In *The Reading Teacher,* (45), 154-155.

Aronson, E., Stephan, C., Sikes J., Blaney, N. & Snapp, M. (1978). *The Jigsaw Classroom.* Beverly Hills, CA: Sage.

Asher, S.R. (1978). *Influence of interest on black children's and white children's reading comprehension.* (Technical Report No. 99). Urbana, IL: University of Illinois Center for the Study of Reading.

Atwell, N. (1987, 1999). *In the Middle: Writing, reading and learning with adolescents.* Portsmouth, NH: Heinemann.

Bamford, R.A. & Kristo, J.V. (Eds.) (1998). *Making Facts Come Alive: Choosing quality nonfiction literature K–8.* Norwood, MA: Christopher-Gordon.

Barr, R., Sadow, M.& Blackowicz, C. (1990). *Reading Diagnosis for Teachers: An instructional approach.* New York, NY: Longman.

Battistich, V., Solomon, D., & Delucchi, K. (1993). "Interaction processes and student outcomes in cooperative learning groups." In *The Elementary School Journal,* 94, 19–32.

Baumann, J.R., Jones, L.A., & Seifert-Kessell. N. (1993). "Using think-alouds to enhance children's comprehension monitoring abilities." In *The Reading Teacher.* (47), 187-199.

Bear, D.R., Invernizzi, M., Templeton, S., & Johnston, F. (2000). *Words Their Way: Word study for phonics, vocabulary, and spelling instruction.* Upper Saddle River, NJ: Merrill.

Beck, I.L. & McKeown, M.G. (1991). "Social studies texts are hard to understand: Mediating some of the difficulties." In *Language Arts,* 68 (6), 482–490.

Beck, I.L., McKeown, M.G., Hamilton, R.L., & Kucan, L. (1997). *Questioning the Author: An approach for enhancing students' engagement with text.* Newark, DE: International Reading Assoc.

Birchak, B., Conner, C., Crawford, K.M., Kahn, L.H., Kaser, S., Turner, S. and Short, K. (1998). *Teacher Study Groups: Building community through dialogue and reflection.* Urbana, IL: National Council of Teachers of English.

Blanton, W.E., Wood, K.D. & Moorman, G.B. (1990). "The role of response in reading instruction." In *The Reading Teacher,* (43), 626-631.

Boomer, G., Lester, C.O. & Cook, J. Eds. (1992). *Negotiating the Curriculum: Educating for the 21st century.* Washington, DC: Falmer Press.

Buehl, D. (2001). *Classroom Strategies for Interactive Learning.* 2nd ed. Newark, DE: International Reading Assoc.

Burke, J. (2000). *Reading Reminders: Tools, tips, and techniques.* Portsmouth, NH: Boyton/Cook.

Calkins, L.M., Montgomery, K., Santman, D. with Falk, B. (1999). *A Teacher's Guide to Standardized Reading Test: Knowledge is power.* Portsmouth, NH: Heinemann.

Cazden, D. (1976). "How knowledge about language helps the classroom teacher—or does it? A personl account" In *The Urban Review* 9, 74–91.

Chall, J.S., & Conrad, S.S. (1991). *Should Textbooks Challenge Students? The case for easier or harder books.* New York, NY: Teachers College Press.

Ciborowski, J. (1992). *Textbooks and the Students Who Can't Read Them: A guide to teaching content.* Boston, MA: Brookline Books.

Clay, M. (1979a). *The Early Detection of Reading Difficulties.* Portsmouth, NH: Heinemann.

Clay, M. (1979b). *Reading: The patterning of complex behavior.* Portsmouth, NH: Heinemann.

Coles, R. (1989). *The Call of Stories: Teaching and the moral imagination.* Boston, MA: Mariner Books.

Colvin, C., & Schlosser, L.K. (2000). "Developing academic confidence to build literacy: What teachers can do." In D.W. Moor, D.E. Alvermann, & K.A. Hinchman (Eds.), *Struggling Adolescent Readers: A collection of strategies.* Newark, DE: The International Reading Assoc.

Cunningham, P.M. & Allington, R.L. (1998). *Classrooms that Work: They all can read and write* (2nd. ed.). New York, NY: Addison-Wesley.

Donnelly, A. (2001). "Living the model." In H. Mills &. A. Donnelly (Eds.), *From the Ground Up: Creating a culture of inquiry.* Portsmouth, NH: Heinemann.

Dowhower, S.L. (1999). "Supporting a strategic stance in the classroom: A comprehension framework for helping teachers help students to be strategic." In *The Reading Teacher* (57), 672-688.

Duffelmeyer, F.A. (1994). "Effective anticipation guide statements for learning from expository prose." In *Journal of Reading* (37), 452-457.

Duke, Nell, K. 2000. "3.6 minutes per day: The scarcity of informational texts in first grade." In *Reading Research Quarterly,* (35), 202-224.

Duvall, R. (2001). "Refining and expanding our notions of inquiry, talk, and classroom community." In H. Mills & A. Donnelly (Eds.), *From the Ground Up: Creating a culture of inquiry.* Portsmouth, NH: Heinemann.

Estes, T.H. & Vaughan, J.L. (1973). "Reading interest and comprehension: Implications." *The Reading Teacher,* (27),149-153.

Estes, T.H., & Vasquez-Levy, D. (2001). "Literature as a source of information and values." In *Phi Delta Kappan.* (82) 7, 507-512.

Evans, K.S. (2001). *Literature Discussion Groups in the Intermediate Grades: Dilemmas and possibilities.* Newark, DE: International Reading Assoc.

Evans, R. (1988). "Teachers' conceptions of history revisited: Ideology, curriculum, and student belief." In *Theory and Research in Social Education,* (28), 101-138.

Fielding, L.G. & Pearson, P.D. (1994). "Reading comprehension: What works." In *Educational Leadership,* 51 (5), 1-7.

Flavell, J.H. (1981). "Cognitive monitoring." In W.P. Dickson, (Ed.), *Children's Oral Communication Skills.* San Diego, CA; Academic.

Fountas, I. & Pinnell, G.S. (1996). *Guided Reading: Good first teaching for all children.* Portsmouth, NH: Heinemann.

Fountas, I. & Pinnell, G.S. (2001). *Guided Readers and Writers (Grades 3–6): Teaching comprehension, genre, and content literacy.* Portsmouth, NH: Heinemann.

Frank, C.R., Dixon, C.N. & Brandts, L.R. (2001). "Bears, trolls, and pagemasters: Learning about learners in book clubs." In *The Reading Teacher,* 54, 448-463.

Fredericks, A.D. (1998). "Evaluating and using nonfiction literature in the science curriculum." In R.A. Bamford & J.V. Kristo, (Eds.), *Making Facts Come Alive: Choosing quality nonfiction literature K–8.* Norwood, MA: Christopher-Gordon.

Freeman, E.B. (1991). "Informational books: Models for students report writing." *Language Arts,* 68 (6), 470-473.

Freeman, E.B. & Person, D.G. (1998). *Connecting Informational Children's Books with Content Area Learning.* Needham Heights, MA: Allyn & Bacon.

Gambrell, L.D. (1996). "What research reveals about discussion." In L.B. Gambrell & J.F. Almasi (Eds.), *Lively Discussions! Fostering engaged reading,* Newark, DE: International Reading Assoc.

Garner, R. (1987). *Metacognition and Reading Comprehension.* Norwood, NJ: Ablex.

Garner, R. (1992). "Metacognition and self-monitoring strategies." In J. Samuels & A. Farstrup (Eds.), *What Research Has to Say about Reading Instruction,* (2nd ed.). Newark, DE: International Reading Assoc.

Garner, R. & Alexander, P. (1989). "Metacognition: Answered and uanswered questions." In *Educational Psychologist.* 24, 143-158.

Gillet, J.W. & Temple, C. (2000). *Understanding Reading Problems: Assessment and instruction.* New York, NY: Longman.

Glickman, C.D. (2000/2001). "Holding sacred ground: The impact of standardization." In *Education Leadership,* 56, 46-51.

Goodlad, J.L. (1994). *Educational Renewal: Better teachers, better schools.* San Francisco, CA: Jossey-Bass.

Goodman, Y. (1985). "Kidwatching: Observing children in the classroom." In A. Jaguar. & M.T. Smith-Burke (Eds.), *Observing the Language Learner.* Newark, DE: International Reading Assoc.

Graves, D.H. (1983). *Writing: Children and teachers at work.* Portsmouth, NH: Heinemann.

Graves, D.H. (1994). *A Fresh Look at Writing.* Portsmouth, NH: Heinemann.

Graves, M.F. & Graves, B.B. (1994). *Scaffolding Reading Experiences.* Norwood, MA: Christopher-Gordon.

Hansen, J. (1987). *When Writers Read.* (1st ed.) Portsmouth, NH: Heinemann.

Hansen, J. (2001). *When Writers Read.* (2nd ed.) Portsmouth, NH: Heinemann.

Harmon, J.M., Hedrick, W.B., & Fox, E.A. (2000). "A content analysis of vocabulary instruction in social science." In *The Elementary School Journal,* (100) 3, 2530271.

Harpaz, Y. & Adam, A. (2000). "Communities of thinking." In *Educational Leadership.* (58) 3, 54-58.

Harvey, S. (1998). *Nonfiction Matters: Reading, writing, and research in grades 3–8.* York, ME: Stenhouse.

Harvey, S. & Goudvis, A. (2000). *Strategies that Work: Teaching comprehension to enhance understanding.* York, ME: Stenhouse.

Heimlich, J.E. & Pittelman, S.D. (1990). *Semantic Mapping: Classroom applications.* Newark, DE; International Reading Assoc.

Herber, H.L. & Nelson, J.B. (1986). "Questioning is not the answer." In E.K. Dishner, T.W. Bean, J.E. Readence, & D.W. Moore (Eds.), *Reading in the Content Areas: Improving classroom instruction,* (2nd ed.). Dubuque, IA: Kendall/Hunt.

Ivey, G. (2000). "Reflections on teaching struggling middle school readers." In D.W. Moor, D.E. Alvermann, & K.A. Hinchman (Eds.), *Struggling Adolescent Readers: A collection of teaching strategies.* Newark, DE: International Reading Assoc.

Keene, E.O. & Zimmerman, S. (1997). *Mosaic of Thought.* Portsmouth, NH: Heinemann.

Klingner, J., Kettmann, S.V. & Schumm. J. S. (1991). "Collaborative strategic reading during social studies in heterogeneous fourth-grade classrooms." In *The Elementary School Journal,* (99) 1, 3-22.

Kohn, A. (1993). "Choices for children: Why and how to let students decide." In *Phi Delta Kappan,* (75) 1, 8-20.

Levstik, L.S. (1998). "To fling my arms wide: Students learning about the world through nonfiction." In *Making Facts Come Alive: Choosing quality nonfiction literature K–8.* R. A., Bamford & J.V. Kristo, (eds.) Norwood, MA: Christopher-Gordon.

Louth, C. & Young, D. (1992). "Negotiating interdisciplinary teaching and learning in secondary English/social studies." In G. Boomer, N. Lester, C. Onore, & J. Cook (Eds.), *Negotiating the Curriculum: Educating for the 21st century.* London: The Routledge Falmer Press.

Lynch-Brown, C.L. & Tomlinson, C. (1999). *Essentials of Children's Literature,* 3rd ed. (4th ed. 2001 available) Needham Heights, MA: Allyn & Bacon.

Manzo, A.V. (1968). *Improving Reading Comprehension Through Reciprocal Questioning.* Unpublished doctoral dissertation. Syracuse University. Primary reference.

Marshall, N., Glock, M. (1978-1979). "Comprehension of connected discourse." In *Reading Research Quarterly* 14, 10-56.

Maxim, D. (1998). "Nonfiction literature as the 'text' of my intermediate classroom: That's a fact." In *Making Facts Come Alive: Choosing quality nonfiction literature K-8.* R. A., Bamford & J.V. Kristo, (eds.) Norwood, MA: Christopher-Gordon.

Mazzoni, S.A. & Gambrell, L.B. (1996). "Text Talk: Using discussion to promote comprehension of information texts" In L.B. Gambrell & J.F. Almasi (Eds.) *Lively Discussions: Fostering engaged reading.* Newark, DE: International Reading Assoc.

McKenna, M.C. & Robinson, R.D. (1990). "Content literacy: A definition and implication." *Journal of Reading,* 34, 184-186.

Meltzer, M. (1993). "Voices from the past." In *The Story of Ourselves: Teaching history through children's literature.* M.O. Tunnell & R. Ammon (Eds.). Portsmouth, NH: Heinemann.

Merkley, D.M. & Jeffries, D. (2000/2001). "Guidelines for implementing a graphic organizer." In *The Reading Teacher,* 54, 350-357.

Meyer & Freedle. (1984). "Effects of discourse type on recall." *American Educational Research Journal.* 21 (1), 121-143.

Miller, K. & George, J. (1992). "Expository passage organizers: Models for reading and writing." In *Journal of Reading,* (35), 372-377.

Minsky, M. (1975). "A framework for representing knowledge." In *The Psychology of Computer Vision,* Winston, P.H. (Ed.). New York, NY: McGraw-Hill.

Moffet, J. (1981). *Active Voice: A writing program across the curriculum.* Portsmouth, NH: Boynton/Cook.

Moore, D.W. (1996). "Contexts for literacy in secondary school." In D.J. Leu, D.J., Kinzer, & K.A. Hinchman (Eds.), *Literacies for the Twenty-first Century: Research and practice,* Chicago, IL: National Reading Conference.

Morris, D., Ervin, C., & Conrad, K. (1998). "A case study of middle school reading disability." In R.L. Allington, Ed., *Teaching Struggling Readers: Articles from the reading teacher,* Newark, DE: International Reading Assoc.

Moss, S. & Fuller, M. (2000). "Implementing effective practices: Teachers' perspectives." In *Phi Delta Kappan,* 82(4), pp. 273-276.

Murray, D.M. (1982). *Learning by Teaching: Selected articles on writing and teaching.* Portsmouth, NH: Boynton/Cook.

Murray, D.M. (1984). *Write to Learn.* New York, NY: Holt, Rinehart and Winston.

Murray, D.M. (1996). *Crafting a Life in Essay, Story, Poem.* Portsmouth, NH: Boynton/Cook.

Nagy, W.E. (1988). *Teaching Vocabulary to Improve Reading Comprehension.* ERIC Clearinghouse, NCTE, and IRA.

National Assessment of Educational Progress (1999) *NAEP 1998 Reading Report Card for the Nation and the States* [Online]. Available on Internet: http://www.ed.gov/NCES/NAEP

Nordstom, V. (1992). "Reducing the Text Burden: Using children's literature and trade books in elementary school science education." *Reference Services Review,* Spring, 57-70.

Ogle, D.M. (1986). "K-W-L: A teaching model that develops active reading of expository text." In *The Reading Teacher,* 39, 564-570.

Ohanian, S. (1999). *One Size Fits Few: The folly of educational standards.* Portsmouth, NH: Heinemann.

O'Neal, S. & Kapinus, B. (2000). "Promoting literacy in grades 4–9." In T.S. Dickinson & K.D. Woods (Eds.), *Standards in the Middle: Moving beyond the basics.* Boston, MA: Allyn & Bacon.

Opitz, M.F. (1998). *Flexible Grouping in Reading.* New York, NY: Scholastic.

Opitz, M.F. & Rasinski, T.V. (1998). *Good-bye Round Robin: 25 Effective oral reading strategies.* Portsmouth, NH: Heinemann.

Owen, D. (1987). "Math discovery." In *Plain Talk: About learning and writing across the curriculum.* Self, J (Ed.) Virginia Department of Education.

Palinscar, A.S. & Brown, A.I. (1984). "Reciprocal teaching of comprehension-fostering and comprehension monitoring strategies." In *Cognition and Instruction,* 1,117-175.

Parker, W.C. (2001). *Social Studies in Elementary Education.* (11th ed.). Upper Saddle River, NJ: Prentice-Hall.

Pauk, W. (1974). "The interest level: That's the thing." In *Journal of Reading,* 16, 459-461.

Pearson, P.D. and Johnson, D. (1978). *Teaching Reading Comprehension.* New York, NY: Holt, Rinehart & Winston.

Pearson, P.D., Roehler, L.R. Dole, J.A. & Duffy, G.G. (1992). "Developing expertise in reading comprehension." In J. Samuels & A. Farstrup, (Eds.), *What Research Has to Say About Reading Instruction,* (2nd ed.). Newark, DE: International Reading Assoc.

Pearson, P.D. (2001). "Life in the radical middle: A personal apology for a balanced view of reading." In R. F. Flippo (Ed.), *Reading Researchers in Search of Common Ground.* Newark, DE: International Reading Assoc.

Pearson, P.D. & Gallgher, M.C. (1983). "The instruction of reading comprehension." In *Contemporary Educational Psychology.* 8, 317-344.

Pettig, K.L. (2000). "On the road to differentiated practice," In *Educational Leadership,* (58) 1, pp. 14-18.

Pierce, K.M. (1990). "Initiating literature discussion groups: Teaching like learners." In K.G. Short & K.M. Pierce (Eds.), *Talking About Books.* Portsmouth, NH: Heinemann.

Popham, James W. (2001). "Teaching to the test?" In *Educational Leadership,* (58) 6, 16-21.

Pressley, M. (2000). "What should comprehension instruction be the instruction of?" In M.L. Kamil, P. Mosenthal, P.D. Pearson, & R. Barr (Eds.) *Handbook of Reading Research,* vol. 3, 545–562. Mahwah, NJ: Erlbaum.

Purcell-Gates, V. (2001). "What we know about readers who struggle." In R.F. Flippo (Ed.), *Reading Researchers in Search of Common Ground.* Newark, DE: International Reading Assoc.

Raphael, T.E., Englert, C.S., & Kirschner, B.W. (1989). "Acquisition of expository writing skills." In J.M. Mason (Ed.), *Reading and Writing Connections.* Boston, MA: Allyn and Bacon.

Readence, J.E., Moore, D.W., & Rickelman, R.J. (2000). *Prereading Activities for Content Area Reading and Learning,* (3rd ed.). Newark, DE: International Reading Assoc.

Readence, J.E., Bean, T.W. & Baldwin, R.S. (1998). *Content Area Reading: An integrated approach,* (6th ed.). Dubuque, IA: Kendall/Hunt.

Richgels, D., McGee, L., Lomax, R. & Sheard, C. (1987). "Awareness of four text structures: Effects on recall of expository texts." In *Reading Research Quarterly,* 22,177-196.

Robb, L (1990). "More poetry, please. In *The New Advocate,* (3) 3, 197-203.

Robb, L. (1993). "A cause for celebration: Reading and writing with at-risk students." In *The New Advocate,* 6 (1), 25-40.

Robb, L. (1994). *Whole Language, Whole Learners: Creating a literature-centered classroom.* New York, NY: Morrow.

Robb, L. (1999). *Easy Mini-Lessons for Building Vocabulary.* New York, NY: Scholastic.

Robb, L. (2000a). *Teaching Reading in Middle School: A strategic approach to teaching reading that improves comprehension and thinking.* New York, NY: Scholastic.

Robb, L. (2000b). *Redefining Staff Development: A collaborative model for teachers and administrators.* Portsmouth, NH: Heinemann.

Robinson, R.D. (2001). "Point of view: George Spache." In R.F. Flippo, (Ed.), *Reading Researchers in Search of Common Ground.* Newark, DE: International Reading Assoc.

Rosenblatt, L.M. (1978). *The Reader, the Text, the Poem: The transactional theory of the literary work.* Carbondale, IL: Southern Illinois University Press.

Rosenblatt, L.M. (1983). *Literature as Exploration.* (4th ed.). New York, NY: The Modern Language Association of America.

Routman, R. (1996). *Literacy at the Crossroads: Critical talk about reading, writing, and other teaching dilemmas.* Portsmouth, NH: Heinemann.

Rudell, R.B. & Unrau, N.J. (1997). "The role of responsive teaching in focusing reader intention and developing reader motivation." In J.T. Guthrie & A. Wigfield (Eds.), *Reading Engagement: Motivating readers through integrated instruction.* Newark, DE: International Reading Assoc.

Salesi, R. (1992). "Reading and writing connections: Supporting content-area literacy through nonfiction trade books." In E.B. Freeman and D.G. Person (Eds.), *Using Nonfiction Trade Books in the Elementary Classroom.* Urbana, IL: National Council of Teachers of English.

Santa, C. (1997). "School change and literacy engagement: Preparing teaching and learning environments." In J.T. Guthrie & A. Wigfield (Eds.), *Reading Engagement: Motivating readers through integrated instruction,* Newark, DE: International Reading Assoc.

Saul, W., Reardon, J., Pearce, C., Dieckman, D., & Newtze, D. (2002). *Science Workshop: Reading, writing and thinking like a scientist.* Portsmouth, NH: Heinemann.

Schallert, D.L. & Reed, J.H. (1997). "The pull of the text and the process of involvement in reading." In J.T. Guthrie & A. Wigfield (Eds.), *Reading Engagement: Motivating readers through integrated instruction.* Newark, DE: International Reading Assoc.

Schunk, D.H. & Zimmerman, B.J. (1997). "Developing self-efficacious readers and writers: The role of social and self-regulatory processes." In J.T. Guthrie & A. Wigfield (Eds.), *Reading Engagement: Motivating readers through integrated instruction.* Newark, DE: International Reading Assoc.

Self, J. (1987). "The picture of writing to learn." In *Plain Talk: About learning and writing across the curriculum.* Virginia Department of Education.

Serafini, F. (2000/2001). "Three paradigms of assesment: Measurement, procedure, and inquiry." In *The Reading Teacher,* 54, 384-393.

Shamlin, M. (2001). "Creating curriculum with and for Children." In H. Mills & A. Donnelly (Eds.), *From the Ground Up: Creating a culture of inquiry.* Portsmouth, NH: Heinemann.

Short, K., Harste, J. & Burke, C. (1995). *Creating Classrooms for Authors and Inquirers.* Portsmouth: NH, Heinemann.

Slavin, R.E. (1986). *Using Student Team Learning* (3rd ed.). Baltimore, MD: Johns Hopkins University, Center for Research on Elementary and Middle Schools. Instruction Manual for Using Jigsaw and Other Team Learning Strategies.

Slavin, R.E. (1996). "Cooperative learning in middle and secondary schools." In *Clearing House,* (69) 4, 200-204.

Smith, F. (2001). "Just a matter of time." In *Phi Delta Kappan,* (82) 8, 573-581.

Smith, F. (1978). *Reading Without Nonsense.* New York, NY: Teachers College, Columbia University.

Stanovich, K.E. (1986). "Matthew effects in reading: Some consequences of individual differences in acquisition of literacy." In *Reading Research Quarterly,* 21, 360-407.

Sywester, R. (2000). "Unconcscious emotions, conscious feelings." In *Educational Leadership,* (58) 3, 20-24.

Taba, H. (1967). *Teacher's Handbook for Elementary Social Studies.* Reading, MA: Addison-Wesley.

Taberski, S. (2001). "Fact & fiction read aloud." In *Instructor,* March, 24–27.

Tannen, D. (1988). "Hearing voices in conversation, fiction, and mixed genres." In *Linguistics in Context: Connecting observation and understanding lectures from the 1985 LSA. TESOL and NEH Institutes.* Ablex Publishing Co.

Taylor, B.T., Harris, L.A., Pearson, P.D. & Garcia, G.E. (1995). *Reading Difficulties, Instruction and Assessment* (2nd ed.). New York, NY: McGraw-Hill.

Tierney, R.J. & Readence, J.E. (2000). *Reading Strategies and Practices: A compendium.* Boston, MA: Allyn and Bacon.

Tomlinson, C. A. (2000). "Reconcilable differences? Standards-based teaching and differentiation." In *Educational Leadership* (58)1, 6-11.

Tomlinson, C. A.. (2001). "Grading for success." In *Educational Leadership,* (58) 6, 12-15.

Topping, K. (1987). "Paired reading: A powerful technique for parent use." In *The Reading Teacher* (40), 608-614.

Tunnel, M.O. & Ammon, R. (Eds.) (1996). *The Story of Ourselves: Teaching history through children's literature.* Portsmouth, NH: Heinemann.

Vacca, R.T. & Vacca, J.A. (2000). *Content Area Reading: Literacy and learcning across the curriculum,* 6th ed. New York, NY: Longman.

Vardell, S. (1998). "Using read-aloud to explore the layers of nonfiction." In R. A., Bamford & J.V. Kristo (Eds.), *Making Facts Come Alive: Choosing quality nonfiction literature K–8,* Norwood, MA: Christopher-Gordon.

Vaughn, J.L. & Estes, T.H. (1986). *Reading and Reasoning Beyond the Primary Grades.* Boston, MA: Allyn and Bacon.

Vygotsky, L. (1978). *Mind in Society: The development of higher psychological processes.* Cambridge, MA: Harvard University Press.

Walpole, P. (1987). "Yes, writing in math." In J. Self (Ed.) *Plain Talk: About learning and writing across the curriculum.* Virginia Department of Education.

Waugh, J.R. (2001). "Becoming reading researchers." In H. Mills & A. Donnelly (Eds.), *From the Ground Up: Creating a culture of inquiry.* Portsmouth, NH: Heinemann.

Weaver, D. & Alvermann, D.E. (2000). "Critical thinking and discussion." In K.D. Wood & T.S. Dickinson (Eds.), *Promoting Literacy in Grades 4-9: A handbook for teachers and administrators.* Boston, MA: Allyn & Bacon.

Wells, G. (1986). *The Meaning Makers: Children learning language and using language to learn.* Portsmouth, NH: Heinemann.

Wigfield, A. (1997). "Children's motivations for reading and reading engagement." In J.T. Guthrie & A. Wigfield (Eds.), *Reading Engagement: Motivating readers through integrated instruction.* Newark, DE: International Reading Assoc.

Whitin, D.J. & Wilde, S. (1992). "Read any good math lately?" In *Children's books for mathematical learning, K–6.* Portsmouth, NH: Heinemann.

Wilde, S. (1998). "Mathematical learning and exploration in nonfiction literature." In R. A. Bamford & J.V. Kristo (Eds.), *Making Facts Come Alive: Choosing quality nonfiction literature K-8.* Norwood, MA: Christopher-Gordon.

Wilhelm, J.D. (2001). *Improving Comprehension with Think-Aloud Strategies: Modeling what good readers do.* New York, NY: Scholastic.

Woodward, A. & Elliot, D.L. (1990). "Textbooks: Consensus and controversy." In D.L. Elliot & A. Woodward (Eds.), *Textbooks and Schooling in the United States.* Chicago, IL: National Society for the Study of Education.

Zarnowski, M. (1998a). "It's more than dates and places: How nonfiction contributes to understanding social studies." In R. A., Bamford & J.V. Kristo (Eds.), *Making Facts Come Alive: Choosing quality nonfiction literature K–8.* Norwood, MA: Christopher-Gordon.

Zarnowski, M. (1998b). "Coming out from under the spell of stories: Critiquing historical narrative." In *The New Advocate,* (11) 4, 345-365.

Zarnowski, M., Kerper, R.M. & Jensen, J.M. (Eds.) (2001). *The Best in Children's Nonfiction.* Urbana, IL: National Council Of Teachers of English.

Appendix

Teaching Reading in Social Studies, Science, and Math

Modeling Reading Strategies with Nonfiction Picture Books

I've selected picture and informational books with short selections, as these are excellent resources for strategy lessons. The books that follow are ones I find effective. However, you will find countless other titles in your school and local libraries. The point to consider is to choose outstanding books with themes that appeal to students in grades 3 to 8.

POSING QUESTIONS

- *Dawn to Dusk in the Galapagos: Flightless Birds, Swimming Lizards, and Other Fascinating Creatures* by Rita Golden Gelman, photographs by Tui De Roy, Little Brown, 1991.
- *Dia's Story Cloth: The Hmong People's Journey of Freedom* by Dia Cha, stitched by Chue and Nhia Thao Cha, Lee and Low, 1996.
- *Surtsey: The Newest Place on Earth* by Kathryn Lasky, photographs by Christopher G. Knight, Hyperion, 1992.
- *My Story* by Ruby Bridges, Scholastic, 2000.

VOCABULARY IN CONTEXT

- *A Boy Named Giotto* by Paolo Guarnieri, pictures by Bimba Landmann, illustrated by Jonathan Galassi, Farrar, Straus, & Giroux, 1998.
- *Born in the Breezes: The Seafaring Life of Joshua Slocum* by Kathryn Lasky, illustrated by Walter Lyon Krudep, Scholastic, 2002.
- *Lives of Extraordinary Women: Rulers, Rebels (and What the Neighbors Thought)* by Kathleen Krull, illustrated by Kathryn Hewett, Harcourt, 2000.
- *Coming to America: The Story of Immigration* by Betsy Maestro, illustrated by Susannah Ryan, Scholastic, 1996.

VISUALIZING

- *Grandfather's Journey* by Allen Say, Houghton Mifflin, 1994.
- *The Librarian Who Measured the Earth* by Kathryn Lasky, illustrated by Kevin Hawkes, Little Brown, 1994.
- *Red Legs: A Drummer Boy of the Civil War* by Ted Lewin, HarperCollins, 2001.
- *The Tomb of the Boy King* by John Frank, Fararr/Foster, 2001.

PARTNER READINGS AND RETELLINGS

- *Animals Who Have Won Our Hearts* by Jean Craighead George, HarperCollins, 1994.
- *Antarctic Journal: Four Months at the Bottom of the World* by Jenniver Owings Dewey, HarperCollins, 2001.
- *Let It Shine: Stories of Black Women Freedom Fighters* by Andrea Davis Pinkney, illustrated by Stephen Alcorn, Harcourt 2000. (104 pages of short biographies)
- *Remember the Ladies: 100 Great American Women* by Cheryl Harness, HarperCollins, 2001.

SUMMARIZING AND SYNTHESIZING

- *The Bald Eagle Returns* by Dorothy Hinshaw Patent, photographs by William Munoz, Clarion, 2001.
- *Herstory: Women Who Changed the World,* edited by Ruth Ashby and Deborah Gore Ohrn, Viking, 1995. (291 pages of one- to two-page biographies)
- *Scholastic Encyclopedia of Animals* by Laurence Pringle, Scholastic, 2001.
- *Thomas Jefferson: A Picture Book Biography* by James Cross Giblin, illustrated by Michael Dooling, Scholastic, 1994.

MAKING CONNECTIONS TO SELF, COMMUNITY, THE WORLD

- *Everglades* by Jean Craighead George, paintings by Wendell Minor, HarperCollins, 1995.
- *The Journey: Japanese Americans, Racism, and Renewal* by Sheila Hamanka, Orchard, 1990.
- *The Way West: Journal of a Pioneer Woman* by Amelia Stewart Knight, illustrated by Michael McCurdy, Simon and Schuster, 1993.
- *The Chimpanzees I Love: Saving Their World And Ours* by Jane Goodall, Scholastic, 2001.

MAKING INFERENCES

- *Flight: The Journey of Charles Lindbergh* by Robert Burleigh, illustrated by Mike Wimmer, Philomel, 1991.
- *The King's Day: King Louis XIV of France* by Aliki, Crowell, 1989.
- *The Wall* by Eve Bunting, illustrated by Ronald Himler, Clarion, 1990.
- *Wounded Knee* by Neil Waldman, Atheneum, 2001.

READ, PAUSE, RETELL, REREAD

- *A Handful of Dirt* by Rayond Bial, Walker, 1998.
- *Egyptian Mummies* by Delia Pemberton, Harcourt, 2001.

- *Gorillas* by Seymour Simon, HarperCollins, 2000.
- *Red, White, Blue, and Uncle Who?: The Stories Behind Some of America's Patriotic Symbols* by Teresa Bateman, illustrated by John O'Brien, Holiday House, 2001.

PAIRED READING AND QUESTIONING

- *If You Made a Million* by David Schwartz, illustrated by Steven Kellogg, Lothrop, Lee & Shepard, 1989.
- *Mandela: From the Life of a South African Statesman,* by Floyd Cooper, Philomel, 1996.
- *Slinky, Scaly, Slithery Snakes* by Dorothy Hinshaw Patent, illustrations by Kendahl Jan Jubb, Walker, 2000.
- *Starry Messenger* by Peter Sis, Farrar, Straus, & Giroux, 1997.

MATH CONCEPTS

- *Anno's Math Games III* by Mitsumasa Anno, Philomel, 1991.
- *The Hershey's Milk Chocolate Multiplication Book* by Jerry Pallotta, illustrated by Rob Bolster, Scholastic, 2001.
- *Fraction Action* by Loreen Leedy, Holiday House, 1994.
- *Twizzlers: Percentages Book* by Jerry Pallotta, illustrated by Rob Bolster, Scholastic, 2001

MAIN IDEA/DETAILS

- *Brave Harriet* by Marissa Moss, illustrated by C.F. Payne, Harcourt, 2001.
- *The North American Rain Forest Scrapbook* by Virginia Wright-Frierson, Walker, 1999.
- *The Voice of the People: American Democracy in Action* by Betsy Maestro and Guilio Maestro, Lothrop, Lee & Shepard, 1996.
- *Waiting for Wings* by Lois Ehlert, Harcourt, 2001.

OBSERVING & THINKING with PHOTOS, MAPS, and ILLUSTRATIONS

- *First on the Moon* by Barbara Hehner, illustrations by Greg Ruhl, Hyperion, 1999.
- *Hidden Under the Ground: The World Beneath Your Feet* by Peter Kent, Dutton, 1998.
- *Land Ho! Fifty Glorious Years in the Age of Exploration* by Nancy Winslow Parker, HarperCollins, 2001.
- *Picturing Lincoln: Famous Photographs That Popularized the President,* Clarion, 2001.

BOOKS TO USE FOR MODELING TEXT STRUCTURES

QUESTION/ANSWER

- *A Drop of Water: A Book of Science and Wonder* by Walter Wick, Scholastic, 1997.
- *Do You Remember the Color Blue? And Other Questions Kids Ask About Blindness* by Sally Hobart Alexander, Viking, 2000.
- *Extraordinary Friends* by Fred Rogers, Putnam, 2000.

SEQUENCE

- *The Amazing Life of Benjamin Franklin* by James Cross Giblin, Scholastic, 2000.
- *The Golden City: Jerusalem's 3,000 Years* by Neil Walkdman, Atheneum, 1995.
- *Fly: A Brief History of Flight* by Barry Moser, HarperCollins, 1993.

PROBLEM/SOLUTION

- *The Man-Eating Tigers of Sundarbans* by Sy Montgomery, Houghton, 2001.
- *Dinosaur Young: Uncovering the Mystery of Dinosaur Families* by Kathleen Weidner Zoehfeld, Clarion, 2001.
- *The Wildlife Detectives: How Forensic Scientists Fight Crimes Against Nature* by Donna Jackson, Houghton, 2000.

DESCRIPTION

- *A Dragon in the Sky: The Story of a Green Darner Dragonfly* by Laurence Pringle, Scholastic/Orchard, 2001.
- *Crocodiles and Alligators* by Seymour Simon, HarperCollins, 2001.
- *Safari Beneath the Sea: The Wonder World of the North Pacific Coast* by Diane Swanson, photographs by the Royal British Columbia Museum, Sierra Club, 1994.

COMPARE/CONTRAST

- *Fantastic Book of Comparisons* by Russell Ash, Dorling Kindersly, 2000.
- *The Great Fire* by Jim Murphy, Scholastic, 1995.
- *One World, Many Religions* by Mary Pope Osbourne, Knopf, 1996.

CAUSE/EFFECT

- *Conestoga Wagons* by Richard Ammon, illustrated by Bill Farnsworth, Holiday House, 2000.
- *The Drop in My Drink: The Story of Water on Our Planet* by Meredith Hooper, illustrated by Chris Coady, Viking, 1998.
- *Fire in the Forest: A Cycle of Growth and Renewal* by Laurence Pringle, paintings by Bob Marshall, Atheneum, 1995.

Teaching Reading in Social Studies, Science, and Math

Questions for Kite Project

by Harry Holloway

Name _____

Group members _____

- Justify all answers
- Be neat and write in complete sentences where appropriate
- Give all answers on a separate paper, all measurements must be in metric units.
- Explain which answers are approximations and why they are approximate.

1. Give the definition of a tetrahedron. Explain why these are called tetrahedral kites.

2. This is a type of "box kite;" what are some other box kites? include drawings and references.

3. What is the surface area and volume of each tetrahedron that your group made? How did you get your answer?

4. How much tissue paper was needed for each tetrahedron? What was the total amount of tissue paper needed for the kite? How much tissue paper had to be wasted? Was there a way to reduce the waste?

5. What percent of each tetrahedron is covered with tissue paper?

6. What percent of the outside surface area of the finished kite is covered with tissue paper?

7. How many planes of symmetry does the kite have?

8. When the four tetrahedrons are put together, a new polyhedron is formed in the middle. What is it? How do you know?

9. What improvements could you add to the kite?

10. Write directions to the kite; include a list of materials and drawings when necessary.

Index

Teaching Reading in Social Studies, Science, and Math

Teaching Reading in Social Studies, Science, and Math